D0931117

WITHDRAWN

KEEPING FAITH WITH THE CONSTITUTION

Not a Suicide Pact
The Constitution in a Time of National Emergency
Richard A. Posner

Supreme Neglect
How to Revive Constitutional Protection for Private Property
Richard A. Epstein

Out of Range
Why the Constitution Can't End the Battle over Guns
Mark V. Tushnet

Unfinished Business
Racial Equality in American History
Michael J. Klarman

Is There a Right to Remain Silent?
Coercive Interrogation and the Fifth Amendment after 9/11
Alan M. Dershowitz

The Invisible Constitution
Laurence H. Tribe

Uninhibited, Robust, and Wide-Open
A Free Press for a New Century
Lee C. Bollinger

From Disgust to Humanity
Sexual Orientation and Constitutional Law
Martha C. Nussbaum

The Living Constitution
David A. Strauss

INALIENABLE RIGHTS SERIES

...

SERIES EDITOR

Geoffrey R. Stone

Keeping Faith with the Constitution

...

Goodwin Liu
Pamela S. Karlan
Christopher H. Schroeder

OXFORD
UNIVERSITY PRESS

2010

OXFORD

UNIVERSITY PRESS

Oxford University Press, Inc., publishes works that further
Oxford University's objective of excellence
in research, scholarship, and education.

Oxford   New York

Auckland   Cape Town   Dar es Salaam   Hong Kong   Karachi
Kuala Lumpur   Madrid   Melbourne   Mexico City   Nairobi
New Delhi   Shanghai   Taipei   Toronto

With offices in

Argentina   Austria   Brazil   Chile   Czech Republic   France   Greece
Guatemala   Hungary   Italy   Japan   Poland   Portugal   Singapore
South Korea   Switzerland   Thailand   Turkey   Ukraine   Vietnam

Published by Oxford University Press, Inc.
198 Madison Avenue, New York, New York 10016
www.oup.com

Oxford is a registered trademark of Oxford University Press

Library of Congress Cataloging-in-Publication Data
Liu, Goodwin.
Keeping faith with the Constitution / Goodwin Liu, Pamela S. Karlan,
Christopher H. Schroeder.
p. cm. (Inalienable rights series)
Includes bibliographical references and index.
ISBN 978-0-19-973877-9
1. Constitutional law—United States.   I. Karlan, Pamela S.
II. Schroeder, Christopher H.   III. Title.
KF4550.Z9L578 2010
342.7302—dc22   2009047949

1 3 5 7 9 8 6 4 2

Printed in the United States of America
on acid-free paper

Contents

...

Acknowledgments

...

IN WRITING THIS book, we have benefited from the guidance and wisdom of many people. For insightful comments on earlier drafts, we thank Judy Appelbaum, Jack Balkin, Lisa Brown, Rebecca Brown, David Lyle, Robert Gordon, Pam Harris, Doug Kendall, Bill Marshall, Martha Minow, John Payton, Andy Pincus, Robert Post, Ted Shaw, Paul Smith, Geoffrey Stone, David Strauss, and Meera Trehan. We are also grateful for the help of Nicole Ries, who provided superb research assistance and editing, and Meredith Dearborn, who sharpened the text with careful editing. Moreover, we could not have completed this project without the encouragement of the American Constitution Society, which published an initial version of this book in April 2009.

More broadly, we are indebted to the many scholars, past and present, whose ideas have shaped the debate over constitutional interpretation for decades. Our work builds on intellectual foundations laid by many friends and colleagues whom we respect and admire. Finally, we are indebted to the many citizens, elected officials, and judges who have worked throughout our history to ensure that we keep faith with the Constitution. Without them, this book quite literally could not have been written.

The views expressed in this book and any errors are of course our own.

Editor's Note

. . .

> We hold these truths to be self-evident, that all men are created
> equal, that they are endowed by their Creator with certain unalien-
> able Rights. . . .

—*The Declaration of Independence*

H<small>OW DO WE</small> "keep faith with the Constitution"? This question has
haunted constitutional lawyers since the earliest days of judicial
review. As judges give meaning to the often vague generalities of
the Constitution, how can they ensure that they protect our essential constitutional liberties in an ever-changing society, without
usurping the legitimate authority of the states or of the democratically elected branches of the federal government?

This challenge has vexed judges and scholars for more than two
hundred years—perhaps most emphatically over the past four
decades. By the end of the 1960s, conservatives were convinced that
the justices of the Warren Court had run amuck and had flagrantly
used the cover of constitutional law to impose their own "liberal"
version of the good society on the nation. Where, they asked, did
the Constitution require the exclusionary rule, *Miranda* warnings,
"one person–one vote," the prohibition of school prayer, the protection of sexually explicit expression, or racial integration? The criticism became even more fervent in the 1970s, after the Burger Court
announced a constitutional right to abortion. Conservative critics
railed that the justices had manipulated the text and design of the

Constitution in order to smuggle their own personal value judgments into constitutional law.

In the 1980s, these critics, led by such figures as Ed Meese, Robert Bork, and Antonin Scalia, insisted that judges should limit themselves to enforcing the "original meaning" of the Constitution. They argued that the judiciary could legitimately hold a law unconstitutional only if the Framers themselves had intended the law to be unconstitutional. By focusing on the original meaning, they argued, judges would remain faithful to the true meaning of the Constitution, resist the temptation to interpret the Constitution to suit their own policy preferences, and exercise judicial review in a more circumscribed and constitutionally appropriate manner.

As Ronald Reagan, the Federalist Society, and other conservative voices popularized this view, they attacked competing theories of constitutional law and sought to discredit decisions that had protected the rights of minorities, dissenters, and the outcasts of society. Advocates of originalism lauded the authority of the elected branches of government and associated their view with such popular catch-phrases as "strict construction," "judicial passivism," "applying rather than making up the law," "judicial restraint," and "calling balls and strikes." Over time, they persuaded many if not most Americans that the proper role of judges is to take a highly mechanical approach to constitutional interpretation. They were largely successful in this campaign, even though many conservative jurists often embraced quite activist interpretations of the Constitution in such controversial areas as federalism, property rights, affirmative action, gun rights, and the First Amendment rights of corporations.

Whether or not originalism is coherent, principled, or restrained, its popularizers effectively put the proponents of a Warren Court–style of jurisprudence on the defensive. Although the critics of original meaning took issue with the logic and practice of the methodology, they found it difficult affirmatively to articulate how they believed judges *should* interpret the Constitution. If the idea of an open-textured and evolving Constitution is legitimate, how can judges give it meaning without injecting their personal values into constitutional law? Is there any credible mode of constitutional interpretation that can both respond to the constantly evolving nature of American society, and at the same time "keep faith" with the Constitution in a principled and coherent manner? This is the most fundamental question of early twenty-first century constitutional law, and it is the central question of this volume.

Goodwin Liu, Pamela Karlan, and Christopher Schroeder attempt in *Keeping Faith with the Constitution* to demonstrate that there is, in fact, a convincing and principled alternative to the view that the Constitution's meaning must be frozen in time—an alternative that interprets the text and aspirations of the Constitution as the Framers understood them, while at the same time ensuring that specific interpretations and applications of the text can change in appropriate ways over time. They argue that such an approach is implicit in the actual practices of American constitutional law, and that without that approach fundamental decisions that the Supreme Court has reached over the years would be simply inexplicable. Whether they succeed in this effort is a judgment that you, the reader, will have to make for yourself. The stakes in this debate are high, for it will help shape the future of constitutional law well into the twenty-first century.

Geoffrey R. Stone

Introduction

...

JUSTICE OLIVER WENDELL HOLMES was right when he said that the words of the Constitution "have called into life a being the development of which could not have been foreseen completely by the most gifted of its begetters. It was enough for them to realize or to hope that they had created an organism; it has taken a century and has cost their successors much sweat and blood to prove that they created a nation."[1]

The reason the United States Constitution is the world's most enduring written constitution is not simply the genius of fifty-five men who met in Philadelphia in 1787. Rather, it is the way that generation after generation of Americans has made the Constitution ours. The Constitution endures because its meaning and application have been shaped by an ongoing process of interpretation. That process includes both judicial interpretation and transformations in constitutional understanding pressed by political leaders and ordinary citizens throughout our history. Our Constitution retains its vitality because it has proven adaptable to the changing conditions and evolving norms of our society. Its words and principles still resonate centuries after they were written because time and again, as

Justice Holmes urged, we have interpreted the Constitution in light of "what this country has become."[2] Americans of all backgrounds can wholeheartedly take an oath to support and defend the Constitution when they are naturalized, join the armed forces, gain admission to the bar, or assume elective office not because of how our founding text was understood in 1789, or even in 1870, but because of how we understand it today.

In recent decades, this common-sense understanding of the Constitution has been eclipsed by alternative conceptions of our founding document and the proper way to interpret it. Originalism—an exclusive reliance on public understandings of the text at the time it was ratified—has been vigorously championed by judges such as Antonin Scalia, Clarence Thomas, and Robert Bork, and by prominent conservatives such as Edwin Meese, who as Attorney General of the United States issued litigation guidelines directing government attorneys to "advance constitutional arguments based only on [the document's] 'original meaning.'"[3] In addition to (and allied with) calls for originalism, a familiar refrain among conservative politicians is their promise to appoint only "strict constructionists" to the bench. Although the meaning of strict construction is far from clear, popular invocations of the term, like appeals to originalism, have served as a powerful polemic in opposition to evolving understandings of individual liberty, equal protection, federalism, and other constitutional principles. Whether applied with rigor or intoned as rhetoric, originalism and strict construction have served to legitimize conservative dominance of the federal judiciary for more than three decades.

In this book, we describe and defend an approach to constitutional interpretation that is richer than originalism or strict construction, more consistent with the history of our constitutional practice, and more persuasive in explaining why the Constitution remains authoritative over two hundred years after the nation's founding. Interpreting the Constitution, we argue, requires adaptation of its text and principles to the conditions and challenges faced by successive generations. The question that properly guides interpretation is not how the Constitution would have been applied at the Founding, but rather how it should be applied today in order to sustain its vitality in light of the changing needs, conditions, and understandings of our society.

We use the term *constitutional fidelity* to describe this approach. To be faithful to the Constitution is to interpret its words and to apply its principles in ways that preserve the Constitution's meaning and democratic legitimacy over time. Original understandings are an important source of constitutional meaning, but so too are the other sources that judges, elected officials, and everyday citizens regularly invoke: the text of the Constitution, its purpose and structure, the lessons of precedent and historical experience, the practical consequences of legal rules, and the evolving norms and traditions of our society. A dynamic process of interpretation informed by these considerations is what enables the American people to keep faith with the Constitution from one generation to the next.

In elaborating this approach, we start from the premise that constitutional interpretation must be faithful to the character of the document itself. Three features are particularly important. First, the Constitution is "the basic charter of our society, setting out in spare but meaningful terms the principles of government."[4] Although some of its provisions establish clear and precise rules—for example, the age of eligibility to serve as a member of Congress or as President[5]—the Constitution, for the most part, does not "partake of the prolixity of a legal code."[6] As Chief Justice Marshall observed, the nature of a constitution "requires that only its great outlines should be marked [and] its important objects designated," and the language of the U.S. Constitution makes clear that "this idea was entertained by [its] framers."[7] Our Constitution was not intended to supply a ready answer for every problem or every question that might arise. The Framers memorialized our basic principles of government with broad language whose application to future cases and controversies would be determined not by a mechanical formula but by an ongoing process of interpretation. The Constitution is "intended to endure for ages to come, and consequently, to be adapted to the various crises of human affairs"; it is a charter of general principles open to "fair and just interpretation" over time.[8] That is "the character of the instrument" that Chief Justice Marshall emphasized when he said "we must never forget that it is a *constitution* we are expounding."[9]

Second, the Constitution is a document designed to be "understood by the public."[10] To quote President Franklin Roosevelt, it is "a layman's document, not a lawyer's contract."[11] Throughout our history, the meaning of the Constitution's text and principles has been the subject of public debate and, at times, intense mobilization among the American people and their representatives. Judges, of course, play a critical role in interpreting the Constitution. But the popular character of the Constitution has meant that constitutional interpretation is not a task for the judiciary alone. Thus it is neither surprising nor illegitimate that judicial doctrine often incorporates the evolving understandings of the Constitution forged through social movements, legislation, and historical practice. Public engagement with the meaning of the Constitution is what has enabled our founding document to retain its democratic authority through changing times.

Third, the Constitution is a declaration of our ideals as well as a set of operational commands. The Constitution does not state our ideals as merely lofty aspirations; it records our commitment to put our ideals into practice. To keep faith with the Constitution is to fulfill its promises "not as a matter of fine words on paper, but as a matter of everyday life in the Natio[n]."[12] What this means for constitutional interpretation is that the application of the Constitution's broad principles to specific controversies must take into account the lived experience and practical consequences of the law. In this way, the task of interpretation serves to realize the Constitution's guarantees "not simply as a matter of legal principle but in terms of how we actually live."[13]

In presenting these ideas, our approach is both descriptive and normative. It is descriptive insofar as it provides an account of our actual constitutional practice. As a historical matter, many of our fundamental constitutional understandings came into being through the adaptation of text and principle to the changing needs and norms of our society. At the same time, our project is normative insofar as it defends the dominant features of our constitutional practice against critics who would reduce the process of interpretation to something more mechanical or formulaic. Unlike alternatives such as originalism, interpretation that strives for constitutional fidelity succeeds over time in preserving the vitality of our founding text and securing the democratic legitimacy that ultimately anchors our continuing allegiance to the Constitution.

We begin in chapter 1 with an overview of the text and historical development of the Constitution. Our discussion starts with the Founding context and the principles set forth in the unamended Constitution, and then examines the concerns that shaped the adoption of the Bill of Rights. From there, we turn to the next burst of additions to the Constitution, the Reconstruction Amendments, whose transformative principles forged what many have called America's Second Founding. We conclude this chapter with a brief discussion of the amendments adopted over the last century. In its entirety, the Constitution charts the centuries-long progress of our nation toward greater liberty and equality and more effective and democratic government. At each critical juncture, the Framers inscribed our fundamental values into the Constitution with broad language and expansive principles open to future interpretation.

Chapter 2 focuses on judicial interpretation of the Constitution. We use the term *constitutional fidelity* to describe an approach to interpretation that sustains the vitality of the Constitution's text and principles over time. This approach does not disavow original understandings as a legitimate source of constitutional meaning. But the overarching question it poses is not simply how the Constitution would have applied during the Framing era, but rather how it should apply today in order to preserve its meaning and authority in the light of evolving precedent, historical experience, practical consequences, and societal change. As many examples show, these considerations inform the constitutional reasoning of judges of all stripes, and their importance and legitimacy are well established in our interpretive tradition. By contrast, neither originalism nor strict construction has proven to be a persuasive or durable methodology, not least because they cannot explain many of the basic constitutional understandings we now take for granted.

In chapters 3 through 9, we illustrate our interpretive approach with historical narratives that show how several constitutional principles have acquired the meaning they have today. Individually and collectively, the narratives provide a textured account of how the Constitution's values have endured through adaptation to contemporary challenges posed by social, economic, and political change. They also demonstrate how our courts interact with the political branches and with the American people in giving practical effect to individual rights and structural guarantees. Finally, the narratives show that the actual practice of constitutional interpretation has never been reducible to a singular inquiry into original understandings or the plain meaning of the text. Throughout our history, judicial and nonjudicial interpreters have rejected such narrow methodologies in favor of a more dynamic and multifaceted approach to interpretation that is faithful to the character of the Constitution itself.

Chapter 3 discusses the interpretive approach underlying *Brown v. Board of Education*, the modern jurisprudence of gender equality, and civil rights protections enacted by Congress as constitutional enforcement measures. Chapter 4 describes the development of Supreme Court doctrine that protects freedom of political expression. Chapter 5 examines the New Deal transformation of constitutional understandings regarding the proper scope of government power to meet our social and economic needs. Chapter 6 discusses the application of the principle of checks and balances to contemporary challenges posed by the war on terrorism. Chapter 7 addresses the interplay of judicial and legislative solutions to malapportionment and vote dilution. Chapter 8 examines the revolution in criminal procedure that now informs our understanding of due process of law. And chapter 9 traces the evolving scope of constitutional protection for individual liberty to make decisions concerning intimate aspects of our lives. Similar narratives could be written on how our society has come to understand free exercise of religion, separation of church and state, cruel and unusual punishment, and other constitutional principles. Our purpose here is not to provide a comprehensive survey but to illustrate a general and widely applicable approach to constitutional interpretation.

In chapter 10, we conclude with a brief summary and a glimpse at future challenges that will continue to require an interpretive approach that adapts the words and principles of our founding document to the evolving conditions and norms of our society and, in so doing, sustains the faith of the American people in our enduring Constitution.

KEEPING FAITH WITH THE CONSTITUTION

CHAPTER ONE

The Constitution's Vision and Values

OUR FOUNDING DOCUMENT establishes a general framework for effective governance of a nation destined to grow and change. It fixes the basic structure of government and some of its important procedures while expressing our commitment to certain core values: liberty, equality, and democracy. This chapter provides an initial grounding in the words and vision of the Constitution and its Framers. The next chapter turns to the role of courts in constitutional interpretation.

THE FOUNDING CONTEXT

As Dr. Martin Luther King observed in his *I Have a Dream* speech, "[w]hen the architects of our republic wrote the magnificent words of the Constitution and the Declaration of Independence, they were signing a promissory note to which every American was to fall heir."[1] Dr. King was right to link these two documents. The Constitution was drafted and ratified against the backdrop of the recent war for independence from Great Britain, and the Declaration expressed Americans' aspirations for the kind of government they sought:

> We hold these truths to be self-evident, that all men are created equal, that they are endowed by their Creator with certain unalienable Rights, that among these are Life, Liberty and the pursuit of Happiness.—That to secure these rights, Governments are instituted among Men, deriving their just powers from the consent of the governed,—That whenever any Form of Government becomes destructive of these ends, it is the Right of the People to alter or to abolish it, and to institute new Government, laying its foundation on such principles and organizing its powers in such form, as to them shall seem most likely to effect their Safety and Happiness.[2]

The Declaration thus expresses a background understanding among the Founding generation that equality, liberty, and opportunity ("the pursuit of Happiness") were fundamental rights; that legitimate government depends on the consent of the governed; and that the powers of government should be organized to enable it to affirmatively "secure" and "effect" the rights and liberties of the people.

At the same time, in its allegations against the King, the Declaration also identified some of the key principles limiting governmental authority. Among the acts justifying America's secession from the British Empire were the King's interference with judicial independence and trial by jury, his elevation of military authority over civilian control, his refusal to respect popular election and legislative authority, and, perhaps most famously, his imposition of taxation without representation.

The Constitution, now more than two hundred years old, was not the first attempt by the thirteen colonies to create a nation. The

Articles of Confederation were ratified in 1781, but they failed after a half-dozen years. A key reason for the failure was that the Articles did not create a national government capable of dealing with the economic and international issues of the times. Not only was the national government's power limited, but two of the three branches—the executive and the judiciary—did not even exist. The desire to create a national government capable of confronting unforeseen and unforeseeable problems was a central motivation behind the Constitution.

The Framers were part of a bold but pragmatic generation. They knew they were creating a nation that would change in important ways over time. The very decision to ratify the proposed Constitution reflected their recognition that America was an expanding nation where commerce and not merely agrarian traditions would play an increasing role. Moreover, the structure of the Constitution reflected the Framers' comfort with innovation as well as their determination to ensure that the government would have sufficient power to deal with the nation's problems as they arose.

At the same time, the Framers understood that dividing power—horizontally within the national government and vertically between the national government and the states—would help protect individual liberty against government abuse. "Ambition must be made to counteract ambition," James Madison wrote, if we are to have "security against a gradual concentration of [power] in the same department."[3] By creating a national government with three interdependent branches, the Framers sought to enlarge the government's capabilities while also limiting the potential for abuse through a system of checks and balances. And by maintaining a federal system, the Framers contemplated "a double security [for] the rights of the people," as the national and state governments "will control each other, at the same time that each will be controlled by itself."[4]

Moreover, although classical republican theory saw the size and diversity of the growing nation as a threat to self-government, Madison argued that these features provide additional protection for individual liberty. In a large, heterogeneous society with a "multiplicity of interests" among its citizens, "the rights of individuals, or of the minority, will be in little danger from interested combinations of the majority."[5] The minority group of primary concern to the Founders may have been wealthy creditors and landowners. And one reason for the system of checks and balances may have been to safeguard property rights by making redistributive measures difficult to enact. But, as a general principle, the republican theory that informs our Constitution is one that values pluralism and diversity, and protects individual rights of all kinds against government abuse.

THE 1789 CONSTITUTION

Even before the addition of any amendments, the Constitution expresses fundamental commitments to democracy, equality, and individual liberty, and to a robust but carefully calibrated system of government power commensurate with the nation's needs. These values are reflected in the text.

The Preamble

The Constitution's opening words describe its ambitions. As the Supreme Court recognized early on, the source of the Constitution's power is the people: "The constitution of the United States was ordained and established, not by the states in their sovereign capacities, but emphatically, as the preamble of the constitution declares, by 'the people of the United States.'"[6] Thus, democratic self-determination is the source of the Constitution's legitimacy, and the Constitution signaled the transformation of the "league of friendship" among sovereign states under the Articles of Confederation[7] into a single nation governed by "the people of the United States."

The language the Constitution uses to describe its purposes is far more capacious than the immediate economic and geopolitical exigencies that prompted the Constitutional Convention. As the Preamble says, the Constitution aims to "establish Justice, insure domestic Tranquility, provide for the common defence, promote the general Welfare, and secure the Blessings of Liberty." These phrases could not then, and cannot now, be defined with precision. But the fact that the phrases are repeated in the text of the Constitution—the Spending Clause of Article I, for example, declares Congress's power to "provide for the common Defence and general Welfare," and the Fifth Amendment prohibits deprivations of "liberty" without due process of law—shows that they were intended to be given real effect.

Government power to address the nation's needs

By expanding the powers of the federal government beyond their limited scope under the Articles of Confederation, the Constitution significantly enhanced the power of government to address the nation's needs. And by creating distinct legislative, executive, and judicial branches within a framework of separated powers, the Framers moderated the exercise of national power through a complex system of checks and balances.

In Article I, the Framers enumerated a broad array of congressional powers—among them, the power to tax and spend for the general welfare, the power to regulate commerce among the states and with foreign nations, the power to establish post offices and roads to link the new nation together, the power to promote scientific progress and innovation through a system of intellectual property, and the power to establish a process for naturalization to welcome immigrants. Further, Article I authorizes Congress to make all laws "necessary and proper" for executing the enumerated legislative powers and all other powers vested in the national government. At the same time, the Framers circumscribed these lawmaking powers through mechanisms such as the presidential veto, judicial power to decide constitutional cases, and the fragmentation of Congress into two chambers, the House and Senate.

Article II creates the office of the President and assigns the President the duty to "take Care that the Laws be faithfully executed." The President also has the power to appoint the principal officers of the government, including federal judges. Article II designates the President as Commander in Chief of the armed forces and assigns the President various diplomatic and foreign policy functions. Importantly, the Constitution makes clear that those powers are shared with Congress. For example, while the President has the power to make treaties and to appoint ambassadors, both require the approval of the Senate, as do the appointments of judges and other principal officers. And while the President serves as Commander in Chief, Article I assigns Congress the power to declare war, to raise and support armies, to provide and maintain a navy, to make rules concerning captures, and to make rules governing land and naval forces.

Article III establishes an independent judiciary with life tenure and protected compensation. The Framers defined the judicial power so that the federal courts would decide cases, such as disputes between states or their respective citizens, that help to ensure uniform application of federal law. In addition, Article III assigns federal courts the power to decide cases arising under the Constitution, a function we discuss throughout this book. As with legislative and executive power, the Framers situated the judicial power within various checks and balances, including presidential appointment and Senate confirmation of federal judges, Congress's impeachment power, and a degree of legislative control over the lower courts and the Supreme Court's appellate jurisdiction.

Liberty and protection against government oppression

In addition to the need for a more effective national government, the Framers were well aware of the awesome power of government to suppress dissent and restrict liberty. Although many of the liberty-protecting features of the 1789 Constitution are structural, the Framers also thought it appropriate to include several specific protections against government abuse. For example, Article III, Section 2 guarantees all defendants in federal criminal cases the right to trial by jury. In addition, Article I, Section 9 guarantees access to habeas corpus and prohibits the enactment of bills of attainder or ex post facto laws. Further, it is significant that even before the Constitution was amended or interpreted to impose general constraints on state governments, Article I, Section 10 prohibited states from passing bills of attainder or ex post facto laws. By creating an independent judiciary, the Framers also sought to ensure that individual rights would not be entirely dependent on current popular will.

Despite its many commitments to individual liberty, the original Constitution was deeply flawed in its express recognition and permission of slavery. Article I, Section 9 prohibited Congress from banning the slave trade until 1808; the Three-Fifths Clause of Article I, Section 2 accounted for slavery in allocating seats in the House of Representatives and the Electoral College; and the Fugitive Slave Clause of Article IV, Section 2 conscripted non–slave states into returning escaped slaves into bondage. Given the glaring incongruity between slavery and the "Blessings of Liberty" mentioned in the Preamble, it is unsurprising that the most far-reaching transformations in our constitutional history—through the amendment process and through judicial, legislative, and popular interpretation—have sought to remedy the Framers' failure to fully secure the promises of liberty and equality.

Democracy and opportunity

The Constitution also responds to democratic values that were central to the Framers' complaints about the British Crown. The qualifications clauses of Article I, for example, set out the exclusive eligibility criteria for members of Congress. They require only that Representatives and Senators be citizens of the United States, residents of the state they represent, and over the age of twenty-five and thirty, respectively. In this respect, the Constitution marked a clear departure from hereditary and class-based leadership, and from many existing state constitutions that restricted eligibility for elected office. Notably, the Framers expressly rejected proposals that would have conditioned eligibility for Congress on property ownership. As Madison explained, "the door of this part of the federal government is open to merit of every description, whether native or adoptive, whether young or old, and without regard to poverty or wealth, or to any particular profession of religious faith."[8]

The prohibition on titles of nobility in Article I, Section 10 and the prohibition on any religious test for public office in Article VI similarly disclaim the idea that family background or faith should affect citizens' ability to participate equally in public life. Further, Article IV, Section 4 requires the United States to guarantee to every state a republican form of government.

To be sure, the 1789 Constitution in some ways did not fully implement democratic values. For example, in order to avoid a potentially fractious disagreement over eligibility to vote, the Framers left the definition of suffrage to the states. In practice, this meant that a majority of Americans were excluded from full participation in self-government based on their race, sex, wealth, literacy, social status, or other criteria that we now understand to be illegitimate in a democratic society. Moreover, the express legalization of slavery could not be reconciled with the ideal of a democratic nation dedicated to freedom and equality.

THE BILL OF RIGHTS

Beyond the original Constitution, subsequent amendments express commitments to a series of fundamental values, beginning with the Bill of Rights. For several reasons, the Framers in 1787 had declined to include a written bill of rights in the Constitution. First, it was broadly understood that fundamental rights of individual liberty were, as the Declaration of Independence had asserted, "inalienable, indefeasible rights inherent in all people by virtue of their humanity"[9] and not dependent upon any express declaration. A bill of rights was thought unnecessary because it would merely affirm the natural existence of rights already in force.[10] A second concern was that a written bill of rights would not, as a practical matter, restrain the will of popular majorities. In a self-governing republic, some argued, respect for individual rights and liberties depends primarily on the checks and balances in a well-structured government and on the virtue of the people and their representatives. Third, many feared that any enumeration of rights would be incomplete and, in future generations, would be vulnerable to the inference that the Constitution does not protect rights that are not enumerated. "Thus a bill of rights might operate as a snare, rather than a protection" when it provides "an enumeration of a great many [rights], but an omission of some."[11]

Important as these arguments were, several states, including Massachusetts and Virginia, refused to ratify the Constitution without an assurance that it would include a national bill of rights. Proponents of such a bill answered the foregoing concerns with compelling arguments of their own. First, they argued, the omission of a bill of rights rendered those rights insecure and ever-vulnerable to factious majorities or unscrupulous leaders who might refuse to recognize their authority. Incorporating rights into the constitutional text would help safeguard their permanence and vitality.

Second, enforcement of a bill of rights would be greatly aided by independent courts that "will consider themselves in a peculiar manner the guardians of those rights" and that "will be naturally led to resist every encroachment upon rights expressly stipulated for in the constitution."[12] The concept of judicial review, though somewhat controversial at the time, provided an important answer to the objection that a written bill of rights would have little practical effect.

Third, the practical importance of a bill of rights also included its educative function. Madison, who initially opposed the idea of a bill of rights, later acknowledged that stating rights explicitly in the Constitution would have "a tendency to impress some degree of respect for them, to establish the public opinion in their favor, and rouse the attention of the whole community... [and thereby serve as] one mean to controul the majority from those acts to which they might be otherwise inclined."[13]

Given the widely shared understanding among the Founding generation that individual rights and liberties are "not annexed to us by parchments and seals" but rather "founded on the immutable maxims of reason and justice,"[14] the concern that enumerating some rights would leave others unprotected had particular weight. In response, Thomas Jefferson argued in a letter to James Madison that "[i]f we cannot secure all our rights, let us secure what we can."[15] Although Madison did not disagree, he thought it crucial to address the concern directly. In 1789, as part of the bill of rights he presented for consideration in the House of Representatives, Madison proposed a specific provision to make clear that the bill of rights did not comprise an exhaustive list of fundamental rights. That provision, ratified as the Ninth Amendment, states: "The enumeration in the Constitution, of certain rights, shall not be construed to deny or disparage others retained by the people."[16]

With this understanding of the context leading to adoption of the Bill of Rights, let us now look briefly at its familiar provisions. Some provisions focus on individual dignity and autonomy—for example, the First Amendment's protection of the free exercise of religion and the Sixth Amendment's guarantee of trial rights for criminal defendants. Other provisions promote democratic account-ability and control—for example, the First Amendment's protection of the rights of assembly and petitioning the government for redress of grievances. Many provisions in the Bill of Rights contribute to both values. Freedom of speech, for example, furthers both indi-vidual dignity and collective democratic activity. So too does the Fourth Amendment's protection against unreasonable searches and seizures, which reflected the Framers' distrust of the King's use of general warrants to attack political dissidents. The militia clause of the Second Amendment and the jury clauses of the Fifth, Sixth, and Seventh Amendments also serve to ensure citizen participation in critical government activity, thereby reinforcing the democratic character of individual rights protections.

Like the original Constitution, the Bill of Rights uses language with varying levels of specificity. Some protections have determinate language—for example, the $20 threshold for the Seventh Amendment right to a jury trial and the warrant requirements specified in the Fourth Amendment. However, other provisions use general language—for example, the Fourth Amendment protection against "unreasonable" searches and seizures, the Fifth Amendment guarantee of "due process of law," and the Eighth Amendment prohibition on "cruel and unusual punishments." The open-textured quality of these phrases is significant because the Framers could have specified, for example, the particular punishments they intended to forbid under the Eighth Amendment. But they chose not to do so, leaving open the punishments that might violate the prohibition in the future. The Framers' choice of general language again demonstrates their concern that a written enumeration of rights should not unduly limit the scope of inalienable rights and liberties we possess.

THE RECONSTRUCTION AMENDMENTS: AMERICA'S SECOND FOUNDING

The amendments ratified after the Civil War worked profound changes in the Constitution. For eight decades, the nation had struggled with the issue of slavery, adopting various legislative compromises and accommodations that, like the slavery provisions in the 1789 Constitution, proved inherently unstable. The Supreme Court's proslavery decisions purporting to resolve the issue only inflamed it further,[17] underscoring the impossibility of any legal or political middle ground. The failure of the Founding-era Constitution to abolish slavery was no mere imperfection; it eventually imperiled the very existence of the Union. As Abraham Lincoln observed in his 1858 *House Divided* speech, the growing nation "cannot endure permanently half slave and half free.... It will become all one thing, or all the other. Either the opponents of slavery will arrest the further spread of it, and place it where the public mind shall rest in the belief that it is in the course of ultimate extinction; or its advocates will push it forward, till it shall become alike lawful in all the States, old as well as new—North as well as South."[18]

The Constitution's most forceful and explicit commitments to human freedom, dignity, and equality emerged from the Civil War, the deadliest conflict in American history. Over four grueling years, what began as a war to preserve the Union became also a war to end slavery. In fact, ending slavery, at least in Confederate territory, became a vital element of the Union strategy to win the war. This was the premise of President Lincoln's Emancipation Proclamation, declaring all slaves in rebel-controlled areas to be "forever free" and calling on the new freedmen to "be received into the armed service of the United States."[19] Some 180,000 black men—over one-fifth of the nation's black male population under age forty-five—served in the Union army and, through their service and sacrifice, "played a crucial role not only in winning the Civil War, but in defining the war's consequences."[20] Having borne arms and given their lives for the Union cause, black soldiers earned for black people throughout the nation not only freedom from bondage, but also a new stature, a new sense of worth and potential, and an incontrovertible claim to be included among "We the People of the United States."

When it came time to memorialize the accomplishments of the war, the Reconstruction Congress moved quickly and decisively to ban slavery. But the constitutional transformation went much further, amounting to what many have called America's Second Founding.

Ratified in December of 1865, eight months after Appomattox, the Thirteenth Amendment declares: "Neither slavery nor involuntary servitude, except as a punishment for crime whereof the party shall have been duly convicted, shall exist within the United States, or any place subject to their jurisdiction." The words the Framers chose are noteworthy in several respects. First, the amendment prohibits not only "slavery," the immediate concern of the Civil War, but also "involuntary servitude," a term "of larger meaning than slavery."[21] Second, the prohibition applies not only "within the United States" but also in "any place subject to their jurisdiction," including U.S. territories. Third, the prohibition is phrased as a direct injunction against slavery and involuntary servitude; it is not limited to state action.[22]

Taken together, the sweeping terms of the Thirteenth Amendment forbid debt peonage and other arrangements, whether private or public, that replicate the conditions of slavery,[23] and they signal the amendment's applicability beyond the specific context of state-sanctioned enslavement of black Americans. As the Supreme Court observed early on, the amendment "forbids any other kind of slavery, now or hereafter. If Mexican peonage or the Chinese coolie labor system shall develop slavery of the Mexican or Chinese race within our territory, this amendment may safely be trusted to make it void."[24] Through the broad language chosen by the Framers, the Thirteenth Amendment expresses a fundamental commitment to human freedom.

Further, the Thirteenth Amendment contains a second sentence: "Congress shall have power to enforce this article by appropriate legislation." The novelty of this provision (and the parallel enforcement provisions of the Fourteenth and Fifteenth Amendments) deserves emphasis. Up to this point, no provision in the Constitution had expressly assigned to Congress the power to enforce a constitutional guarantee, and the first twelve amendments were adopted largely to limit the scope of federal authority.[25] Now, instead of limiting federal power in order to protect individual rights, the Framers sought to protect individual rights by *expanding* federal power. And instead of leaving enforcement of the ban on slavery and involuntary servitude up to the courts, the Framers—many of whom had witnessed the debacle of *Dred Scott*[26]—envisioned that Congress would play a leading role.

Signaling the breadth of the new power, the Framers chose the familiar phrase "Congress shall have power" used throughout the Constitution to define broad grants of lawmaking authority.[27] Moreover, the reference to "appropriate legislation" echoes the term that Chief Justice Marshall used in *McCulloch v. Maryland* to define the expansive scope of Congress's power under the Necessary and Proper Clause.[28] As the Supreme Court has made clear, Congress's enforcement power under the Thirteenth Amendment extends not only to state action but also to private conduct, and not only to eradicating slavery but also to "determin[ing] what are the badges and the incidents of slavery, and...translat[ing] that determination into effective legislation."[29]

With this new power, the Reconstruction Congress took aim at the Black Codes enacted by many southern states to keep newly freed blacks from exercising basic civil rights. Four months after the Thirteenth Amendment was ratified, Congress passed the Civil Rights Act of 1866 over President Johnson's veto.[30] The act provided that "all persons born in the United States and not subject to any foreign power, excluding Indians not taxed, are hereby declared to be citizens of the United States." It further declared that all citizens "shall have the same right...to make and enforce contracts, to sue, be parties, and give evidence, to inherit, purchase, lease, sell, hold, and convey real and personal property, and to full and equal benefit of all laws and proceedings for the security of person and property, as is enjoyed by white citizens, and shall be subject to like punishment, pains, and penalties, and to none other, any law, statute, ordinance, regulation, or custom, to the contrary notwithstanding."

Before and after the Civil Rights Act was passed, however, there were doubts as to whether it exceeded Congress's power under the

Thirteenth Amendment. To resolve those doubts, Congress considered a series of new proposals that would eventually become the Fourteenth Amendment in 1868. Although the immediate object of the Fourteenth Amendment was to place the Civil Rights Act on a secure constitutional footing, the Framers once again chose general language to establish a set of fundamental principles with broader applicability.

The first sentence of the Fourteenth Amendment declares: "All persons born or naturalized in the United States, and subject to the jurisdiction thereof, are citizens of the United States and of the State wherein they reside." With these words—"the first explicit *constitutional* definition of American citizenship"[31]—the Fourteenth Amendment overturned the *Dred Scott* decision and significantly expanded the political community comprising the new postwar nation. Importantly, this definition of citizenship "codified a profound nationalization of American identity."[32] Whereas national citizenship was widely thought to be derivative of state citizenship before the Civil War, the Fourteenth Amendment nationalizes our political identity as "citizens of the United States" and makes the federal government the ultimate guarantor of our most fundamental rights.

The Fourteenth Amendment goes on to say: "No State shall make or enforce any law which shall abridge the privileges or immunities of citizens of the United States...." Whereas the Bill of Rights protects individual liberty against national power, the Privileges or Immunities Clause protects the fundamental rights of American citizens against *state* power. Further, the leading sponsors of the Fourteenth Amendment explained that, in addition to the rights specified in the Civil Rights Act of 1866, the "privileges" and "immunities" of American citizens include the various rights and freedoms protected by the Bill of Rights.[33] In choosing to use general language, the Framers of the Fourteenth Amendment—like the Founding-era Framers before them—also understood that the fundamental rights we possess cannot be exhaustively enumerated and thus left the scope of such rights open to future interpretation.[34] The same is true of the general wording of the Fourteenth Amendment's additional injunctions: "nor shall any State deprive any person of life, liberty, or property, without due process of law; nor deny to any person within its jurisdiction the equal protection of the laws." The extension of due process and equal protection guarantees to all "persons," not only to citizens, further illustrates the Framers' intent to establish broad principles that transcend the specific applications encompassed at the time of their enactment.

As with the Thirteenth Amendment, the Fourteenth Amendment gives Congress the "power to enforce, by appropriate legislation, the provisions of this article." Through this enforcement clause, "the draftsmen sought to grant to Congress, by a specific provision applicable to the Fourteenth Amendment, the same broad powers expressed in the Necessary and Proper Clause."[35] By authorizing Congress to enforce explicit limitations on state power, the Fourteenth Amendment fundamentally revised the balance of power between the federal government and the states. As the principal author of the amendment observed, "the powers of the States have been limited and the powers of Congress extended."[36] Equally important, the enforcement clause altered the horizontal separation of powers by empowering Congress, independently of the courts, to give concrete, practical meaning to the broadly worded guarantees of citizenship and its "privileges or immunities," "due process of law," and "equal protection of the laws." Not only did the Framers understand that these general principles would require interpretation in order to be made effective; they recognized that the process of interpretation and application must include both judicial elaboration and democratic lawmaking if the principles are to retain their vitality over time.

The last of the Reconstruction Amendments was ratified in 1870. The Fifteenth Amendment provides: "The right of citizens of the United States to vote shall not be denied or abridged by the United States or by any State on account of race, color, or previous condition of servitude." The amendment also empowers Congress "to enforce this article by appropriate legislation." The Fourteenth Amendment had indirectly supported black suffrage by including a federal apportionment penalty for state denial of the franchise to any adult male citizen.[37] But the Fourteenth Amendment's core guarantee of equal citizenship was thought at the time to apply only to *civil* rights as distinguished from the *political* right of voting.[38] To secure black suffrage and thereby integrate the national political community, the Reconstruction Congress, with President Grant's vigorous support, adopted the Fifteenth Amendment. And yet, by banning voting discrimination "on account of race, color, or previous condition of servitude," the Framers again chose broad language transcending the specific context of enactment. As the Supreme Court has explained, the term "race" was understood during the Reconstruction era to apply not only to black Americans but also to ethnic and even some religious minorities.[39]

For all that was accomplished during Reconstruction, however, the task of giving practical effect to the Constitution's bold promises has been and continues to be a challenging work-in-progress. Moreover, the constitutional commitment to equal citizenship was incomplete at its inception: the Fourteenth Amendment secured the status of women as citizens, but the rights of citizenship did not yet disturb the laws of coverture or otherwise protect women against gender discrimination. Indeed, the federal apportionment provision of the Fourteenth Amendment wrote gender inequality into the Constitution by privileging the vote of adult "male citizens."[40] Although women had played leading roles in the struggle for abolition and black suffrage, it would be another fifty years before their own right to equal suffrage gained constitutional recognition, and still another fifty years before women began to enjoy more fully the promise of equal citizenship.

Despite these shortcomings, the Reconstruction Amendments fundamentally transformed both substantive rights and constitutional structure. They established broad principles of liberty and equality, and they codified the nationalization of citizenship and its privileges and immunities. They limited state power while enhancing federal power in order to protect individual rights. And they created a framework of overlapping legislative and judicial power in the enforcement of constitutional rights. Through the Thirteenth, Fourteenth, and Fifteenth Amendments, the nation forged from the crucible of war the central tenets of its Second Founding.

POST-RECONSTRUCTION AMENDMENTS

Since Reconstruction, many constitutional amendments have been more narrowly targeted. For example, the Eighteenth Amendment adopted prohibition, and the Twenty-First Amendment repealed it. The Twentieth Amendment changed the date of the presidential inauguration. The Twenty-Second Amendment limits the President to two terms in office. The Twenty-Fifth Amendment addresses presidential succession in the event of death, resignation, or incapacity. And the Twenty-Seventh Amendment regulates congressional pay.

Even so, several twentieth-century amendments expand constitutional rights and modify constitutional structure in ways that reflect and deepen the principles of the Reconstruction Amendments. Four amendments removed additional barriers to voting and political participation. With language parallel to the

Fifteenth Amendment, the Nineteenth Amendment secured equal voting rights for women in 1920, "mark[ing] the single biggest democratizing event in American history."[41] The Twenty-Third Amendment enfranchised citizens of the District of Columbia in national elections for President and Vice President. The Twenty-Fourth Amendment abolished the poll tax in elections for federal office. And the Twenty-Sixth Amendment lowered the age qualification for voting to eighteen years old.

Moreover, several amendments continued the nationalization of the American polity and the expansion of congressional power. The Sixteenth Amendment authorized Congress to use the taxing power as a vehicle for national redistribution, overruling an 1895 precedent that invalidated a progressive federal income tax.[42] The Seventeenth Amendment superseded the Article I provision for election of Senators by state legislatures and instead mandates the direct election of Senators by statewide popular vote, thereby increasing the democratic accountability of Congress. In addition, each of the four voting rights amendments just mentioned includes a congressional enforcement provision equivalent to those in the Reconstruction Amendments.

. . .

Overall, the Constitution is a profoundly visionary document. It advanced a new model of effective governance and democratic rule. Its text and structure express general principles that further the guiding purposes stated in the Preamble. And the amendment process has enlarged our basic commitments to liberty, equality, and democracy. Our Constitution thus reflects, in a spare outline, the trajectory of a nation continually striving for greater justice.

During each major transformation, the Framers memorialized their constitutional understandings with broad language setting forth expansive principles open to future interpretation. While the

Constitution in 1789 made clear that the national government is one of enumerated powers, the Framers included the Necessary and Proper Clause in order to give Congress wide latitude to execute those powers and thereby meet the nation's needs. The debate over whether to include a national bill of rights reveals as much about the Framers' thinking on fundamental rights as the rights they ultimately chose to specify. In the end, the enumeration of certain rights left open the recognition and protection of others retained by the people, and many of the enumerated rights were themselves phrased as general principles applicable to the challenges and concerns of each new generation. Similarly, the Reconstruction-era Framers established broad and powerful principles that went beyond the goal of ending slavery and securing equal citizenship for black Americans. The authors of the Reconstruction Amendments committed the nation to new promises of liberty, equality, and citizenship, but they did not pretend to know all that those principles would entail. As the country has matured, these broad principles have naturally been the subject of ongoing debate. Each generation has sought to remain faithful to these constitutional commitments through a process of interpretation and enforcement by Congress and the courts. Those institutions, in turn, have been informed by public deliberation and engagement.

With this brief overview of the Constitution's vision and values, we now turn to the subject of constitutional interpretation. As the next chapter will make clear, our central theme is that the practice of constitutional interpretation must be faithful to what the Constitution is: not a legal code, not a lawyer's contract, but a basic charter of government whose practical meaning arises from the continual adaptation of its enduring text and principles to the conditions and challenges facing each generation.

CHAPTER TWO

Judicial Interpretation of the Constitution

THE CONSTITUTION SPEAKS its values and commands to a variety of public officials and to the public at large. Throughout our history, political leaders have taken seriously their sworn duty to uphold the Constitution. Consider, for example, Thomas Jefferson's pardon of those convicted under the Alien and Sedition Acts, Andrew Jackson's veto of legislation reauthorizing the national bank, Harry Truman's executive order desegregating the U.S. military, and the administrative enforcement of *Brown v. Board of Education* under Lyndon Johnson. Or consider Congress's enactment of voting rights legislation during Reconstruction, civil rights legislation during the 1960s and 1970s, or protections for religious freedom in recent decades. In each instance, nonjudicial actors acted on their best understanding of the Constitution's broad principles to uphold individual rights or to define the proper scope of governmental powers and responsibilities.

Still, the judiciary has a special role in our system with respect to constitutional interpretation, even though the Constitution does not explicitly provide for judicial review. The reason is not simply that "[i]t is emphatically the province and duty of the judicial department to say what the law is."[1] That famous line from *Marbury v. Madison*, in the context of 1803, was not an assertion of interpretive supremacy but a claim of interpretive parity: the courts "as well as other departments" are bound by the Constitution and must interpret it when a dispute so requires.[2] Yet two centuries later, the judiciary's unique (though not exclusive) competence and authority to interpret the Constitution have become widely accepted "as a permanent and indispensable feature of our constitutional system."[3] In this way, judicial review itself exemplifies the adaptation of our constitutional system to the structural principle of checks and balances and to the Constitution's purposes of "establish[ing] Justice" and "secur[ing] the Blessings of Liberty."[4]

The interpretive authority of the courts is rooted in a familiar duality. On the one hand, the judiciary by virtue of life tenure enjoys independence from the political branches and public passions of the moment. Insulated from partisan pressures, the judiciary bears a responsibility to render decisions without fear or favor toward the political majority. As Alexander Hamilton said, independent courts serve as an "excellent barrier to the encroachments and oppressions of the representative body," and they play a "peculiarly essential" role in safeguarding individual rights and liberties.[5] On the other hand, the judiciary "has no influence over either the sword or the purse"; it has "neither FORCE nor WILL, but merely judgment."[6] As a practical matter, the voice of the judiciary on constitutional questions must ultimately draw its authority from the public's acceptance of its institutional role, even when its specific decisions are controversial. The Court's judgment must reflect the nation's best understanding of its fundamental values, "[f]or the power of the great constitutional decisions rests upon the accuracy of the Court's perception of this kind of common will and upon the Court's ability, by expressing its perception, ultimately to command a consensus."[7]

Constitutional adjudication thus combines both countermajoritarian and majoritarian elements. In interpreting and applying the Constitution, the judiciary must exercise independence from politics and reflect the common will in order to secure the democratic legitimacy of its decisions. These institutional features frame the challenge that the judiciary uniquely faces in interpreting the Constitution.

CONSTITUTIONAL FIDELITY

The methodology that judges use to interpret the Constitution has garnered significant public attention in recent decades, as judicial nominations, confirmation hearings, and constitutional controversies have enlarged the issue's political salience. In the simplest terms, the debate over methodology has been framed as a contest between two views.

On one side are those who argue that the text of the Constitution should be interpreted and applied as the people who drafted, proposed, and ratified the Constitution would have interpreted and applied it. On this view, modern constitutional controversies should be resolved on the basis of what the framing generation understood the text to mean in application because that understanding is what the people of the United States, acting in their sovereign capacity, endorsed as the supreme law of the land. When judges interpret a constitutional provision, the argument goes, they are bound by this original understanding, which can only be changed through the formal process of constitutional amendment under Article V.

By contrast, others have argued in favor of treating the Constitution as a living document. On this approach, the Constitution is understood to grow and evolve over time as the conditions, needs, and values of our society change. Proponents of this view contend that such evolution is inherent to the constitutional design because the Framers intended the document to serve as a general charter for a growing nation and a changing world. Thus, constitutional interpretation must be informed by contemporary norms and circumstances, not simply by its original meaning.

In this book, we develop a different approach to interpretation that respects the endurance of our written Constitution and explains how its text and principles retain their authority and legitimacy over decades and centuries. Preserving the document's meaning and its democratic legitimacy requires us to interpret it in light of the conditions and challenges faced by succeeding generations. We use the term *constitutional fidelity* to describe this approach. To be faithful to the Constitution is to interpret its words and to apply its principles in ways that sustain their vitality over time. Fidelity to the Constitution requires judges to ask not how its general principles would have been applied in 1789 or 1868, but rather how those principles should be applied today in order to preserve their power and meaning in light of the concerns, conditions, and evolving norms of our society. As Jack Balkin has put it, "if each generation is to be faithful to the Constitution and adopt the Constitution's text and principles as its own, it must take responsibility for interpreting and implementing the Constitution in its own era."[8]

In our legal culture, it is often argued that fidelity to the Constitution requires constancy in interpretation whereas "change betrays infidelity."[9] This rendition of fidelity can be valid when the object of interpretation is one of the Constitution's concrete and precise commands. For example, all bills for raising revenue must originate in the House of Representatives, military appropriations cannot last more than two years, the seat of the national government may not exceed ten square miles, and no person can be elected President more than twice.[10] But many of the Constitution's commitments are not expressed in this way. When it comes to the many provisions that are phrased as broad and general principles, change in application may be necessary to preserve constitutional meaning over time. "Sometimes change is essential for fidelity" whereas "refusing to change in light of changed circumstances would be infidelity."[11]

Justice Brandeis powerfully articulated this point in his famous dissent in *Olmstead v. United States*,[12] a case examining whether the protections of the Fourth and Fifth Amendments apply to private telephone conversations intercepted by law enforcement through wiretapping. The Court held that, because wiretapping did not involve physical trespass upon the defendant's person or property, it did not implicate a search or seizure as those terms were understood when the Fourth Amendment was adopted.[13] "The amendment itself shows that the search is to be of material things—the person, the house, his papers, or his effects" and not "voluntary conversations secretly overheard," the Court said.[14]

Although this view is historically correct insofar as the Framing generation understood Fourth Amendment "searches" to apply only to physical spaces, and "seizures" to apply only to physical things, Justice Brandeis was nonetheless right to reject it. He explained the notion of constitutional fidelity this way:

"We must never forget," said Mr. Chief Justice Marshall in *McCulloch v. Maryland*, "that it is a Constitution we are expounding." Since then this court has repeatedly sustained the exercise of power by Congress, under various clauses of that instrument, over objects of which the fathers could not have dreamed. We have likewise held that general limitations on the powers of government, like those embodied in the due process clauses of the Fifth and Fourteenth Amendments, do not forbid the United States or the states from meeting modern conditions by regulations which a century ago, or even half a century ago, probably would have been rejected as arbitrary and oppressive. Clauses guaranteeing to the individual protection against specific abuses of power, must have a similar capacity of adaptation to a changing world. It was with reference to such a clause that this court said in *Weems v. United States*:

> "Legislation, both statutory and constitutional, is enacted, it is true, from an experience of evils, but its general language should not, therefore, be necessarily confined to the form that evil had theretofore taken. Time works changes, brings into existence new conditions and purposes. Therefore a principle to be vital must be capable of wider application than the mischief which gave it birth. This is peculiarly true of Constitutions. They are not ephemeral enactments, designed to meet passing occasions. They are, to use the words of Chief Justice Marshall, 'designed to approach immortality as nearly as human institutions can approach it.' The future is their care and provision for events of good and bad tendencies of which no prophecy can be made. In the application of a Constitution, therefore, our contemplation cannot be only of what has been but of what may be. Under any other rule a Constitution would indeed be as easy of application as it would be deficient in efficacy and power. Its general principles would have little value and be converted by precedent into impotent and lifeless formulas. Rights declared in words might be lost in reality."[15]

Applying these precepts to the issue of wiretapping, Justice Brandeis continued:

When the Fourth and Fifth Amendments were adopted, "the form that evil had theretofore taken" had been necessarily simple.

Force and violence were then the only means known to man by which a government could directly effect self-incrimination. It could compel the individual to testify—a compulsion effected, if need be, by torture. It could secure possession of his papers and other articles incident to his private life—a seizure effected, if need be, by breaking and entry. Protection against such invasion of the sanctities of a man's home and the privacies of life was provided in the Fourth and Fifth Amendments by specific language. But "time works changes, brings into existence new conditions and purposes." Subtler and more far-reaching means of invading privacy have become available to the government. Discovery and invention have made it possible for the government, by means far more effective than stretching upon the rack, to obtain disclosure in court of what is whispered in the closet. Moreover, "in the application of a Constitution, our contemplation cannot be only of what has been, but of what may be." The progress of science in furnishing the government with means of espionage is not likely to stop with wire tapping. Ways may some day be developed by which the government, without removing papers from secret drawers, can reproduce them in court, and by which it will be enabled to expose to a jury the most intimate occurrences of the home. Advances in the psychic and related sciences may bring means of exploring unexpressed beliefs, thoughts and emotions.... Can it be that the Constitution affords no protection against such invasions of individual security?[16]

Justice Brandeis's reasoning in *Olmstead*, later vindicated in *Katz v. United States*,[17] demonstrates how a changed interpretation in response to changed circumstances can be an act of fidelity to the Constitution. The text of the document must be construed to have the "capacity of adaptation to a changing world"; otherwise, "[r]ights declared in words may be lost in reality."[18]

Of course, any method of constitutional interpretation can be abused. But when the method of constitutional fidelity just illustrated is conscientiously applied, it does not give judges unchecked power to determine what society's values are or to impose their own values on society. Further, the idea that the meaning of the Constitution in application is capable of evolving over time is not license to disregard text or precedent or to undermine the rule of law. As we explain below, these criticisms are more often based on caricatures of judicial decision-making than on a careful examination of the methodology that judges actually use. More fundamentally, they misapprehend the character of the Constitution and the role of courts in maintaining its authority and legitimacy as the nation and the world continually change.

Rather than acknowledge the need to adapt the Constitution's text and principles to evolving social conditions, critics of this approach have sought to reduce constitutional interpretation to something more mechanical or formulaic. Originalism is one such effort; so-called strict construction is another. The first Justice Roberts once described the task of judicial review as requiring nothing more than "lay[ing] the article of the Constitution which is invoked beside the statute which is challenged and...decid[ing] whether the latter squares with the former."[19] The current Chief Justice Roberts declared in his confirmation hearing that "[j]udges are like umpires" whose job is simply "to call balls and strikes."[20]

Although these attempts to simplify constitutional interpretation may have a surface appeal, they do not withstand scrutiny, as we show in this chapter and beyond. Ironically, the significance of Chief Justice Roberts's baseball analogy is actually the opposite of what he intended. Just as baseball players and many fans know that umpires over time have interpreted the strike zone differently in response to changing aspects and contemporary understandings of the game,[21] so too do lawyers, judges, and ordinary citizens know that the faithful application of constitutional principles to new and specific circumstances demands attention to evolving social context.

At the same time, the claim that ours is a "living Constitution" has been vulnerable to the criticism that our Constitution is a written document and, as such, does not grow or evolve except by formal amendment. The metaphor of a "living Constitution" misleadingly suggests that the Constitution itself is the primary site of legal evolution in response to societal change and that the Constitution can come to mean whatever a sufficient number of people think it ought to mean. Describing our Constitution as a "living" document unduly minimizes the fixed and enduring character of its text and principles. We approach the Constitution quite differently. In our view, interpretations, applications, and understandings of the Constitution's text and principles may change, but the Constitution itself does not change unless properly amended. Our approach explains the dynamic character of constitutional law by focusing on how courts, political leaders, and everyday citizens interpret, apply, and adapt our written Constitution.

There has never been one and only one legitimate, mechanical, and timeless way to derive constitutional meaning, and notably the Constitution itself does not prescribe a specific method of interpretation. The 1789 Founders, over half of whom were lawyers or had some legal education, were no doubt aware of long-standing debates over how to interpret legal texts, yet they declined to specify any interpretive rules or guidelines. It is thus no surprise that, from the Founding to the present day, arguments about what the Constitution requires, permits, and prohibits have always looked to multiple sources of wisdom and authority: the Constitution's text and structure, the framing and ratification history, the broad purposes and principles reflected in the document, the lessons of precedent and historical experience, our shared and evolving popular understandings of the Constitution, and the practical consequences of any given interpretation. Throughout our history, these sources have been invoked by judges of every stripe, even those who purportedly adhere to originalism or strict construction. In our interpretive tradition, reading the Constitution's text and principles in light of changing norms and societal consequences is not radical. What is radical is an insistence that the Constitution's meaning is static and divorced from contemporary context. That approach, as we illustrate throughout this book, cannot explain many of the constitutional understandings we cherish today. When static interpretation fails to preserve the vitality of the Constitution's text and principles, our nation's judges have typically rejected it in favor of the method of constitutional fidelity.

AN EXAMPLE: INTERPRETING THE SECOND AMENDMENT

A recent case, *District of Columbia v. Heller*,[22] illustrates the multifaceted approach to constitutional interpretation that is routinely applied by judges across the ideological spectrum. As *Heller* shows, it is caricature to say that conservative judges decide cases based only on text and original meaning, without considering social context or practical consequences,[23] or that liberal judges ignore text and history, and instead decide cases based on contemporary values or their own policy preferences. What divided the Court in *Heller* was not interpretive methodology but rather the substantive accounts of text, history, structure, precedent, contemporary norms, and social consequences that the dueling Justices offered. We do not weigh the merits of the contrasting opinions in *Heller* here. Instead, we simply describe the opinions in order to elucidate the methodology our courts have commonly used in constitutional interpretation.

Heller involved the Second Amendment, which says: "A well regulated Militia, being necessary to the security of a free State, the right of the people to keep and bear Arms, shall not be infringed." The issue before the Court was whether the amendment barred the District of Columbia from enforcing its law prohibiting handgun possession against individuals who wish to keep handguns in their homes for self-defense.

All of the Justices—the five in the majority as well as the four dissenters—devoted a great deal of attention to parsing the text of the amendment. Both sides relied on dictionaries, contemporaneous commentaries, and the work of grammarians and linguists to unpack the words of the amendment. The majority read "the right of the people" to refer to a right possessed by individuals acting on their own, akin to the Fourth Amendment "right of the people to be secure...against unreasonable searches and seizures." And it read the phrase "keep and bear Arms" to refer generally to the possession and use of weapons, including for hunting and individual self-defense. The dissenters, by contrast, read "the right of the people" to protect individuals engaged in collective action through participation in the militia, akin to the First Amendment "right of the people peaceably to assemble," which also protects a collective activity. And it construed "keep and bear Arms" as a reference to military use of weapons.

Each side also defended its reading by invoking historical evidence, including English antecedents of the Second Amendment, the amendment's drafting history, analogous provisions in state constitutions and statutes during the colonial and Founding eras, and postratification commentary in case law and other published sources. The majority argued that the amendment's opening clause simply "announces the purpose for which the right was codified" and "does not suggest that preserving the militia was the only reason Americans valued the ancient right."[24] Among other sources, it cited contemporaneous state constitutional provisions expressly protecting an individual right to keep and bear arms for self-defense to demonstrate the prevailing understanding of the scope of the right.[25] Meanwhile, the dissenters observed that the Framers considered but rejected more expansive language concerning the right to keep and bear arms, including several proposals from state ratifying conventions that would have clearly protected civilian use and possession of weapons.[26] According to the dissenters, the drafting history and the language that was ultimately adopted reflected the Founding generation's "overriding concern about the potential threat to state sovereignty that a federal standing army would pose, and a desire to protect the States' militias as the means by which to guard against that danger."[27]

Both sides also grappled with precedent, especially the 1939 case *United States v. Miller*, in which a unanimous Court held that possession of a sawed-off shotgun is not protected by the Second Amendment "[i]n the absence of any evidence tending to show that [its] possession or use...at this time has some reasonable relationship to the preservation or efficiency of a well regulated militia."[28] The dissenters understood *Miller* to turn "on the basic difference between the military and nonmilitary use and possession of guns,"[29] with the latter falling outside the scope of Second Amendment protection. The majority, by contrast, read *Miller* to say that the Second Amendment right "extends only to certain types of weapons," namely, "those weapons...typically possessed by law-abiding citizens for lawful purposes."[30]

Moreover, in applying the Second Amendment to the District of Columbia handgun ban, both sides in *Heller* demonstrated that the modern-day application of a constitutional principle must take into account contemporary social practices and anticipated social consequences. Despite Justice Scalia's insistence elsewhere that the Constitution's meaning is determined by how members of the

Founding generation would have applied it,[31] his opinion for the Court in *Heller* ultimately adopts an interpretation that depends on current social norms and conditions. This is apparent from the Court's answers to two questions arising under its view that the Second Amendment protects a right to bear arms for self-defense as well as military purposes: What kinds of arms are covered by the amendment? And what constitutes a forbidden infringement?

As to the first question, the Court squarely rejected the idea that the word "Arms" covers only those weapons that would have been covered in 1791:

> Some have made the argument, bordering on the frivolous, that only those arms in existence in the 18th century are protected by the Second Amendment. We do not interpret constitutional rights that way. Just as the First Amendment protects modern forms of communications, *e.g.*, *Reno v. American Civil Liberties Union*, 521 U.S. 844, 849 (1997), and the Fourth Amendment applies to modern forms of search, *e.g.*, *Kyllo v. United States*, 533 U.S. 27, 35–36 (2001), the Second Amendment extends, prima facie, to all instruments that constitute bearable arms, even those that were not in existence at the time of the founding.[32]

Why is that so? It is because many words in the Constitution are properly read to stand for broad principles—here, the right to use technology, or "instruments," for self-protection—whose practical meaning depends on interpretation that is responsive to evolving social conditions, including advances in technology.

At the same time, the Court recognized that not all weapons available today fall within the Second Amendment's scope. As a historical matter, the Court explained, the amendment accommodated the tradition of prohibiting the carrying of "dangerous and unusual weapons" and covered only arms "of the kind in common use at the time," since those were the arms that men called for militia service would have brought with them.[33] With this reading, the Court reaffirmed its holding in *Miller* that the Second Amendment does not protect possession of a sawed-off shotgun.[34] But what distinguishes protected handguns from unprotected sawed-off shotguns? Nothing straightforwardly textual or historical. Instead, the difference lies in contemporary social practice—or, as Justice Scalia put it, the fact that "handguns are the most popular weapon chosen by Americans for self-defense in the home."[35] By limiting the Second Amendment's protection to weapons "in common use at the time," the Court interpreted the constitutional principle to have the "capacity of adaptation to a changing world."[36] Indeed, just as a sawed-off shotgun is not what "the American people have considered...to be the quintessential self-defense weapon,"[37] the American people might some day reach the same conclusion about handguns perhaps believing that the risks they present inside the home exceed their potential benefits to self-defense. Evolving social norms can change the ambit of the Second Amendment's protection as interpreted by the Court.

Moreover, even with respect to handguns, the Court in *Heller* indicated its receptivity to a broad range of government regulation, including "longstanding prohibitions on the possession of firearms by felons and the mentally ill, or laws forbidding the carrying of firearms in sensitive places such as schools and government buildings, or laws imposing conditions and qualifications on the commercial sale of arms."[38] Although the amendment itself gives no indication whether such regulations "infringe" the right to bear arms, their validity does not appear to be in doubt. Why? The most plausible reason is that such regulations reflect an acceptable balance between "the interests protected by the Second Amendment on one side and the governmental public-safety concerns on the other."[39] As the Framers understood, and as the Court has recognized in many areas, no right has absolute applicability regardless of how severely it may clash with other important values.[40] Thus, attention to real-world consequences—or to the reasonableness of legislative judgments concerning real-world consequences[41]—is an ordinary part of constitutional adjudication. The Court's readiness to uphold various firearms regulations simply illustrates this point, despite Justice Scalia's purported disavowal of an "interest-balancing" approach.[42] Although the majority and the dissenters ultimately disagree on the validity of the District of Columbia handgun ban, the difference between the two sides is not that one engages in interest-balancing while the other does not. It is that one side does so "explicitly"[43] while the other does not.

JUDICIAL METHODOLOGY: FIVE OBSERVATIONS

From *Heller* and other cases we discuss throughout this book, we see that judges generally look to a variety of sources to elucidate the meaning of the Constitution. These sources include the document's text, history, structure, and purposes, as well as judicial precedent. They also include contemporary social practices, evolving public understandings of the Constitution's values, and the societal consequences of any given interpretation. The latter sources of meaning, no less than the former, are legitimate components of the methodology that courts use when applying the Constitution's general principles to present-day problems.

Five observations help to summarize the essential features of this methodology. First, constitutional meaning is a function of both text and context. In many instances, a court cannot be faithful to the principle embodied in the text unless it takes into account the social context in which the text is interpreted. The relevant context includes not only social conditions and facts about the world, but also public values and social understandings as reflected in statutes, the common law, and other parts of the legal landscape. Just as the range of "Arms" protected by the Second Amendment and the types of "searches and seizures" covered by the Fourth Amendment depend upon social norms and practices, so too do the definitions of interstate "commerce" under Article I, "cruel and unusual punishment" under the Eighth Amendment, and "equal protection" and "liberty" under the Fourteenth Amendment. In these and other areas, a court that ignores changes in context will end up changing—and defeating—the meaning of the text.[44] The words of the Constitution must be read in context, and interpretations must sometimes change as the context changes, if the meaning of the text is to be preserved over time. That is what fidelity to the Constitution requires.

Second, constitutional fidelity serves not only to preserve the Constitution's meaning over time, but also to maintain its authority and legitimacy. The words and principles of the Constitution endure as our fundamental law because they have been made relevant to the conditions and challenges of each generation through an ongoing process of interpretation. As we show in later chapters, an interpretive approach that takes into account social context has been central to the process by which each generation of Americans comes to see the Constitution's text and principles as its own.

Third, in legitimizing the consideration of evolving norms and practical consequences in constitutional interpretation, the method of constitutional fidelity is not a license for judicial activism, for such considerations have often served to constrain, not enlarge, the judicial role in our democracy. Consider, for example, the demise of the *Lochner* doctrine and the erosion of judicially imposed limits on federal power as our courts came to understand the severity of the Great Depression and the government response required to ensure a fair and efficient economy.[45] Consider also the judicial deference to popular and legislative understandings of constitutional equality in the 1960s and 1970s that undergird our transformative civil rights laws.[46] *Heller*, too, demonstrates the constraining effect of judicial attention to social practice and widely shared understandings. While recognizing an individual right to bear arms for self-defense, the Court limited the right to cover only weapons "in common use" today and to exempt "long-standing" regulations on commercial sales, possession by felons and the mentally ill, and the carrying of firearms in sensitive places.[47]

Fourth, the interpretive methodology we describe does not dictate a single "right answer" in every case. As the contrasting opinions in *Heller* demonstrate, the multiple sources of constitutional meaning do not always yield unambiguous inferences as to how a given constitutional provision or principle should be applied. But once we recognize that it is appropriate for judges to examine those sources, we can free ourselves from distracting debates over methodology and instead focus our attention on the substantive reasoning in support of one interpretation or another. Thus, in *Heller*, the key questions are not whether it is important to parse the text, but rather who offers the best reading of the text; not whether it is appropriate to consult the drafting history, but rather who marshals the strongest historical evidence; not whether it is necessary to acknowledge precedent, but rather who provides the most faithful reading of precedent; and not whether contemporary context and consequences must be taken into account, but rather who provides the most persuasive account of the context and consequences. As the Framers understood, the application of constitutional principles to difficult problems often involves conflict among important values and requires an irreducible element of judgment.[48] What is important is that courts exercise their judgment with "transparency" and "lay[] bare [their] reasoning for all to see and criticize."[49] Such transparency enables the citizenry to assess the correctness or wisdom of judicial decision-making and is therefore central to the legitimacy of constitutional interpretation by independent courts.

Fifth, our view of constitutional fidelity is not at odds with originalism if originalism is understood to mean a commitment to the underlying principles that the Framers' words were publicly understood to convey, as opposed to the Framers' expectations of how those principles would have applied at the time they were adopted. In explaining this view of originalism, a number of scholars have distinguished between "the [original] expected application of constitutional texts, which is not binding law, and the original meaning, which is."[50] When "original meaning" refers to the core principles that underlie the Constitution's broad and general terms, fidelity to the Constitution requires that its original meaning be preserved over time. Adherence to original expected applications often fails to preserve original meaning because it is "[b]lind to the effect of context on meaning."[51] Applications of constitutional text and principles must be open to adaptation and change if the Constitution's original meaning is to retain its vitality as the conditions and norms of our society become ever more distant from those of the Founding generation.

Originalism, however, is not widely understood as a commitment to original meaning as defined above. The significance of originalism as a polemic in ongoing debates over judicial methodology is rooted in the claim that judges should adhere to a historically fixed understanding of what principles the Constitution contains *and* how the Framing generation would have applied those principles to specific situations. We thus conclude this chapter by discussing the problems with originalism so understood and also by examining the oft-heard calls for "judicial restraint" and "strict construction" in constitutional interpretation.

ORIGINALISM

In the hands of some judges, most notably Justice Scalia, originalism requires a judge confronted with a constitutional dispute to ask how informed individuals living at the time the Constitution was ratified would have applied it to a similar dispute. This methodology has led Justice Scalia to conclude, for example, that the Eighth Amendment prohibits only those punishments considered cruel and unusual according to the "moral perceptions *of the time*" and not to ones "we consider cruel today."[52] It has also led to the claim that the Establishment Clause merely bars Congress from establishing a national church and does not declare a general principle of separation between church and state.[53] In deciding whether a posting of the Ten Commandments in a county courthouse violates the First Amendment, Justice Scalia recently argued, "[w]hat is more probative of the meaning of the Establishment Clause than the actions of the very Congress that proposed it, and of the first President charged with observing it? ... [T]hese official actions show *what it meant*."[54] Originalism thus posits that the best way to ascertain the Constitution's meaning in particular cases is to explore how the members of the Framing generation would have applied them to such cases.

As mentioned earlier, the original understanding of a particular constitutional provision, no less than the text of the provision itself, is an important consideration in constitutional interpretation. For example, it is surely relevant to contemporary debates over affirmative action that the same Congress that enacted the Fourteenth Amendment also enacted a variety of social welfare programs expressly designed to benefit black Americans.[55] It is likewise relevant to modern questions of executive power that the Founding generation crafted our system of checks and balances largely to avoid concentrating too much power in executive hands.[56] But original understandings such as these cannot alone be dispositive, for originalism as a complete and exclusive theory of constitutional interpretation founders on two decisive objections.

The first is a problem of indeterminacy, which itself has several layers. To begin with, it is unclear how a judge is to decide whose original understanding should be controlling.[57] In deciding what "due process of law" means in a particular case, should a judge examine what James Madison meant when he drafted the Fifth Amendment, what the House and Senate meant when they passed it and sent it to the states, what the ratifiers in each state meant when they voted for it, what the phrase meant when used in other legal settings at the end of the eighteenth century, or something else? Another choice has to do with the information to be examined when determining those persons' understanding. In making sense of an open-ended phrase like "the privileges or immunities of citizens of the United States," should a judge look to how the relevant persons understood the general concept, what specific rights they thought were covered by the term, how they thought a future judge should interpret the term, or something else?

Different originalists have proposed different answers to these questions. But even if there were consensus on whose understanding to consult and what information to seek, an additional layer of indeterminacy arises from the fact that members of the Framing generation did not always share the same understanding of particular constitutional provisions. For example, the question whether Congress had power under the Necessary and Proper Clause to establish a national bank famously produced divergent views among constitutional Framers such as Hamilton, Madison, and Randolph. Likewise, the question whether the Senate can or must approve the removal of officers who have been appointed subject to its advice and consent produced disagreement within each chamber of the First Congress and also between the Senate and the House. In short, the Constitution in several places embodies principles and ideas whose application was indeterminate even among the document's contemporaries.

The problem of indeterminacy is further compounded by the fact that no original understanding could have existed with respect to many modern controversies. For example, the Founding generation could not have foreseen the Fourth Amendment implications of modern surveillance technology. Because many technologies do not involve physical trespass into a protected space, they go beyond the ambit of unlawful intrusions that the Framers apparently had in mind.[58] In response, some originalists argue that historically fixed principles in the Constitution ought to extend to new circumstances that are analogous to original applications. But in that case, why isn't a punishment that is viewed as cruel in contemporary times sufficiently analogous to punishments viewed as cruel in 1791, such that the Eighth Amendment prohibits the former as well as the latter? Opening the door to analogies across generations is premised on treating the Constitution's provisions as expressions of general principle and not as shorthand for a list of specific applications. That is the right way to think about the Constitution, and it underscores why an originalism of expected applications cannot serve as a complete and exclusive method of constitutional interpretation. A principle functions as a mapping of an idea onto the world in which we live. As our world changes, the aspects of the world that give practical meaning to a principle are susceptible to change as well.

A second objection to originalism is that it cannot account for many of the constitutional understandings that Americans take for granted today. The most obvious example is *Brown v. Board of Education*. The Framing generation most likely did not believe the Fourteenth Amendment outlawed segregation; at best, they had no clear view on the issue. Further, it is doubtful that the Framers believed the Fourteenth Amendment protected women against gender discrimination. However, these elementary propositions are now settled features of our constitutional law. An originalism of expected applications cannot explain the legitimacy of these basic understandings and instead regards them either as mistakes or as exceptions to sound constitutional interpretation.[59]

More broadly, the history of our country has been marked by an enlarging appreciation of the individuality and equal dignity of all persons, of the pernicious effect of stereotypes and intolerance in limiting human potential, of the role of government in addressing the nation's challenges, and of the need to continually update the protection of individuals from arbitrary government action. It is no surprise that our society's understanding of the proper application of many constitutional principles has enlarged as well. Originalism would create a wide divergence between how many constitutional principles are widely understood today and how those principles are implemented as a matter of constitutional doctrine.

The infirmities of originalism serve to underscore that the Framers' act of constitutional creation was also an important act of delegation—an expectation that future generations would ascertain the specific meaning of concepts and principles only dimly specifiable at the time of ratification. Perhaps for this reason, Madison recognized that many provisions of the Constitution would be considered "more or less obscure and equivocal, until their meaning be liquidated and ascertained by a series of particular discussions and adjudications."[60] Similarly, Hamilton said that only time "can mature and perfect so compound a system, liquidate the meaning of all the parts, and adjust them to each other in a harmonious and consistent whole."[61]

Madison and Hamilton's view that the specific meaning of the Constitution's provisions would develop through a process of interpretation coheres with the Framers' decision to make the Constitution difficult to amend. Under Article V, constitutional amendments can be enacted only with the approval of large supermajorities.

The Framers understood that "maintaining stable agreement on the fundamental organizing principles of government has a number of clear political advantages over a system whose basic structure is always up for grabs."[62] Madison explained that the amendment process should be reserved "for certain great and extraordinary occasions" because "frequent appeals [to the popular amendment process] would, in a great measure, deprive the government of that veneration which time bestows on every thing, and without which perhaps the wisest and freest governments would not possess the requisite stability."[63]

The Framers succeeded in creating a remarkably stable document. Aside from the ten amendments comprising the Bill of Rights, which were introduced in the First Congress to fulfill a commitment made during the ratification debates and essentially comprise part of the original document, the Constitution has been amended formally only seventeen times, while our nation has continued to evolve and change, often in dramatic ways that the Framers did not anticipate. By using broad language to set forth basic principles of government, the Framers ensured that ongoing interpretation, not formal amendment, would be the primary way that the Constitution would retain its relevance, legitimacy, and authority over time. In our actual constitutional practice, judicial decisions as well as important legislation have played a much larger role than formal amendments in preserving the Constitution's vitality and practical significance as the nation has grown and changed.[64]

Ironically, originalism—by invoking the Framers' understanding of how the Constitution should apply to specific situations—actually diminishes their accomplishment. In writing the Constitution, the Framers sought to vest a set of fundamental principles with authority and permanence. At the same time, they understood that the Constitution could not spell out answers to every important controversy. As revolutionaries themselves, they were not so parochial as to bind future generations to their own specific understandings of broad principles.[65] They chose general language to anchor a set of basic values that the nation could adapt as it grew and changed in unforeseeable ways.[66] The genius of the Framers' accomplishment is not that they had answers to every imaginable challenge facing our society. It is that they correctly anticipated that a constitution written in general terms, open to interpretation and adaptation by succeeding generations, would endure and retain its legitimacy even as the nation experienced profound social, economic, and political transformations.

JUDICIAL RESTRAINT

In addition to originalism, the lexicon of judicial critique has long included calls for "judicial restraint" and condemnation of "judicial activism."[67] These terms have been variously defined, but whatever the definition, it is evident that judicial activism—long wielded as a critique of judicial liberals—appropriately characterizes many decisions of judicial conservatives in recent years.[68] This is true whether judicial activism is defined as lack of deference to democratic decision-making,[69] failure to adhere to constitutional text[70] or original meaning,[71] lack of deference to judicial precedent,[72] selective provision of access to the courts,[73] or the use of judicial power to achieve partisan objectives.[74]

Judicial restraint is an important value, and as mentioned above, the method of constitutional fidelity has served to promote judicial restraint in areas where originalism or strict construction would have licensed antidemocratic judicial activism.[75] But judicial restraint, by itself, is not a meaningful guide to constitutional interpretation. Although we rightly expect unelected judges to be cautious in exercising their power, we also expect an independent judiciary to serve as a crucial bulwark against majoritarian abuse of individual rights. Judicial restraint requires judges to refrain from enacting their own policy preferences into law, but it does not clarify how judges should interpret and apply broad principles such as "liberty," "property," "freedom of speech," or "equal protection of the laws." Faithful application of these and other principles may sometimes require a robust judicial role. Moreover, a commitment to democratic decision-making itself may call for a strong judicial role in circumstances where the democratic process does not function properly.[76] Thus, while the notion of judicial restraint instructs judges to be vigilant against abuses of their own power, it does not provide much guidance as to what interpretive methods or substantive judgments properly fall within the scope of judicial power.

That is why criticizing a decision as judicial activism, whether liberal or conservative, often conveys little of substance beyond the fact that the decision has produced a result with which the critic disagrees. Judges across the ideological spectrum believe in good faith that it is their duty to uphold the Constitution and to apply its principles according to their best understanding of the law. More important than whether a decision exhibits activism or restraint is whether it persuasively construes text, history, structure, and precedent, and properly takes into account social context and practical consequences.

STRICT CONSTRUCTION

At least since Richard Nixon, numerous Presidents and presidential candidates have promised to appoint "strict constructionists" to the bench. President Nixon used the term to indicate his opposition to court-ordered busing and to the Warren Court's interpretation of the rights of criminal defendants. His successors have invoked the term to signal opposition to abortion rights, affirmative action, and government regulation. While campaigning in 2000, George Bush promised to appoint "strict constructionists" in the mold of Justice Scalia and Justice Thomas.[77] In 2008, presidential candidate John McCain cited Chief Justice Roberts and Justice Alito as his models for judicial nominees who will "strictly interpret" the Constitution.[78]

Like critics who denounce judicial activism, however, proponents of strict construction rarely provide a clear definition of the term. It is often said that judges should not "legislate from the bench" and should not "make law" but apply it. Beyond these agreeable platitudes, strict construction seems to suggest a method of interpretation that takes the words of the Constitution literally. In other words, judges must read the Constitution to mean simply what it says, nothing more and nothing less. In this way, its proponents say, strict construction limits judicial discretion.

The problems with this approach are apparent on a moment's reflection. For one thing, the Constitution contains phrases that do not bear a literal reading. The First Amendment, for example, says "Congress shall make no law...abridging the freedom of speech." Does "no law" really mean *no* law, *no* exceptions?[79] And does the directive to "Congress" mean that the First Amendment should not be read to apply to the President or the states?[80] If constitutional interpretation were simply an exercise in literalism, much of First Amendment doctrine would be unnecessary. As another example, consider the Necessary and Proper Clause in Article I. Does the term "necessary" mean that Congress's power is limited to what is truly *necessary*, indispensable, or essential to carrying out the powers of government enumerated in the Constitution? Here again, strict construction has long been rejected.[81]

An additional difficulty has to do with phrases whose meaning is indeterminate. "Equal protection of the laws," for example, may be understood in a variety of ways. What does it mean to strictly construe those words? Justices who are so-called strict constructionists have found the phrase to be compatible with unequal funding of public schools and unequal rates of capital sentencing associated with the race of the crime victim[82]—even though a strictly literal construction of the term "equal" might well be thought to cast constitutional doubt on such disparities. Because the Framers stated the equal protection guarantee in general terms, it is difficult to see how courts could faithfully interpret the phrase without seeking guidance from the Constitution's history, purpose, and structure as well as precedent and evolving social understandings. The same is true of other words in the Constitution such as "due process of law," "unreasonable searches and seizures," and "cruel and unusual punishment." As Justice Holmes explained, the application of constitutional text in specific cases "must be considered in the light of our whole experience and not merely in that of what was said a hundred years ago."[83] Historically, the process of interpreting the broadly worded provisions of the Constitution has more closely resembled common-law adjudication than statutory interpretation.[84] Our constitutional practice has generally heeded Chief Justice Marshall's admonition to treat the Constitution as a charter of general principles lacking "the prolixity of a legal code."[85]

Alternatively, strict construction may mean an interpretive approach that is not literal but narrow. That is, courts should give a narrow construction to the Constitution's general phrases in order to avoid overreaching. But here, too, there are obvious problems. Most important, there is no reason to think that the substantive meaning of the Constitution's open-textured language should always have a narrow scope. The "separate but equal" doctrine is a strict (both literal and narrow) construction of the Equal Protection Clause; the doctrine itself incorporates the constitutional term "equal." Yet all agree that the Equal Protection Clause means something more. The fallacy of "separate but equal" lies not in its implausibility as a parsing of constitutional text, but in its deliberate inattention to the social meaning of segregation and the irreconcilability of that meaning with the Fourteenth Amendment's promise of equal citizenship.[86]

The same objection applies in the context of enumerated powers, where the Supreme Court considered and rejected strict construction early in our constitutional history. In 1824, the Court in *Gibbons v. Ogden* explained:

> What do gentlemen mean, by a strict construction?...If they contend for that narrow construction which, in support or [*sic*] some theory not to be found in the constitution, would deny to the government those powers which the words of the grant, as usually understood, import, and which are consistent with the general views and objects of the instrument; for that narrow construction, which would cripple the government, and render it unequal to the object for which it is declared to be instituted, and to which the powers given, as fairly understood, render it competent; then we cannot perceive the propriety of this strict construction, nor adopt it as the rule by which the constitution is to be expounded.[87]

Notably, the Justices who are most often cited as strict constructionists themselves reject the term. Justice Scalia has called strict constructionism "a degraded form of textualism," declaring: "I am not a strict constructionist, and no one ought to be....A text should not be construed strictly, and it should not be construed leniently; it should be construed reasonably, to contain all that it fairly means."[88] Justice Thomas considers himself an originalist and has not hesitated to construe the text of the Constitution broadly, not strictly, when it comes to executive power and state sovereign immunity.[89] Indeed, even as they decry judicial recognition of unenumerated rights, Justice Thomas, Justice Scalia, and Chief Justice Rehnquist did not flinch when they said that the Eleventh Amendment, which bars *federal* courts from hearing suits "against one of the United States by Citizens of *another* State," merely exemplifies a broader principle of sovereign immunity that "extends beyond the literal text of the Eleventh Amendment" to bar suits under federal law against a state by citizens of the *same* state, even in *state* court.[90]

President Nixon revealed the hollowness of his concern with judicial methodology when, six years before promising to appoint strict constructionists to the bench, he complained that the Supreme Court "had followed its usual pattern of interpreting the Constitution rigidly" in striking down school prayer.[91] Nixon knew well what is now transparent in debates over judicial methodology: strict construction, at bottom, is a political calling card and not a genuine method of constitutional interpretation.

. . .

Ultimately, what accounts for our enduring faith in the Constitution is not that we have rigidly adhered to original understandings frozen in amber or to so-called strict construction of the text. It is that we have continually interpreted the Constitution's language and applied its principles in ways that are faithful to its original purposes and to the social context in which new challenges arise. As we said in chapter 1, the Constitution should be read for what it is—not a legal code or a lawyer's document, but "the basic charter of our society, setting out in spare but meaningful terms the principles of government."[92] As such, the Constitution does not supply a ready answer for every problem or every question that our nation might face. But the American people have kept faith with the Constitution because its text and principles have been interpreted in ways that keep faith with the needs and understandings of the American people.

The balance of this book further describes and defends the interpretive approach we call constitutional fidelity. In chapters 3 through 9, we explain how several constitutional principles have acquired concrete and widely shared meaning throughout our history. We focus on the role of the Supreme Court in the development of constitutional meaning across a variety of areas. In each area, we see how the Court has adapted and applied the Constitution's general principles to the specific challenges that have confronted our nation. In interpreting the Constitution, the Court analyzes text, history, structure, and precedent, but it does not do so in a legal vacuum. It also considers social practices, evolving norms, and practical consequences in order to give concrete, everyday meaning to text and principle. And it looks to the constitutional understandings forged by ordinary Americans and their representatives through vigorous debate and engagement. As we show, many of the fundamental constitutional understandings that we take for granted today came into being through this dynamic process of interpretation.

CHAPTER THREE

. . .

Equality

IN THIS CHAPTER, we illustrate our interpretive approach with examples from the Supreme Court's jurisprudence of equality. We begin with *Brown*, then discuss the evolution of gender equality norms, and conclude with Congress and the Court's shared responsibility for enforcing civil rights.

BROWN

Perhaps no single decision better exemplifies an interpretive approach faithful to the Constitution's vision and values than *Brown v. Board of Education.*[1] For decades, *Brown* has stood as the most honored decision in the Supreme Court's jurisprudence. Today, no judicial nominee could win confirmation, and no legal theory could gain wide acceptance, without embracing the correctness and stature of *Brown*. Thus it is a telling contrast that *Brown* is an easy case from the standpoint of our interpretive approach, whereas

Brown cannot be explained easily, if at all, under originalism or strict construction.

The unanimous *Brown* opinion authored by Chief Justice Earl Warren provides a rich account of constitutional interpretation and the meaning of equality as a constitutional value. What stands out in the Court's reading of the Fourteenth Amendment is its explicit rejection of originalism in favor of an interpretive approach sensitive to historical change and social context. Through *Brown*, we come to understand constitutional equality not as an abstract formula or a narrow idea limited by history, but as a moral principle that guides our public values and responds to the lived reality of contemporary social practices.

Chief Justice Warren began the opinion by noting that the *Brown* cases had been argued in the 1952 Term but then, at the Court's request, reargued in the 1953 Term to address "the circumstances surrounding the adoption of the Fourteenth Amendment in 1868" and, in particular, whether the Congress or the states ratifying the Fourteenth Amendment understood it to abolish segregation in public schools.[2] Although the ratification history was "exhaustively" examined by the parties, by the United States as amicus curiae, and by the Court's own investigation, the Court ultimately found the inquiry into original understanding to be "[a]t best...inconclusive."[3] Because public education in the North and South was rudimentary or nonexistent at the time, the Court explained, "it is not surprising that there should be so little in the history of the Fourteenth Amendment relating to its intended effect on public education."[4]

Chief Justice Warren went on to observe that, although *Plessy v. Ferguson* had upheld the doctrine of "separate but equal," the Court had never resolved the doctrine's applicability to public education. In clear and explicit terms, the Court explained that the answer to the issue presented must come not from an indeterminate quest for original understanding but from a reading of the

Fourteenth Amendment that situates its guarantee of "equal protection of the laws" within a social context that had evolved considerably since its ratification:

> In approaching this problem, we cannot turn the clock back to 1868 when the Amendment was adopted, or even to 1896 when *Plessy v. Ferguson* was written. We must consider public education in the light of its full development and its present place in American life throughout the Nation. Only in this way can it be determined if segregation in public schools deprives these plaintiffs of the equal protection of the laws.[5]

This declaration of interpretive approach served as prologue to *Brown*'s familiar passage describing the contemporary significance of public education for each individual and for our democratic society.[6]

With this historical and social backdrop, the Court then analyzed the constitutionality of school segregation by reference to its actual consequences for black schoolchildren: "To separate them from others of similar age and qualifications solely because of their race generates a feeling of inferiority as to their status in the community that may affect their hearts and minds in a way unlikely ever to be undone."[7] The Court went on to quote the district court's finding that segregation "is usually interpreted as denoting the inferiority of the negro group" and that the sense of inferiority redounds to the educational detriment of black children.[8]

Although the *Brown* opinion focused on the importance of education and the stigmatic harms that segregation imposed on black children, the significance of the decision went further. The Justices clearly understood *Brown* to rest not only on the educational harms of segregation but more broadly on the incompatibility of racial caste with the constitutional meaning of equality. For equality, if it means anything, must mean that it is untenable for "a whole race of people [to find] itself confined within a system which is set up and continued for the very purpose of keeping it in an inferior station."[9] Thus, in the ensuing years, the Court issued a series of unanimous judgments summarily invalidating segregation in public transportation and places of recreation on the authority of *Brown*.[10]

Brown may be faulted for not fully articulating how legalized segregation undermined the full and equal citizenship that the Fourteenth Amendment promised to former slaves and their descendants.[11] But this omission does not obscure its jurisprudential legacy. As an interpretive matter, *Brown* did what *Plessy* refused to do: the Court treated the social meaning of segregation as a relevant—indeed determinative—factor in appraising whether it fulfilled the Constitution's principle of equality. In upholding "separate but equal," *Plessy* artificially distinguished between legal and social equality. Under *Plessy*, so long as the law (in theory) guaranteed equal facilities, racial separation had no legal consequence because whatever stigma it caused was a matter of antecedent attitudes and affinities unstructured by law.[12] The Constitution, *Plessy* held, guaranteed legal but not social equality.

By contrast, *Brown* understood the Constitution to guarantee equality not as an abstract formalism, but as a lived experience in social context. The lived experience can be framed narrowly (e.g., the educational harms to black schoolchildren) or broadly (e.g., the systemic subordination of blacks in a regime of racial caste). The overarching point is that the patent illegality of segregation depends on a principle of constitutional equality concerned not only with law's reason and logic but also with its social consequences and social meanings. The Court in *Brown* recognized that merely formal equality is not genuine equality at all. Once the constitutional meaning of equality is understood this way, *Brown* is—as it should be—an easy case.

Why, then, has the correctness of *Brown* been the subject of so much hand-wringing in some legal circles? The short answer is that *Brown* is a difficult case under interpretive theories that disavow the relevance of contemporary social understandings to the application of the Constitution's general principles. To justify *Brown*, originalism must posit that the federal and state legislators who ratified the Fourteenth Amendment understood it to abolish segregated schools. Given the widespread practice of school segregation in the states and the paucity of evidence that the enacting Congress believed the Amendment would radically transform public schooling, it is no wonder that the unanimous Court in *Brown* found the original intent "[a]t best...inconclusive."[13] Indeed, for over half a century, a scholarly consensus across the ideological spectrum has recognized that *Brown* cannot be explained on originalist grounds.[14] Even the most ambitious and labored effort to reconcile *Brown* with originalism[15] comes up short for reasons lucidly elaborated by one of the nation's leading civil rights historians.[16]

In recent years, some have read *Brown* to stand for the neutral principle that the Constitution requires government to be color-blind. In 2007, four Justices, led by Chief Justice Roberts, asserted that the violation in *Brown* was that "schoolchildren were told where they could and could not go to school based on the color of their skin" and that the Constitution requires "'admission to the public schools on a nonracial basis.'"[17] But the superficial neutrality of this phrasing paints a false portrait of history by implying that segregation imposed equal burdens on blacks and whites alike. As Justice Stevens observed, "it was only black schoolchildren who were so ordered; indeed, the history books do not tell stories of white children struggling to attend black schools."[18] Neither history nor common sense supports Chief Justice Roberts's conclusion that "assign[ing] black and white students to *different* schools in order to *segregate* them" presents the same constitutional evil as "assign[ing] black and white students to the *same* school in order to *integrate* them."[19]

Moreover, in what sense is colorblindness "neutral" when its foreseeable result is, as it is in many communities, the assignment of schoolchildren to racially separate and unequal schools? The same criticism applies to another entailment of so-called neutral principles—the intent doctrine of *Washington v. Davis*—which provides a safe harbor for policies that, while not demonstrably motivated by race, show deliberate indifference to the racial inequalities they produce.[20] The lesson of *Plessy*, revealed in *Brown*, is that "the seduction of 'neutral principles' must be tempered by an honest accounting of relevant social facts."[21] In other words, the constitutional meaning of equality cannot be forged in a vacuum of legal formalism.

In sum, the authority of *Brown* lies in the Court's candid recognition that the true test of constitutional equality must be the lived experience of the American people. Justice Breyer put it well when he described "the hope and promise of *Brown*" this way:

> For much of this Nation's history, the races remained divided. It was not long ago that people of different races drank from separate fountains, rode on separate buses, and studied in separate schools. In this Court's finest hour, *Brown v. Board of Education* challenged this history and helped to change it. For *Brown* held out a promise. It was a promise embodied in three Amendments designed to make citizens of slaves. It was the promise of true racial equality—not as a matter of fine words on paper, but as a matter of everyday life in the Nation's cities and schools. It was about the nature of a democracy that must work for all Americans. It sought one law, one Nation, one people, not simply as a matter of legal principle but in terms of how we actually live.[22]

GENDER EQUALITY

The evolution of constitutional protection against gender discrimination likewise demonstrates how contemporary social understandings legitimately influence the task of interpreting the principles stated in the Constitution's text. For more than a generation, the nation has recognized the equal citizenship of men and women as a core constitutional value. This is true even though our well-accepted norms of gender equality were not widely shared when the nation ratified the Fourteenth Amendment or even the Nineteenth Amendment. Fidelity to the Constitution's commitment to equality, informed by our society's increasingly egalitarian perspectives on the roles and capabilities of women and men, legitimizes modern gender equality jurisprudence.

Although suffragists during the nineteenth century actively fought for the abolition of slavery, their own claim to equal citizenship was not part of the original understanding of the Fourteenth Amendment. The text of Section 1 applies to "citizens" and "persons" regardless of gender, but the Framers did not expect the Fourteenth Amendment's guarantees to apply to women. In particular, the amendment was not intended to disturb common-law coverture rules that merged a woman's legal identity into that of her husband upon marriage and effectively disabled women from owning property, making contracts, or keeping their own wages if they were permitted to work.

Moreover, Section 2 of the Fourteenth Amendment indicates that the Framers assumed the continued validity of state laws limiting the right to vote to men. In apportioning representatives among states by population, Section 2 reduces the apportionment of any state that denies the franchise to any noncriminal "male" citizen. By contrast, state denial of the franchise to women resulted in no corresponding reduction in the apportionment of representatives.

The unmistakable premise of Section 2—that states may lawfully disenfranchise women—was affirmed by a unanimous Supreme Court in 1875.[23]

Other decisions confirm that few members of the Framing generation understood the Fourteenth Amendment to apply to gender discrimination. In *Bradwell v. Illinois*, the Court affirmed an Illinois Supreme Court decision denying Myra Bradwell admission to the bar, rejecting her claim that the privileges and immunities of national citizenship include the right to practice law.[24] *Bradwell* was decided at the same time as the *Slaughter-House Cases*, which held that federal privileges and immunities do not encompass the right to pursue an occupation.[25] Although four Justices dissented from the holding in *Slaughter-House*, three of them nonetheless voted against Bradwell's claim for reasons stated by Justice Bradley:

> It certainly cannot be affirmed, as an historical fact, that [the right to pursue employment] has ever been established as one of the fundamental privileges and immunities of the sex. On the contrary, the civil law, as well as nature herself, has always recognized a wide difference in the respective spheres and destinies of man and woman. Man is, or should be, woman's protector and defender. The natural and proper timidity and delicacy which belongs to the female sex evidently unfits it for many of the occupations of civil life. The constitution of the family organization, which is founded in the divine ordinance, as well as in the nature of things, indicates the domestic sphere as that which properly belongs to the domain and functions of womanhood.[26]

Justice Bradley affirmed the vitality of common-law coverture rules and went on to treat the circumstances of unmarried women as "exceptions to the general rule," explaining that "[t]he paramount destiny and mission of woman are to fulfil the noble and benign offices of wife and mother. This is the law of the Creator. And the rules of civil society must be adapted to the general constitution of things, and cannot be based upon exceptional cases."[27] Two decades later, in *Ex parte Lockwood*, a unanimous Court, citing *Bradwell*, reaffirmed that states may exclude women from the practice of law.[28]

In 1920, the Nineteenth Amendment finally extended the franchise to women, fifty years after it had been extended to black men. But the amendment was not understood to work a broad change in women's legal status or to embody a general principle against sex discrimination. Many state courts continued to uphold laws barring women from serving as jurors,[29] and even as late as 1961, the U.S. Supreme Court upheld a state law exempting women from jury service on the ground that the "woman is still regarded as the center of home and family life."[30]

Moreover, as women entered the paid workforce in increasing numbers during the early twentieth century, states enacted legislation setting maximum hours and minimum wages for women only. Although these laws made it possible for many low-income mothers to participate in the labor market, they also tended to perpetuate stereotypes concerning gender roles and differences. In *Muller v. Oregon*, for example, the Supreme Court pointed to "the inherent difference between the two sexes" and, in particular, a woman's "physical structure and a proper discharge of her maternal functions" in sustaining a women-only maximum hours law.[31]

In *West Coast Hotel v. Parrish*, the Court upheld a women-only minimum wage law as a reasonable response to "the fact that [women] are in the class receiving the least pay, that their bargaining power is relatively weak, and that they are the ready victims of those who would take advantage of their necessitous circumstances."[32] But the Court in subsequent cases failed to develop a coherent doctrine distinguishing beneficial protective legislation from discriminatory laws based on gender stereotypes. In *Goesaert v. Cleary*, the Court upheld a Michigan law prohibiting a woman from bartending unless she was the wife or daughter of a bar's male owner, reasoning that "bartending by women may, in the allowable legislative judgment, give rise to moral and social problems" that may be minimized with "the oversight assured through ownership of a bar by a barmaid's husband or father."[33] After *Goesaert*, numerous state courts invoking traditional gender roles upheld ordinances that prohibited the sale of liquor to women or limited women's employment in bars and taverns.[34]

Remarkably, "[f]or the first century of the Fourteenth Amendment's life, no court interpreted the Constitution to prohibit state action favoring men over women."[35] It was not until 1971, in *Reed v. Reed*, that the Supreme Court for the first time invalidated a gender classification under the Equal Protection Clause.[36] Although spare in its reasoning, *Reed* inaugurated a line of precedents that closely scrutinized gender stereotypes and struck down laws treating men and women unequally. As a result, "the American constitution now has something very much like a constitutional ban on sex discrimination—not because of the original understanding of its text but because of new judicial interpretations."[37]

The modern transformation of gender equal protection doctrine shows how judicial interpretation of the Constitution can legitimately incorporate evolving social understandings. *Reed* and subsequent cases were decided against the backdrop of a social movement that powerfully challenged traditional gender roles and stereotypes.[38] Throughout the late 1960s and 1970s, popular mobilization behind the cause of gender equality sought not only to eliminate overtly discriminatory practices but also to remake the social organization of the family and to eradicate structural barriers to women's full participation in economic and political life. Through sustained advocacy and public debate, the women's movement called into question the social and legal structures that perpetuated the gendered divide between breadwinning and homemaking and the unequal citizenship that division entailed.

The claims of the women's movement found tangible expression in a raft of federal legislation. Not only did Congress include "sex" among the prohibited bases of employment discrimination under Title VII of the Civil Rights Act of 1964,[39] it also invoked its power under Section 5 of the Fourteenth Amendment, the enforcement clause, to extend that prohibition to state employers in 1972,[40] even though the Supreme Court at that point had never found sex discrimination in employment to be unconstitutional. In the same session, Congress banned sex discrimination in federally funded educational programs[41] and in a host of other federally supported programs.[42] In addition, Congress passed the Equal Rights Amendment on March 22, 1972, and sent it to the states for ratification.

The constitutional significance of this intense period of popular mobilization and lawmaking was not lost on the Court. In 1973, a four-Justice plurality in *Frontiero v. Richardson* identified gender as a suspect classification under the Equal Protection Clause.[43] In an opinion by Justice Brennan, the plurality observed that "over the past decade, Congress has itself manifested an increasing sensitivity to sex-based classifications," citing Title VII of the Civil Rights Act of 1964, the Equal Pay Act of 1963, and the Equal Rights Amendment as examples.[44] "Thus," the plurality said, "Congress itself has concluded that classifications based upon sex are inherently invidious, and this conclusion of a coequal branch of Government is not without significance to the question presently under consideration."[45]

Frontiero invalidated federal statutes that imposed more onerous requirements on husbands than on wives for claiming housing and medical benefits as dependents of uniformed servicemembers. In reaching this judgment, the plurality reviewed the nation's history of discrimination against women and observed that the "practical effect" of policies "rationalized by an attitude of 'romantic paternalism'" was to "put women, not on a pedestal, but in a cage."[46] Despite improvements in recent decades, "women still face pervasive, although at times more subtle, discrimination in our educational institutions, in the job market and, perhaps most conspicuously, in the political arena."[47] Statutory gender classifications deserve heightened scrutiny under the Equal Protection Clause, the plurality explained, because "the sex characteristic frequently bears no relation to ability to perform or contribute to society."[48]

After *Frontiero*, a solid Court majority began to invalidate a wide range of policies premised on overbroad or outdated sex stereotypes. In *Weinberger v. Weisenfeld*, the Court struck down a statute entitling a widowed mother, but not a widowed father, to Social Security benefits based on the earnings of the deceased spouse.[49] The Court faulted the policy for its "archaic and overbroad generalization...that male workers' earnings are vital to the support of their families, while the earnings of female wage earners do not significantly contribute to their families' support."[50] In *Stanton v. Stanton*, the Court voided a state law requiring parents to provide support until age twenty-one for boys, but only until age eighteen for girls, because it reflected "old notions" that "the female [is] destined solely for the home and the rearing of the family, and only the male for the marketplace and the world of ideas."[51]

In *Craig v. Boren*, the Court struck down a statute prohibiting the sale of nonintoxicating beer to boys under the age of twenty-one and to girls under the age of eighteen, explaining that "the gender-based difference [was not] substantially related to achievement of the statutory objective" in promoting traffic safety.[52] In *Mississippi University for Women v. Hogan*, the Court held that a state nursing school may not limit enrollment to women because such an "admissions policy lends credibility to the old view that women, not men, should become nurses."[53] And in *United States v. Virginia*, the Court invalidated the exclusion of women from the Virginia Military Institute on the ground that gender "classifications may not be used, as they once were, to create or perpetuate the legal, social, and economic inferiority of women."[54]

Through these and other cases, the Court has transformed constitutional doctrine on gender equality from a deferential approach premised on "inherent" differences between men and women to a modern rule of careful and rigorous skepticism. Today, gender classifications must have a "direct, substantial relationship" to an "important" state objective so that they reflect "reasoned analysis rather than...the mechanical application of traditional, often inaccurate, assumptions about the proper roles of men and women."[55] "Parties who seek to defend gender-based government action must demonstrate an 'exceedingly persuasive justification' for that action."[56] The application of heightened scrutiny to gender classifications is now a firmly settled principle of constitutional law.[57]

Heightened scrutiny has not uniformly led to invalidation of gender distinctions. The Court has upheld sex-based classifications that remedy prior discrimination against women in economic or employment opportunity[58] or that arguably reflect "real" differences between men and women.[59] The line between protective and paternalistic legislation, or between "real" and socially constructed differences between the sexes, can be difficult to discern because the distinctions are dynamic and informed by society's changing attitudes and perceptions. The Court's jurisprudence properly recognizes the role of evolving social understandings in shaping a responsive constitutional doctrine of gender equality. The expression of those understandings through federal legislation, in particular, can have considerable constitutional significance, as the plurality acknowledged in *Frontiero*[60] and as the Court more recently confirmed in *Nevada Department of Human Resources v. Hibbs.*[61]

In sum, our modern doctrine of gender equality has not resulted from adherence to the Framers' original understanding of how the Fourteenth Amendment's commitment to equality applies to gender discrimination. Nor did the doctrinal transformation occur through a formal process of constitutional amendment; although Congress passed the ERA in 1972, it was not ratified by the states. Instead, in a series of decisions over several decades, the Court managed to integrate contemporary understandings of gender equality into Fourteenth Amendment doctrine, producing results virtually equivalent to what the ERA would have accomplished.[62] The widespread acceptance of the Court's gender equality jurisprudence in our legal and public culture attests to the legitimacy of interpreting the Constitution in the context of contemporary understandings. This interpretive approach is central to the process by which the Constitution's broad principles are given practical meaning and, from generation to generation, made our own.

CONGRESSIONAL ENFORCEMENT POWER AND THE EVOLVING SCOPE OF CIVIL RIGHTS

Although we typically look to the courts to interpret the Constitution, we have seen that the courts often interpret the Constitution by looking to the widely held understandings of constitutional principle reflected in our legal and public culture. The absorption of democratically articulated norms into constitutional law is not only an aspect of sound judicial practice. It is also an explicit feature of our constitutional design.

The Thirteenth, Fourteenth, and Fifteenth Amendments include enforcement clauses that authorize Congress "to enforce...by appropriate legislation" the substantive guarantees of those amendments. The provisions mark the first instances in the constitutional text where enforcement authority is expressly assigned to Congress. While the Framers of the Reconstruction Amendments did not intend to preclude judicial enforcement, it is unsurprising that they placed "their primary faith...in Congress"[63] since their generation had witnessed the debacle of *Dred Scott*. As a historical matter, it turns out the Framers were prescient in their design. When judicial interpretation of Congress's enforcement powers has embraced the democratic implementation of constitutional rights, the nation has made progress toward greater liberty and equality. By contrast, when courts have restricted Congress's enforcement powers, the result has been to stifle democratic understandings and to impede the progress of civil rights.

The latter dynamic characterized the immediate decades after the Civil War, when the scope of legislative enforcement power was a frequent source of conflict between Congress and the Supreme Court. Congress passed the Enforcement Act of 1870 and the Ku Klux Klan Act of 1871 to protect the new constitutional rights of black citizens. These laws criminalized conduct that interfered with the right to vote, the right to serve on a jury, or the enjoyment of the privileges of citizenship and the equal protection of the laws. In a series of decisions, the Court held that the statutes exceeded Congress's enforcement power because they applied to conduct beyond overt racial discrimination[64] or because they applied to private conduct and not state action.[65] Further, after Congress passed the Civil Rights Act of 1875 banning racial discrimination in public accommodations, the Court struck it down because it covered private acts of discrimination and applied to conduct that, in the Court's view, did not amount to "badges and incidents of slavery."[66]

These decisions reflected the Court's narrow view of the substantive guarantees of the Thirteenth, Fourteenth, and Fifteenth Amendments. But they also reflected the Court's disregard for the interpretive judgments of Congress, a co-equal branch of government expressly authorized by the Constitution to enforce those guarantees. The Reconstruction Congress understood that racial discrimination in voting could take ostensibly race-neutral forms, such as poll taxes and literacy tests. It also understood that black citizens were denied the privileges of citizenship and equal protection of the laws when state inaction or passivity facilitated private acts of violence by the Ku Klux Klan and others. Yet the Court ignored these constitutional judgments by Congress.

These congressional judgments were clearly sensible. The Civil Rights Act of 1875, for example, was readily understood as legislation to enforce the Fourteenth Amendment guarantee of citizenship for black Americans. As Justice Harlan observed in his dissent in the *Civil Rights Cases*, the Citizenship Clause "is of a distinctly affirmative character" and is not merely a prohibition on the states. Thus, Harlan reasoned, Congress may enforce the citizenship guarantee through "legislation of a primary direct character" and not merely through legislation targeting state action.[67] By limiting Congress's enforcement authority, the Court in these early cases stunted the implementation of constitutional civil rights and paved the way for Jim Crow.

Congress's enforcement power lay dormant for decades until the civil rights movement breathed new life into the Reconstruction Amendments in the wake of *Brown*. *Brown*, of course, was a judicial triumph. But the implementation of *Brown* occurred through a mutually reinforcing dynamic of judicial and legislative activity that reflected the equality claims of a powerful popular movement.[68] In this period, as in the first Reconstruction, Congress used its enforcement power to play a leading role in defining the substantive contours of the Constitution's equality guarantees. This time the

Supreme Court was willing to acknowledge Congress's role in interpreting constitutional principles in contemporary contexts.

A leading example is the Voting Rights Act of 1965 (VRA), "[a]n Act to enforce the fifteenth amendment to the Constitution of the United States."[69] Congress passed the VRA against a backdrop of judicial decisions that had upheld poll taxes and literacy tests in some instances as permissible voting requirements.[70] The Act established a nationwide prohibition on the use of literacy tests in order "[t]o assure that the right of citizens of the United States to vote is not denied or abridged on account of race or color," as provided by the Fifteenth Amendment.[71] The Act also declared that "the constitutional right of citizens to vote is denied or abridged in some areas by the requirement of the payment of a poll tax as a precondition to voting" and authorized the U.S. Attorney General to challenge poll taxes in federal court.[72] Further, the VRA required certain states and political subdivisions to seek preclearance from the Attorney General or a federal district court before enacting any change in voting qualifications, prerequisites, standards, practices, or procedures.[73]

In several decisions, the Supreme Court validated Congress's role under the enforcement clauses in defining the scope of constitutional guarantees. In *Katzenbach v. Morgan*, a suit challenging one provision of the VRA ban on literacy tests, the Court rejected the view that Congress's powers under Section 5 of the Fourteenth Amendment are limited to proscribing conduct that a court would find unconstitutional. "A construction of § 5 that would require a judicial determination that the enforcement of the state law precluded by Congress violated the Amendment, as a condition of sustaining the congressional enactment, would depreciate both congressional resourcefulness and congressional responsibility for implementing the Amendment."[74] Upholding the VRA ban on literacy tests, the Court explained that the Framers chose the phrase "appropriate legislation" in Section 5 of the Fourteenth Amendment and Section 2 of the Fifteenth Amendment in order "to grant to Congress...the same broad powers expressed in the Necessary and Proper Clause" as interpreted by *McCulloch v. Maryland*.[75]

The Court likewise upheld the preclearance requirements of the VRA in *South Carolina v. Katzenbach*, explaining:

> Congress had found that case-by-case litigation was inadequate to combat widespread and persistent discrimination in voting, because of the inordinate amount of time and energy required to overcome the obstructionist tactics invariably encountered in these lawsuits. After enduring nearly a century of systematic resistance to the Fifteenth Amendment, Congress might well decide to shift the advantage of time and inertia from the perpetrators of the evil to its victims.[76]

Moreover, one year after Congress passed the VRA, the Court finally declared the poll tax unconstitutional, overruling prior precedent.[77]

Yet the Court during this period declined to revisit other precedents that limited Congress's enforcement power—in particular, the *Civil Rights Cases*. When faced with identifying the source of Congress's authority to ban racial discrimination in public accommodations in the Civil Rights Act of 1964, the Court looked to the Commerce Clause instead of the Fourteenth Amendment.[78] As a result, the Civil Rights Act of 1964 is treated, somewhat anomalously, as merely economic legislation from the perspective of constitutional doctrine, even as it is widely understood in our legal and public culture as the crowning legislative achievement that made the principle of *Brown* "more firmly law."[79]

In areas beyond race, Congress has also exercised its enforcement power to broaden the scope of civil rights. In 1972, Congress made the prohibition on sex discrimination in employment applicable to the states[80] and banned sex discrimination in federally funded educational programs[81]—five years before the Supreme Court held that sex discrimination warrants heightened scrutiny under the Equal Protection Clause.[82] Congress also passed the Pregnancy Discrimination Act (PDA) in 1978, declaring pregnancy discrimination to be discrimination on the basis of sex.[83] As applied to the states, the PDA is Section 5 legislation expressing Congress's interpretation of the constitutional principle of gender equality. Further, Congress passed the Family and Medical Leave Act (FMLA) in 1993 and the Violence Against Women Act (VAWA) in 1994 to enforce the Constitution's protections against sex discrimination.[84]

Congress also established protections against age discrimination in the Age Discrimination in Employment Act (ADEA) of 1967 and extended the antidiscrimination requirements to state employers in 1974.[85] Moreover, in 1990, Congress overwhelmingly passed the bipartisan Americans with Disabilities Act (ADA), banning discrimination against people with disabilities and requiring reasonable accommodations in wide-ranging areas of civic life, including public services and public employment.[86] Through the ADA, Congress established a new baseline for measuring equality of opportunity for persons with disabilities.

In recent years, however, the Supreme Court has again sought to circumscribe Congress's enforcement power in several ways. First, the Court has limited Congress to enforcing constitutional rights only as those rights have been interpreted by the Court.[87] Second, it has sometimes insisted on a detailed legislative record of state constitutional violations as a predicate for enforcement legislation.[88] Third, it has required "congruence and proportionality between the injury to be prevented or remedied and the means adopted to that end"[89]—a tailoring requirement more stringent than the deferential *McCulloch* standard approved in *Katzenbach v. Morgan*.

Employing these tests, the Court has invalidated the application of significant civil rights legislation to the states. In 1997, the Court held that Congress exceeded its Section 5 power when it enacted the Religious Freedom Restoration Act, a statute designed to increase protection for religious liberty in response to a prior decision by the Court weakening such protection under the Free Exercise Clause.[90] In 2000, the Court held that Congress lacked power under Section 5 to establish a damages remedy under the ADEA for state employees because the statute "prohibits substantially more state employment decisions and practices than would likely be held unconstitutional" by a court applying rational basis review.[91] Also in 2000, the Court held that a provision of VAWA authorizing victims of gender-motivated violence to sue their assailants in federal court is not proper Section 5 legislation because it sought to remedy state inaction rather than state action.[92] And in 2001, the Court invalidated the ADA's provision for civil damages against state employers who fail to provide reasonable accommodation for persons with disabilities, reasoning that Congress had not demonstrated a "pattern of unconstitutional discrimination" by the states and that "the accommodation duty far exceeds what is constitutionally required" by judicially established equal protection standards.[93]

In these cases, the Court failed to recognize the distinctive institutional capacities for fact-finding, remedial innovation, and policy judgment that Congress brings to the task of enforcing constitutional rights. In particular, Congress, as a politically accountable body, does not operate under the institutional limitations that counsel restraint when unelected courts interpret the Constitution. When the Court insists that legislative enforcement of constitutional rights conform to judicial standards for enforcing those rights, the Court effectively treats Congress as if it were a lower federal court instead of a co-equal branch of government with its own democratically legitimate interpretive authority. Further, as Michael McConnell has explained,

> the Court's conclusion that judicial interpretations of the provisions of the Amendment are the exclusive touchstone for congressional enforcement power finds no support in the history of the Fourteenth Amendment. Members of Congress felt they had a responsibility to read and to interpret the Constitution for themselves, and they expected that their judgments regarding the reach of the Constitution would be given the same presumption of correctness that any other legislative determinations were given in the ordinary course of judicial review. This did not mean that Congress had plenary power to decide what rights should be given federal protection; Congress was limited to enforcing preexisting constitutional rights. But in determining what those preexisting constitutional rights are, Congress would engage in independent interpretation.
>
> Section Five was born of the conviction that Congress—no less than the courts—has the duty and the authority to interpret the Constitution.[94]

In short, the Reconstruction Amendments envision that Congress and the judiciary would each bring its own institutional capacities and perspectives to bear on enforcing constitutional rights. The Court's recent Section 5 cases depart from this understanding.

In 2003, the Court appeared to modulate its Section 5 doctrine in *Nevada Department of Human Resources v. Hibbs*.[95] In an opinion by Chief Justice Rehnquist, the Court upheld the FMLA guarantee of twelve weeks of unpaid caregiving leave as valid Section 5 legislation to combat gender discrimination in the provision of leave by state employers. Although gender-neutral administration of leave benefits, including a state policy of providing no leave at all, would

presumably pass muster under the Court's equal protection jurisprudence, Chief Justice Rehnquist observed that such an alternative
"would not have achieved Congress' remedial object.... Where
'[t]wo-thirds of the nonprofessional caregivers for older, chronically
ill, or disabled persons are working women,' and state practices
continue to reinforce the stereotype of women as caregivers,
[a gender-neutral no-leave policy] would exclude far more women
than men from the workplace."[96]

Hibbs thus suggests that sex-based disparate impact in public
employment, while not actionable under judicially articulated equal
protection standards,[97] nevertheless constitutes a legitimate target
of constitutional concern for Congress. Indeed, Congress has long
treated disparate impact as an actionable basis for claiming employment discrimination, including discrimination by state employers,
under Title VII of the Civil Rights Act of 1964. *Hibbs* demonstrates
how remedial statutes such as Title VII and the FMLA give practical shape, beyond the contours of judicial doctrine, to the constitutional guarantee of equality.

In sum, the enforcement clauses, properly understood, serve as
structural devices that enable the practical meaning of constitutional principles to evolve through a dynamic interplay of judicial
and popular understandings. Because the Reconstruction-era
Framers did not presume to know what citizenship, equality, and
liberty would entail from one generation to the next, the Thirteenth, Fourteenth, and Fifteenth Amendments expressly provide
for the enforcement of those fundamental guarantees through a
continual process of doctrinal and democratic articulation. When
this structural design has operated as intended, it has strengthened
the core of civil rights protections that we enjoy today. But when the
design has been perverted by an overreaching Court, the result has
been to retard the progress of civil rights and to suppress democratic
understandings of constitutional principle

CHAPTER FOUR

Freedom of Speech

AMONG THE RIGHTS guaranteed under the Constitution, perhaps none is more familiar to Americans than freedom of speech. We cherish the liberty to express ideas and dissent without fear of government reprisal. Constitutional protection for dissenting speech is especially important to the functioning of democracy, since the quality and legitimacy of government decision-making depend on free and vigorous debate. That is why "expression of dissatisfaction with the policies of this country" is "expression situated at the core of our First Amendment values."[1] As Justice Brennan put it: "If there is a bedrock principle underlying the First Amendment, it is that the government may not prohibit the expression of an idea simply because society finds the idea itself offensive or disagreeable."[2] This principle is, for many Americans, the essence of what it means to live in a free society.

Yet the "bedrock principle" Justice Brennan described was hardly settled when the First Amendment was ratified. The Founding generation agreed that freedom of the press encompassed freedom from prior restraint. But there was little agreement on whether the First Amendment protected seditious speech once uttered or published. Many of the Framers adhered to the common-law principle summarized by Blackstone:

> The liberty of the press is indeed essential to the nature of a free state; but this consists in laying no previous restraints upon publications, and not in freedom from censure for criminal matter when published. Every freeman has an undoubted right to lay what sentiments he pleases before the public: to forbid this is to destroy the freedom of the press: but if he publishes what is improper, mischievous, or illegal, he must take the consequences of his own temerity.[3]

By contrast, James Madison called it "a mockery to say that no laws should be passed preventing publications from being made, but that laws might be passed for punishing them in case they should be made."[4] The fierce controversy over the Sedition Act of 1798 underscored the indeterminacy of the First Amendment's original meaning. Benjamin Franklin, discussing freedom of the press, candidly observed in 1789 that "few of us, I believe, have any distinct ideas of its Nature and Extent."[5]

Today we understand freedom of speech differently than the Founding generation did. We are more certain of its protective reach, more vigilant against restrictive measures, and more aware of the harms to individuals, to government, and to democracy when this essential liberty is violated. The evolution of our understanding has not occurred through ever-deeper excavation of original meanings. It has occurred through a dynamic process of argument, interpretation, and reinterpretation as the nation has grappled with some of its most divisive challenges. And it has occurred not only through judicial exegesis of constitutional text, but through an ongoing interplay among our courts, political institutions, and citizenry at large.

In this chapter, we discuss how our understanding of the First Amendment has been shaped by periods when serious threats to national security led to restrictions on dissenting speech. In times of threat, dissenting speech may seem disloyal or subversive. Public criticism of our government or empathy for our enemies has often sparked demands to silence or punish dissenting voices. As Justice Holmes once said, "[p]ersecution for the expression of opinions seems to me perfectly logical. If you have no doubt of your premises or your power and want a certain result with all your heart you naturally express your wishes in law and sweep away all opposition."[6]

But Holmes believed that the First Amendment rejected this logic. Our system, he said, is grounded in the belief that "the best test of truth is the power of the thought to get itself accepted in the competition of the market.... That at any rate is the theory of our Constitution."[7] Although those words were written in dissent in 1919, we have since come to embrace "a profound national commitment to the principle that debate on public issues should be uninhibited, robust, and wide-open, and that it may well include vehement, caustic, and sometimes unpleasantly sharp attacks on government and public officials."[8] We focus on two examples from our history—the Sedition Act of 1798 and the World War I era—to illustrate the interpretive process through which our nation has forged strong protections for freedom of speech. In addition, we briefly trace the contemporary understandings of those protections and the challenges that demand continued vigilance.

EARLY UNDERSTANDINGS AND THE SEDITION ACT OF 1798

At the core of early controversies over freedom of speech was whether the First Amendment abolished the crime of seditious libel. At common law, seditious libel "consisted of defaming or contemning or ridiculing the government: its form, constitution, officers, laws, conduct, or policies, to the jeopardy of the public peace."⁹ The vagueness of the crime meant that "any malicious criticism about the government that could be construed to have the bad tendency of lowering it in the public's esteem, holding it up to contempt or hatred, or of disturbing the peace was seditious libel, exposing the speaker or writer to criminal prosecution."¹⁰ Whether speech was seditious was a question reserved to judges; the jury decided only whether the defendant had uttered or published the statement at issue. Truth was not a defense, for "the greater the truth, the greater the libel."¹¹ At bottom, the law of seditious libel reflected the notion that "[i]f people should not be called to account for possessing the people with an ill opinion of the government, no government can subsist. For it is very necessary for all governments that the people should have a good opinion of it."¹²

Despite the law, open political discussion existed to an "astonishing degree" in America throughout the eighteenth century.¹³ The 1735 trial of John Peter Zenger heralded the virtual collapse of common-law prosecutions for seditious libel.¹⁴ Zenger, a newspaper printer, had published articles criticizing the reviled royal governor of New York. When Zenger's lawyers sought to prove that the criticisms were true, the court responded that truth was no defense. But the jury, nominally charged with deciding whether Zenger had printed the material, returned a verdict of not guilty. Throughout the colonies, Zenger's acquittal fortified an emerging understanding that truthful criticism of unjust and unpopular government should not be a crime.

Nevertheless, freedom of speech in eighteenth-century America did not resemble what we understand the concept to mean today. The Zenger case showed that juries, reflecting public sentiment, were prepared to disregard the law in order to protect speech that criticized unpopular Crown authorities. But criticism of the locally elected colonial legislatures was a different matter. The power of local assemblies to summon, interrogate, and punish their critics was "the most efficacious of all colonial press controls."[15] Although legislative prosecutions were "merely sporadic," the threat of prosecution "was sufficiently restrictive to have a dampening effect on the free expression of opinion on legislative measures and matters."[16] During the revolutionary era, the colonists continued to suppress dissent from alleged Tory sympathizers or anyone who questioned the revolutionary cause.[17] As Arthur Schlesinger put it, "liberty of speech belonged solely to those who spoke the speech of liberty."[18] Tellingly, after the colonies achieved independence, all of them except Connecticut expressly adopted the common-law system of which seditious libel was a part; none abolished the crime, and no state court read the free press clause of a state constitution to void a prosecution for libel.[19]

Given the legal context in which the First Amendment was written and ratified, freedom of speech meant something narrower to the Founding generation than it means to us now. According to Leonard Levy, the leading historian of the free speech and press guarantees,

> no evidence suggests an understanding that a constitutional guarantee of free speech or press meant the impossibility of future prosecutions of seditious utterances.... The security of the state against libelous advocacy or attack outweighed any social interest in open expression, at least through the period of the adoption of the First Amendment.[20]

Other scholars have argued that the original understanding of the First Amendment incorporated significant reforms to the law of seditious libel, including truth as a defense, and a growing recognition of free speech as a check on abusive government.[21] But even if the Framers did not fully embrace the old common law, they did not fully repudiate it either. The fact that Congress passed the Sedition Act of 1798 less than seven years after ratification of the First Amendment underscores that many leaders of the Founding era saw no inconsistency between the First Amendment and criminal prosecution for criticizing the government.

The Sedition Act was the product of tensions over the United States' potential involvement in growing hostilities between England and France. The Federalists, who controlled all three branches of government, feared that France was about to invade the United States and sought to prepare for war; the Republicans urged neutrality and accused the Federalists of exaggerating the security threat for partisan ends. The debate reached a fevered pitch in the spring of 1798, with leading Federalists charging their Republican critics with disloyalty and treason. In a swell of patriotic fervor, the Federalists proposed the Sedition Act as a necessary response to what they saw as lies, slander, and deceptions published by Republican newspapers. The Act criminalized "any false, scandalous, and malicious" speech or writing against the United States government, Congress, or the President.[22] A violation was punishable by a fine of up to $2,000 and imprisonment for up to two years.[23]

The debate over the legislation and subsequent experience under it "played a central role in shaping the future of American constitutional law."[24] In Congress, both sides plumbed the meaning of the First Amendment.[25] The Federalists argued that the free speech and press guarantees were informed by common-law concepts and analogous state constitutional provisions, all of which contemplated the punishment of seditious libel. The Sedition Act, the Federalists noted, was actually more protective than the common law: it made truth a defense, it assigned the ultimate question of guilt to the jury, and it required proof of intent to defame.[26] But the reforms failed to assuage Republican concerns, especially since the availability of truth as a defense afforded no protection to expressions of opinion.

More broadly, the Republicans denied that government was "superior to the people and must not be subjected to censure that might diminish [its] authority," and instead argued that "the governors were servants of the people, who therefore had a right and a responsibility to question and criticize their judgments."[27] By clarifying the proper relationship between government and the people, the Republicans illuminated an essential feature of American democracy and laid bare the constitutional infirmities of the Sedition Act. Not only did the Act suppress criticism of government; it did so in a transparently partisan way. By setting an expiration date of March 3, 1801, the last day of Adams's presidency, the statute effectively "criminalized libel of incumbents, but not of challengers."[28] Thus the legislation doubly subverted democratic principle by stifling debate on important issues *and* by enabling partisan self-dealing.

The Sedition Act passed on a party-line vote. Between July 1798 and March 1801, the Federalist administration arrested twenty-five prominent Republicans, including politicians, lawyers, and journalists. Fifteen were indicted, ten cases went to trial, and all ten were convicted.[29] Federalist judges made no pretense of impartiality and rejected arguments attacking the constitutionality of the statute.[30] True to its partisan design, no Federalist was ever indicted under the Act.[31]

But the Federalists' tactics only served to galvanize their critics and to hasten the party's demise. The Sedition Act was deeply offensive to a substantial majority of Americans; thousands took part in protests and rallies to express their opposition. The statute became a major issue in the election of 1800, and freedom of political expression supplied a potent principle for Republicans seeking to end twelve years of Federalist rule. Although the election was close, President Jefferson's victory marked a decisive repudiation of the Sedition Act: in one of his first acts in office, he pardoned everyone who had been convicted under the Act and set free those who were still imprisoned.[32] In 1840, Congress repaid all fines levied under the Act, declaring it "conclusively settled" that "the law...was unconstitutional, null, and void, passed under a mistaken exercise of undelegated power."[33] Although the Supreme Court never ruled on the constitutionality of the Sedition Act, it has acknowledged that "the attack upon its validity has carried the day in the court of history."[34]

The debate over the Sedition Act "first crystallized a national awareness of the central meaning of the First Amendment."[35] For many Americans, the practical controversies surrounding the Act's enforcement strengthened their conviction that freedom of speech is essential to the democratic process and that criticism of government may not be silenced simply because it is false, unpopular, or obnoxious. This conviction did not emerge through discovery of original meanings. Instead, the Sedition Act engaged the American people and their elected representatives in the process of constitutional interpretation. In subsequent periods of national security threat, similar public engagement has enlarged our understandings of the role of dissent in our constitutional democracy. Those understandings, informed by lessons of experience, have in turn shaped the development of First Amendment doctrine.

WORLD WAR I AND THE RED SCARE

The Supreme Court did not review the validity of any federal laws under the First Amendment until the twentieth century. That is not to say that the nineteenth century was devoid of important disputes over free speech,[36] but it is to say that the Court's jurisprudence remained largely undeveloped for a long time. In 1907, more than a century after the Sedition Act had been decisively condemned, the Court still endorsed the view that freedom of speech and press bars only prior restraint and not "subsequent punishment of [speech] as may be deemed contrary to the public welfare."[37] In a series of cases, the Court accepted that government could punish speech merely if it tended to bring about a substantive evil that government could otherwise legitimately prevent.[38] Thus, judicial doctrine was hardly hospitable to dissenting speech as the nation entered another era of repression driven by the felt imperatives of war.

In the run-up to American involvement in World War I, President Wilson faced a skeptical public. Wilson himself had won reelection in 1916 on the platform that he had kept the nation out of war, and many Americans believed that U.S. involvement would serve primarily the interests of the wealthy. But after a German submarine blockade sank American ships in early 1917, Wilson sought a declaration of war to make the world "safe for democracy" and moved aggressively to build public support. He warned of German spies within the United States; he established a government agency to spread prowar propaganda; his Department of Justice asked Americans to report on neighbors and coworkers whom they suspected of disloyalty; and he encouraged voluntary groups, such as the American Protective League, to observe and ferret out purportedly suspicious individuals.[39] Amid the fear, mistrust, and intolerance fomented by these efforts, Wilson urged Congress to pass the Espionage Act of 1917.

The Espionage Act made it a crime "when the United States is at war" to "willfully make or convey false reports or false statements with the intent to interfere with the operation or success of the military or naval forces of the United States or to promote the success of its enemies," to "willfully cause or attempt to cause insubordination, disloyalty, mutiny, or refusal of duty, in the military or naval forces of the United States," or to "willfully obstruct the recruiting or enlistment service of the United States."[40] A violation was punishable by a fine of up to $10,000 or imprisonment for up to twenty years, or both.[41] The Act also excluded from the mails any writing or publication "in violation of any of the provisions of this Act" or "containing any material advocating or urging treason, insurrection or forcible resistance to any law of the United States."[42]

In passing this legislation, Congress rejected broader language proposed by the Wilson administration to authorize censorship of information that the President deemed "useful to the enemy," to criminalize statements that "cause or attempt to cause disaffection" in the military, and to exclude from the mails any material of "treasonable or anarchistic character."[43] Even without those expansive terms, however, the Department of Justice brought over two thousand Espionage Act prosecutions during World War I. The climate of hostility toward nonconformers meant that "[w]hatever the offending language, surrounding circumstances, or jury instructions, almost all prosecutions led to guilty verdicts."[44]

Most federal courts during this period interpreted the Espionage Act as broadly as possible to facilitate convictions. The prevailing approach held that a defendant "must be presumed to have intended the natural and probable consequences of what he knowingly did."[45] On this view, the prosecution did not need to prove a specific intent to cause insubordination or obstruct enlistment; it was enough to show that a defendant's speech had a tendency to produce those results. For example, a minister who urged that Christians should not kill in wars was convicted of attempt to cause insubordination, and a man who mailed a book describing the war as "murder" and "a crime" was convicted of willfully obstructing enlistment.[46] So long as unlawful intent could be inferred from the "bad tendency" of dissenting speech, it was risky for anyone to criticize the war.

But a few courageous judges recognized that constitutional principles demanded a narrower interpretation of the Act. In a case involving the *Masses*, a leading journal that featured social satire and political criticism, federal district judge Learned Hand enjoined the postmaster from excluding the periodical from the mails.[47] The journal had published several items criticizing the war, among them a cartoon with provocative images depicting conscription as "the destruction of youth, democracy, and labor, and the desolation of the family"[48] and an article reprinting anguished letters from imprisoned conscientious objectors in England.[49] Judge Hand held that none of the prohibitions in the Espionage Act covered the published materials.

First, he found that the attacks on the war did not involve willfully false statements because they were "all within the range of opinion and of criticism" and "all certainly believed to be true by the utterer."[50] Next, he refused to extend the Act's prohibition on "caus[ing]" insubordination or disloyalty to cover the publications at issue: "to interpret the word 'cause' so broadly would…involve necessarily as a consequence the suppression of all hostile criticism, and of all opinion except what encouraged and supported the existing policies, or which fell within the range of temperate argument."[51] Finally, Judge Hand held that the published materials could not be construed as willful obstruction of military recruitment.[52] Explaining that tolerance of political agitation "is a safeguard of free government," he concluded that the Espionage Act had to be limited to punishing "direct advocacy" of unlawful conduct.[53] Otherwise, "every political agitation which can be shown to be apt to create a seditious temper is illegal"—a result that "would contradict the normal assumption of democratic government that the suppression of hostile criticism does not turn upon the justice of its substance or the decency and propriety of its temper."[54]

Judge Hand understood that a clear, objective test is necessary, especially in times of passion, to ensure that legitimate dissent is not punished or chilled by reflexive accusations of unlawful intent. First Amendment doctrine has vindicated this view, but it had few adherents in 1917. Judge Hand's opinion was reversed on appeal,[55] and the *Masses* soon went out of business.

Freedom of speech fared no better in the Supreme Court. In its first major decisions interpreting the First Amendment, the Court issued three opinions in March 1919 upholding Espionage Act convictions of antiwar socialists based on the "tendency" of their speech to cause disloyalty or obstruct enlistment.[56] Justice Holmes wrote for a unanimous Court in each case. In *Schenck*, the defendant, who was general secretary of the Socialist Party, had sent a pamphlet to drafted men declaring conscription "a monstrous wrong against humanity in the interest of Wall Street's chosen few" and urging readers "to assert your opposition to the draft" and "not [to] submit to intimidation."[57] Justice Holmes's analysis included these famous lines:

> [T]he character of every act depends upon the circumstances in which it is done. The most stringent protection of free speech would not protect a man in falsely shouting fire in a theatre and causing a panic.... The question in every case is whether the words used are used in such circumstances and are of such a nature as to create a clear and present danger that they will bring about the substantive evils that Congress has a right to prevent. It is a question of proximity and degree.[58]

Although "clear and present danger" sounds to modern ears like a speech-protective standard, Holmes's initial usage signaled no departure from the bad tendency test since Schenck's conviction was sustained without evidence of imminent danger that distribution of the pamphlet would actually obstruct the draft.

In the next case, *Frohwerk*, the defendant had published articles in a German-language newspaper praising Germany and opposing the draft and the war.[59] Justice Holmes's opinion cited *Schenck* but never mentioned clear and present danger. Instead, he said that despite no evidence of "special effort to reach men who were subject to the draft," the record permitted an inference that the defendant knew "circulation of the paper was in quarters where a little breath would be enough to kindle a flame."[60] In the third case, the Court applied *Schenck* and *Frohwerk* to sustain a jury finding that an antiwar speech by Socialist Party leader Eugene Debs "had as [its] natural tendency and reasonably probable effect to obstruct the recruiting service."[61] Again, there was no mention of clear and present danger.

But experience and reflection soon began to undermine the interpretation of the First Amendment in *Schenck*, *Frohwerk*, and *Debs*. The fighting in Europe ended in November 1918, and public debate over the Versailles Treaty in the summer of 1919 left many Americans questioning whether the war had really made the world "safe for democracy." Emerging doubts made the earlier criticisms of antiwar activists seem less radical or threatening. Moreover, a postwar economic downturn and labor unrest led to worsening hysteria over domestic subversion and even more repressive government measures. For many people, the Palmer raids, federal surveillance, and enactment of state criminal syndicalism laws during the Red Scare overstepped so far that they provoked new sensitivity to freedom of speech. On a personal level, Justice Holmes received swift criticism of his Espionage Act opinions in private letters from Learned Hand and in influential articles by scholars Zechariah Chafee and Ernst Freund.[62]

A transformation in Justice Holmes's thinking surfaced in November 1919. In *Abrams v. United States*, the Supreme Court upheld five convictions under the Sedition Act of 1918, an amendment to the Espionage Act that broadened its criminalization of antigovernment or antiwar speech.[63] The defendants had distributed leaflets opposing American intervention in the Russian revolution, and the Court's ruling was a straightforward application of *Schenck*. But Justice Holmes dissented. In an opinion joined by Justice Brandeis, he wrote:

> [W]e should be eternally vigilant against attempts to check the expression of opinions that we loathe and believe to be fraught with death, unless they so imminently threaten immediate interference with the lawful and pressing purposes of the law that an immediate check is required to save the country.... Only the emergency that makes it immediately dangerous to leave the correction of evil counsels to time warrants making any exception to the sweeping command, "Congress shall make no law abridging the freedom of speech."[64]

With this passage, Justice Holmes set forth what we conventionally understand clear and present danger to mean. Holmes's dissent in *Abrams* gave the principle of free speech its first strongly protective articulation in Supreme Court jurisprudence.

In subsequent cases, the Court continued to sustain convictions under the Sedition and Espionage Acts and under state criminal syndicalism laws.[65] But additional dissents by Holmes and Brandeis strengthened the foundation for doctrinal reform. In *Gitlow v. New York*, Justice Holmes underscored that clear and present danger requires an element of immediacy; it protects speech that is not "an attempt to induce an uprising against government at once" but "at some indefinite time in the future."[66] In *Whitney v. California*, Justice Brandeis explained that "no danger flowing from speech can be deemed clear and present, unless the incidence of the evil apprehended is so imminent that it may befall before there is opportunity for full discussion."[67] Further, he said, "even imminent danger cannot justify resort to [a speech] prohibition...unless the evil apprehended is relatively serious"; such prohibition "would be inappropriate as the means for averting a relatively trivial harm to society."[68] More fundamentally, Justice Brandeis tied freedom of speech to the effective functioning of democracy:

> [The Founding generation] believed that freedom to think as you will and to speak as you think are means indispensable to the discovery and spread of political truth; that without free speech and assembly discussion would be futile; that with them, discussion affords ordinarily adequate protection against the dissemination of noxious doctrine; that the greatest menace to freedom is an inert people; that public discussion is a political duty; and that this should be a fundamental principle of the American government.[69]

Although attributing all of these ideas to the Founding generation is questionable history, Justice Brandeis's opinion in *Whitney* is justly celebrated because it powerfully captures the reasons we value freedom of speech.[70]

Outside the Court, postwar developments also reflected the direction of change. In May 1920, Zechariah Chafee, Ernst Freund, Felix Frankfurter, Roscoe Pound, and eight other distinguished lawyers and scholars issued a document entitled *Report upon the Illegal Practices of the United States Department of Justice.*[71] With fifty-seven pages of affidavits, exhibits, and government papers, the report documented widespread abuses "committed by the highest legal powers in the United States" in searches, arrests, detentions, interrogations, and prosecutions of alleged radicals.[72] The next month, the *Christian Science Monitor* declared that "in light of what is now known it seems clear that what appeared to be an excess of radicalism...was certainly met with...an excess of suppression."[73] Moreover, many turn-of-the-century progressives emerged from the war as civil libertarians, and with the leadership of Roger Baldwin, the American Civil Liberties Union was founded in 1920.[74] The movement also benefited from a growing body of scholarship on freedom of speech by Chafee, Freund, John Dewey, and others.[75]

Congress repealed the 1918 Sedition Act in March 1921.[76] As for those who had been convicted under the Sedition or Espionage Act, President Wilson accepted the recommendation of Attorney General Thomas Gregory to release or reduce the sentences of two hundred prisoners. In 1921, President Harding pardoned twenty-five additional prisoners, including Eugene Debs. In 1923, President Coolidge released all the remaining prisoners. And in 1933, President Franklin Roosevelt, in a Christmas Amnesty Proclamation, granted a full pardon to all convicted individuals who had completed their sentences under the Sedition or Espionage Act.[77]

CONTEMPORARY UNDERSTANDINGS AND
CONTINUING CHALLENGES

Over time, the nation and the Supreme Court have come to accept the central tenets of the Holmes and Brandeis dissents. In 1969, a unanimous Court held in *Brandenburg v. Ohio* that government may not "forbid or proscribe advocacy of the use of force or of law violation except where such advocacy is directed to inciting or producing imminent lawless action and is likely to incite or produce such action."[78] This standard goes beyond the distinction that Judge Hand in *Masses* sought to draw between the bad tendency of speech and direct advocacy of unlawful conduct. By requiring incitement and likelihood of "imminent lawless action," the Court recognized that "mere advocacy" of unlawful conduct, without more, is simply one point along a continuum of protected speech.[79] Holmes and

Brandeis had urged the same view decades earlier,[80] and *Brandenburg* noted that the precedents from which they dissented have been "thoroughly discredited by later decisions."[81]

But the trajectory of First Amendment doctrine from the Holmes and Brandeis dissents to the unanimous opinion in *Brandenburg* was hardly linear. In the 1930s, the Court decided at least three cases in favor of free speech without mentioning the clear and present danger test.[82] Throughout the 1940s, the Court invoked clear and present danger in several cases upholding free speech claims,[83] including one decision reversing an Espionage Act conviction that almost certainly would have been sustained under *Schenck*.[84] But the Court did not consistently use the test, as evidenced by cases where free speech claims were rejected with no mention of clear and present danger.[85]

The malleability of the test became evident in the Cold War–era case *Dennis v. United States*, in which the Court upheld the convictions of eleven Communist Party leaders for conspiring to advocate the overthrow of the United States government.[86] The case arose under the Smith Act, which Congress enacted in 1940 in response to a growing Nazi and Communist threat.[87] In a plurality opinion for four Justices, Chief Justice Vinson reviewed the case law since *Schenck* and observed that "the Holmes-Brandeis rationale"—requiring clear and present danger before advocacy of unlawful conduct may be punished—had become the majority view.[88] But Vinson went on to say that "a shorthand phrase should [not] be crystallized into a rigid rule."[89] Adopting language from the appeals court opinion below, he interpreted clear and present danger to mean that a court "must ask whether the gravity of the 'evil,' discounted by its improbability, justifies such invasion of free speech as is necessary to avoid the danger."[90] Forcible overthrow of the government is certainly a substantial evil, Vinson explained, and the government need not "wait until the putsch is about to be executed, the plans have been laid and the signal is awaited."[91] Here, "there was a group that was ready to make the attempt."[92]

By allowing the gravity of a danger to offset its lack of imminence, *Dennis* sapped the clear and present danger test of its protective force. As Justice Black noted in dissent, the Court sustained the conviction of individuals not charged with saying or writing anything or with doing any overt act designed to overthrow the government; the only charge "was that they agreed to assemble and to talk and publish certain ideas at a later date."[93] Justice Douglas later opined, in light of *Dennis*, that the clear and present danger test had become too "free-wheeling" to anchor First Amendment jurisprudence.[94] More broadly, *Dennis* illustrated once again the vulnerability of free speech to a climate of fear and officially sanctioned intolerance. The rise of Joe McCarthy, investigations by the House Un-American Activities Committee, zealous loyalty programs, public intimidation of scholars and authors, and blacklisting of Hollywood figures conspired to produce another harshly repressive period in our history.

The Supreme Court, however, retreated from *Dennis* and ultimately played a key role in ending the McCarthy era. In 1957, with public hysteria subsiding, the Court in *Yates v. United States* reversed the convictions of fourteen Communist Party leaders under circumstances that closely resembled those in *Dennis*.[95] Justice Harlan's opinion for the Court distinguished "advocacy of abstract doctrine" from "advocacy directed at promoting unlawful action" and interpreted the Smith Act to reach only the latter.[96] By reading the statute to target advocacy of "concrete action" and not abstract ideas,[97] the Court effectively ended prosecutions under the Smith Act. Subsequent decisions invalidated a broad range of anti-Communist loyalty programs,[98] sharply limited government-compelled disclosure of organizational membership lists,[99] and narrowed the ability of government to criminalize membership in a subversive organization or to deny employment on that basis.[100]

As with earlier controversies, the nation emerged from the Cold War with a deeper understanding of the perils of suppressing dissent. This time, the Supreme Court developed a sturdier bulwark of doctrines that paved the way for some of the most eminent decisions in First Amendment law. In addition to *Brandenburg*, the Court in *New York Times Co. v. Sullivan* severely restricted the reach of libel law in cases involving statements about the conduct of public officials.[101] *Tinker v. Des Moines Independent Community School District* upheld the right of students to peacefully express their opposition to the Vietnam War in public schools.[102] In the *Pentagon Papers* case, the Court refused to enjoin publication of a classified report on the history of U.S. policy in Vietnam because it would have worked an unconstitutional prior restraint.[103] More recently, the Court has held that flag-burning, however odious or unpopular, is expressive conduct entitled to First Amendment protection.[104]

Thus we have come to value strong protections for political speech and dissent—protections far stronger than many leaders of the Founding generation or even jurists of the early twentieth century ever imagined. Our commitment has evolved through a dynamic process that integrates public deliberation on major controversies with the gradual accretion of judicial precedent to give meaning to the spare text of the First Amendment. Our history shows that the interpretive process assimilates our country's experiences, that current understandings may yield to new challenges, and that the law is susceptible to taking two steps forward and one step back.

As today's war on terrorism nears its first decade, it is notable that the federal government has refrained from prosecuting anyone for merely criticizing its tactics or policies. Immediately after September 11, 2001, President Bush publicly warned against hostile reactions against American Arabs and Muslims[105]—a stark contrast to President Wilson's rhetoric against German Americans during World War I and to President Franklin Roosevelt's complicity in the propaganda that facilitated the Japanese internment. At the same time, we have learned that government can silence dissent in myriad ways, including surveillance, investigation, detention, deportation, and interrogation or the threat to use those tactics. Moreover, it was not long ago that the Attorney General of the United States, appearing before the Senate Judiciary Committee, attacked the government's critics by likening dissent to disloyalty. "[T]o those who scare peace-loving people with phantoms of lost liberty," he said, "my message is this: Your tactics only aid terrorists, for they erode our national unity and diminish our resolve. They give ammunition to America's enemies, and pause to America's friends. They encourage people of good will to remain silent in the face of evil."[106]

Hence the need for constant vigilance, affirmation, and reaffirmation of our core freedoms in the context of contemporary challenges. We cannot avoid the ongoing process of constitutional interpretation in the hope of discovering a transcendent original meaning. For "the framers of the First Amendment had no common understanding of its 'true' meaning. They embraced a broad and largely undefined constitutional principle, not a concrete, well-settled legal doctrine."[107] Our nation's experience confirms that freedom of speech "was an aspiration to be given meaning over time."[108]

CHAPTER FIVE

Promoting the General Welfare

ONE OF THE purposes of the Constitution, stated in the Preamble, is to "promote the General Welfare." Promoting the general welfare has two dimensions. One concerns the duty of government to provide for the basic needs of the citizenry. In general, our Constitution has not been interpreted to encompass positive rights to social or economic provision,[1] although there are good arguments that the Constitution is properly read (at least by the political branches if not by the courts) to secure the material conditions necessary for full citizenship and equal opportunity.[2] The other dimension concerns the scope of government authority to respond to the nation's needs. In this chapter, we examine the development of our constitutional understandings in this latter dimension.

Today, Americans do not think twice about the authority of government to respond to economic needs. Social Security, Medicare, collective bargaining and minimum wage laws, disaster assistance, regulation of the financial markets, and robust initiatives to stabilize the economy comprise large parts of the work we expect our federal and state governments to do. Reasonable people may disagree about the specific policies needed to deal with various economic conditions, with regulation of the marketplace, and with the economy as a whole. But there is no question that developing, enacting, and implementing such policies are an important and legitimate part of what government does.

It was not always so. Until 1937, two lines of judicial doctrine often prevented government from responding to pressing economic problems. First, the Supreme Court interpreted the principle of federalism to limit Congress's power to regulate the economy, reserving much of that sphere for state governments. The principle of federalism is implicit in Article I's enumeration of limited federal powers, and it is made explicit in the Tenth Amendment's reservation to the states of powers not delegated to the federal government. However, the Constitution does not state the principle with the precision necessary to resolve particular disputes over the scope of federal power. Consider, for example, Congress's power to regulate interstate commerce.[3] Before 1937, the Supreme Court often applied the federalism principle by adhering to the eighteenth-century understanding of the term "commerce." As Justice Thomas has explained, "[a]t the time the original Constitution was ratified, 'commerce' consisted of selling, buying, and bartering, as well as transporting for these purposes.... [T]he term 'commerce' was used in contradistinction to productive activities such as manufacturing and agriculture."[4] Applying this definition, the Court repeatedly struck down federal regulation of manufacturing, mining, agriculture, and other "local" activities on the ground that they occurred "prior to" commerce and affected commerce only "indirectly."[5]

Under this reading of the Commerce Clause, the federal government could not enact laws to address labor inequities or to establish minimum wages or maximum hours in vast parts of the American economy. Moreover, the Court took a similarly narrow view of the Taxing and Spending Clause, disabling Congress from imposing taxes on businesses in part to implement regulatory policy unless some other enumerated power authorized the objectives Congress sought to achieve.[6] This limitation cast serious doubt on the validity of the 1935 Social Security Act for workers in manufacturing, mining, and other activities occurring "prior to" interstate commerce. The National Labor Relations Act, which established procedures for collective bargaining, was also constitutionally suspect before 1937.

The second doctrinal roadblock to enacting social and economic policy was the Supreme Court's interpretation of the Due Process Clause in *Lochner v. New York*.[7] Just as narrow construction of the commerce and spending powers limited Congress's ability to regulate the economy, so too did the Court's construction of Fourteenth Amendment "liberty" to encompass "freedom of contract" disable state governments from enacting various labor laws, price regulations, maximum hours and minimum wage laws, and other economic regulations.[8] On this view, the state had to leave workers free to accept any terms of employment they were offered, even if it meant, as a practical matter, that workers had to accept unfavorable terms dictated by their employers or else remain unemployed.

The Court's federalism and contractual freedom jurisprudence was not a marginal development. It significantly affected the power of government to meet society's needs. As the nation became more industrialized and as the national economy became more integrated, the impact of the Court's doctrines on government's ability to respond to economic conditions became more pronounced in the everyday life of the nation. In turn, both state and federal governments came to conclude that a market economy was vulnerable to serious distortions and inequities if left largely unregulated.

One of those conditions was the increasing concentration of corporate power through trusts and monopolies. In 1890, Congress passed the Sherman Antitrust Act, which prohibits contracts or combinations in restraint of trade.[9] When the federal government sued the American Sugar Refining Company for "acquir[ing] nearly complete control of the manufacture of refined sugar within the United States," the Supreme Court held that Congress had no power to regulate contracts governing activities that supposedly precede commerce, such as sugar production, even though the evident purpose of the production monopoly was to control the price of sugar in the national marketplace.[10]

The sweatshop conditions facing wage laborers who migrated from rural areas into the cities exposed the vulnerabilities of an unprotected workforce. When Congress responded by prohibiting the interstate shipment of goods produced by child labor, the Supreme Court invalidated the law, again on the ground that manufacturing occurred prior to interstate commerce and thus the working conditions associated with manufacturing were outside of Congress's control.[11] Such matters were left to individual states, the Court said, because the Commerce Clause gave Congress no authority to set a national baseline of fair competition among states with respect to child labor, minimum wages, or maximum hours.[12]

And yet, when states attempted to establish minimum wages or maximum hours pursuant to their authority to regulate local employment conditions, they encountered judicial resistance based on the doctrine of freedom of contract. Although the decisions were not uniformly antiregulation,[13] the freedom of contract doctrine prevailed for more than three decades after *Lochner* and prohibited many government efforts to ensure equitable terms and conditions of employment. Striking down a New York minimum wage law for women in 1936, the Court continued to state the doctrine in broad terms:

> The right to make contracts about one's affairs is a part of the liberty protected by the due process clause. Within this liberty are provisions of contracts between employer and employee

fixing the wages to be paid. In making contracts of employment, generally speaking, the parties have equal right to obtain from each other the best terms they can by private bargaining. Legislative abridgement of that freedom can only be justified by the existence of exceptional circumstances. Freedom of contract is the general rule and restraint the exception.[14]

In these and other ways, the Supreme Court articulated a restrictive view of federal and state authority that blocked measures to reduce some of the inequities, hardships, and economically harmful conditions that accompanied the industrialization and urbanization of the economy. While these doctrinal roadblocks were consequential even before 1929, they deepened the genuine crisis facing the nation after the economy fell into the grip of the Great Depression. When President Roosevelt took office in 1933, he voiced the American people's widely shared belief that "the economy would almost certainly remain debilitated without substantial government intervention" and that "government had an affirmative obligation to do whatever was necessary to restore a healthy economy."[15]

In the first hundred days of his administration, President Roosevelt proposed and Congress enacted ambitious programs to stabilize the supply side of the economy. The cornerstones of his early efforts were the National Industrial Recovery Act (NIRA) and the Agricultural Adjustment Act (AAA), each intended to prevent destructive competition, to establish equitable wages, and to maintain stable supplies and profitability. In 1935, the Supreme Court struck down the core provisions of the NIRA and, in the next year, invalidated the AAA.[16] In the latter decision, *United States v. Butler*, the Court ruled that despite the apparently broad authority of the federal government to tax and spend for the "general welfare,"[17] the tax-and-subsidy provisions of the AAA were beyond the powers of Congress. "Coming on top of the 1935 opinions, the *Butler* verdict appeared to indicate a determination by the Court to wipe out all of the New Deal."[18] With these decisions as well as others that invalidated the federal railroad workers' pension law[19] and provisions of the Bituminous Coal Conservation Act,[20] the Supreme Court thwarted the focused response of the President and Congress to the most pressing economic crisis the country had ever faced.

On June 2, 1936, the day after the Court invalidated New York's minimum wage law for women, President Roosevelt said: "It seems to be fairly clear, as a result of this decision and former decisions, using this question of minimum wage as an example, that the 'no-man's-land' where no Government—State or Federal—can function is being more clearly defined. A State cannot do it, and the Federal Government cannot do it."[21] The impasse with the Court deeply frustrated President Roosevelt and his supporters. They could not believe that the Constitution forbade government from improving the working and living conditions of millions of Americans mired in poverty and hopelessness, or from regulating the marketplace to stabilize important industries and to stimulate growth. Constitutional authorities inside and outside of Roosevelt's administration debated whether the problem lay with the Constitution itself or with the current composition of the Court. In the end, President Roosevelt saw the prospect of amending the Constitution as remote if not impossible[22] and decided to pursue the course he thought most feasible to reform the Court's misguided doctrines.

On February 5, 1937, the President proposed the Judiciary Reorganization Act of 1937. It contained a provision to add one judge or Justice to any federal court on which a judge or Justice over the age of seventy and one half was sitting. The impact on the Supreme Court would have been dramatic and immediate: the bill would have enabled Roosevelt to appoint six new Justices. Despite widespread dissatisfaction with the Court, the court-packing plan met fierce and widespread resistance even among members of Roosevelt's party in Congress.

But before its validity could be tested legally or politically, the Supreme Court handed down a remarkable series of decisions dismantling the jurisprudence that had stymied federal and state legislative action. On March 29, 1937, the Court rejected a freedom-of-contract challenge to a minimum wage law from the state of Washington that was in all material respects identical to the New York law struck down a year earlier.[23] Two weeks later, the Court interpreted the Commerce Clause to sustain federal protections for labor organizing provided in the National Labor Relations Act,[24] and six weeks after that, it construed the Spending Clause to uphold the unemployment compensation provisions of the Social Security Act.[25] In each of these five-to-four decisions, Justice Owen Roberts abandoned the pre-1937 jurisprudence that he had previously endorsed, providing the so-called switch in time that saved the nine-person composition of the Court. The court-packing plan was never enacted, as congressional support for the bill dwindled. In the ensuing years, several departures from the Court enabled President Roosevelt to solidify, through new appointments, the change in direction that the 1937 decisions had signaled. Ultimately, the Court repudiated all significant aspects of its earlier doctrine blocking federal and state initiatives to promote equity, fair competition, and stability in the market economy.[26]

The legitimacy of the specific sequence of events by which the doctrinal transformation occurred has been much debated by constitutional scholars, with one leading theorist arguing that the 1937 change was an unorthodox but valid amendment of the Constitution outside of the Article V process.[27] Through all of the scholarly debate, the Court's changed understanding of the scope of federal and state power to oversee the economy has endured with the support of a broad national consensus. Today, as the nation emerges from its most severe economic crisis perhaps since the Great Depression, that understanding informs proposals for aggressive government action to stimulate growth and to cushion the free market's effects on individuals and corporate entities. Far from requiring a formal amendment to the Constitution, the legitimacy of such government action rests comfortably on a proper reading of the Constitution as written—that is, as a declaration of general principles "intended to endure for ages to come, and consequently, to be adapted to the various *crises* of human affairs"[28] and not as a set of narrow legalisms that "would cripple the government, and render it unequal to the object for which it is declared to be instituted."[29] In short, the constitutional history of the New Deal reveals the inadequacy of the Court's pre-1937 interpretive methodology rather than any shortcoming of the Constitution itself.

The error of the Court's jurisprudence on the scope of federal power lay in its adherence to formal conceptions of "commerce" that failed to correspond to the economic reality of the challenges Congress tried to address. The contrived distinctions between activities that "precede" or "succeed" commerce, or between activities with "direct" or "indirect" effects on commerce, disabled Congress from responding to problems, such as anticompetitive practices and unfair labor standards, with clearly national dimensions. Whatever resonance such distinctions might have had in a smaller nation comprised of distinct local economies, they bore little relationship to the functional realities of the integrated national economy that was emerging as the forces of industrialization and urbanization, the rise of large corporations, and advances in transportation and communication progressed and interacted.[30] In applying eighteenth-century definitions of commerce to the twentieth-century economy, the Court's conception of federalism failed to account for the more interdependent nation that the United States had become. As Justice Souter has observed, " '[t]he first call of a theory of law is that it should fit the facts,'" and "[t]he facts that cannot be ignored today are the facts of integrated national commerce and a political relationship between States and Nation much affected by their respective treasuries and constitutional modifications adopted by the people."[31] The lesson of the New Deal is thus similar to the lesson of *Brown:* constitutional interpretation that is untethered to social context and unresponsive to the lived experience of the American people cannot keep faith with a charter of government designed to endure and meet the challenges facing each generation, and will not long command legitimacy.

The *Lochner* doctrine was also grounded in an implausible account of economic and social realities. Whatever the merits of construing "liberty" in the Due Process Clause to encompass a right of contractual freedom, the Court's recurring portrait of state regulation as unwarranted interference with supposedly voluntary and consensual relationships between employers and employees or between businesses and consumers[32] often ignored the conditions of hardship, privation, and unequal bargaining power in the face of ascendant corporatism that made true freedom of contract illusory. Moreover, the doctrine of contractual freedom failed to recognize that market ordering under the common law is itself a social and legal construct rather than a natural baseline from which to evaluate the validity of government action.[33] Once the Court recognized that traditional market mechanisms were "state-created, hardly neutral, and without prepolitical status," government regulation of market exchange could no longer be deemed suspect on the ground that it disturbed the purportedly "natural" outcome of private choices.[34]

After 1937, the Court generally applied minimal scrutiny under the Fourteenth Amendment to "regulatory legislation affecting ordinary commercial transactions" and reserved "more searching judicial inquiry" for legislation that may reflect "prejudice against discrete and insular minorities."[35] And with respect to congressional power, the Court, appropriately pressed by the nation's needs and experiences, found a new equilibrium that adapted the principle of federalism to accommodate national authority to facilitate a productive and fair economy. As the Court eventually explained, "the Framers chose to rely on a federal system in which special restraints on federal power over the States inhered principally in the workings of the National Government itself, rather than in discrete limitations on the objects of federal authority. State sovereign interests, then, are more properly protected by procedural safeguards inherent in the structure of the federal system than by judicially created limitations on federal power."[36]

Events since 1937 illustrate how these procedural safeguards of federalism function, as well as how the national dialogue about federalism continues. Without undermining the consensus supporting federal authority on economic and other matters, Congress regularly enacts provisions respecting state and local primacy through programs in which the states decide how national standards are to apply to local conditions. State and local governments also continue to take the lead in many areas of traditional state concern, such as education, land use planning, and law enforcement. When Congress funds programs, it often does so in the form of block grants to states and in a manner that reflects state-determined priorities. The state- and district-based nature of congressional representation ensures that state concerns are heard and understood. In both congressional debates and the larger national dialogue, the balance between federal and state authority continues to be negotiated.

In recent years, the Court has re-entered the dialogue regarding this balance in several contexts, including limits on the federal commerce power. Its recent decisions invalidating federal laws under the commerce clause caused some to worry about "a return to the untenable jurisprudence from which the Court extricated itself [over]

60 years ago."[37] These decisions render certain subjects off-limits to federal regulation by attempting to draw a line between "economic" and "noneconomic" activity[38]—a line that "looks much like the old distinction between what directly affects commerce and what touches it only indirectly" in its incoherence and inefficacy in advancing federalism values.[39] Later decisions, however, seem to indicate that the Court's new federalism is not heading toward a jurisprudence incompatible with the demands of contemporary society.[40] Perhaps this shows the continuing influence of Justice Cardozo's observation years ago when he rejected the distinction between "direct" and "indirect" effects, that "a great principle of constitutional law is not susceptible of comprehensive statement in an adjective."[41] That admonition remains as pertinent today as it was then in pointing the way toward faithful interpretation of constitutional text and principle.

The principle of federalism is another of our Constitution's commitments that is informed by the actual experiences and changing conditions facing the American people. Neither original understandings nor static, formal categories provide an adequate account of what we understand today as the legitimate scope of government power and responsibility to promote the general welfare. The application of the Constitution's text and principles to authorize government to address contemporary economic challenges provides another illustration of what we mean by constitutional fidelity.

CHAPTER SIX

Separation of Powers

SEPARATING THE POWERS of the federal government and dividing them among the House and Senate, the President, and the Judiciary were decisions fundamental to the Constitution's design. With fresh memories of the Crown's exercise of autocratic authority over the colonies, the Founding generation was determined to prohibit the concentration of government power in the hands of one person or one body. As an "essential precaution in favor of liberty,"[1] the Framers created a government that separates the power to make law from the power to execute the law and further separates those powers from the power to try individuals for violating the law. While departing from the Articles of Confederation to create the office of the President, our Constitution conspicuously omits any analog to the dispensing power invoked by British monarchs to disregard acts of Parliament and instead directs the President to "take Care that the Laws be faithfully executed."[2]

In the aftermath of September 11, 2001, President Bush repeatedly claimed that the Constitution gave him authority to act contrary to duly enacted federal statutes. He asserted the right to engage in domestic electronic surveillance despite restrictions in the Foreign Intelligence Surveillance Act.[3] He claimed the power to apply so-called enhanced interrogation techniques to persons in U.S. custody despite statutes prohibiting torture.[4] He argued that Congress cannot extend the habeas corpus jurisdiction of federal courts to alien detainees held abroad because it would interfere with the President's authority to conduct the military campaign against al Qaeda.[5] And upon passage of the McCain amendment in 2005 banning cruel, inhuman, or degrading treatment of any person under U.S. custody or control anywhere in the world, President Bush issued a signing statement declaring that he would construe the prohibition subject to his authority as Commander in Chief to protect the nation from further terrorist attacks.[6]

An August 2002 memorandum on torture by the Office of Legal Counsel set out the purported basis for the President's ability to disregard statutory law.[7] The Department of Justice subsequently withdrew this "torture memo" but did not disclaim its bold assertion of executive authority until five days before President Bush left office.[8] "In wartime," the memo stated, "it is for the President alone to decide what methods to use to best prevail against the enemy."[9] When the enemy is not the Taliban or Saddam Hussein but rather "international terrorist organization[s],"[10] with whom we might be at war for our lifetimes,[11] the upshot of reserving to the President alone the authority to decide what methods to use against the enemy would be to grant unfettered discretion to the President, notwithstanding statutory constraints, to pursue any action he believes conducive to interdicting, retaliating against, or gaining intelligence about terrorist activities.

Throughout the world, there are examples of governments led by a strongman with such unchecked powers. But our nation's Founders made a different choice. A key premise of our Constitution, as James Madison explained, is that "[t]he accumulation of all powers, legislative, executive, and judiciary, in the same hands, whether of one, a few, or many, and whether hereditary, self-appointed, or elective, may justly be pronounced the very definition of tyranny."[12] Our system disperses power among three branches of government, and it does so not by making them "wholly unconnected with each other" but by "giv[ing] to each a constitutional control over the others."[13] In other words, ours is a system of checks and balances.

This fundamental principle applies even in times of war. The Founders recognized that the executive must act with dispatch and strength in times of war, but they were deeply concerned about the risk of concentrating too much power in executive hands. The text of the Constitution reflects that concern. It contains seven clauses assigning significant war powers to Congress—the powers to declare war, grant letters of marque and reprisal, and make rules concerning captures on land and water; to raise and support armies; to provide and maintain a navy; to make rules governing land and naval forces; to call forth the militia; to provide for the organizing, arming, and disciplining of the militia; and to define and punish piracies and felonies committed on the high seas and offenses against the law of nations.[14] By contrast, the war powers committed to the President derive solely from his designation as Commander in Chief of the armed forces and the militia.[15]

In times of emergency, the President is naturally inclined toward robust action in the nation's defense, and the Commander in Chief authority ensures unified control of our armed forces. While reserving to Congress the power to declare war, the Founders certainly expected the President to have the power to repel sudden attacks without prior congressional authorization.[16] Such power is meant to authorize the President not to create a state of war but to use force to defend the nation when conditions of exigency make prior approval by Congress impractical and when the President reasonably anticipates that Congress will support the action after the fact. But nothing in the Constitution's text or framing history suggests that the President's power to repel sudden attacks displaces Congress's authority under its war powers (or other powers) to make law that is binding on the Executive after the emergency has passed.

In recent years, the most aggressive claims of executive authority have relied not on the well-established power to respond to exigencies but instead on the President's prerogative as Commander in Chief to make strategic and tactical decisions in wartime. As the August 2002 memorandum by the Office of Legal Counsel put it, "Congress lacks authority under Article I to set the terms and conditions under which the President may exercise his authority as Commander-in-Chief to control the conduct of operations during a war."[17] Under this theory, "Congress may no more regulate the President's ability to detain and interrogate enemy combatants than it may regulate his ability to direct troop movements on the battlefield."[18] And so, "[j]ust as statutes that order the President to conduct warfare in a certain manner or for specific goals would be unconstitutional, so too are laws that seek to prevent the President from gaining the intelligence he believes necessary to prevent attacks upon the United States."[19]

These assertions go beyond the claim that the President has inherent power to conduct military operations in the nation's defense absent congressional authorization. The latter claim is an interpretation of presidential power within what Justice Jackson called the "zone of twilight," where the "absence of either a congressional grant or denial of authority" invites the President to "rely upon his own independent powers" even as "he and Congress may have concurrent authority, or . . . its distribution is uncertain."[20] Justice Jackson recognized that presidential claims of inherent power in this zone of twilight (Category Two in his tripartite analytical framework) are often controversial, with "any actual test of power...likely to depend on the imperatives of events and contemporary imponderables rather than on abstract theories of law."[21] Even more controversial, then, are Category Three cases—such as the recent examples above—where the President claims "preclusive" power to "take[] measures incompatible with the expressed or implied will of Congress."[22] Here the President's power "is at its lowest ebb."[23] Such claims of executive authority "must be scrutinized with caution" lest they undermine "the equilibrium established by our constitutional system."[24]

Throughout our nation's history, the equilibrium to which Justice Jackson referred is one that has eschewed any broad assignment of preclusive power to the President in his role as Commander in Chief. Textually, the Constitution's designation of the President as Commander in Chief does suggest some limits on congressional control. For example, Congress may not alter the military hierarchy by assigning ultimate command of the armed forces to a military officer or to anyone other than the President. Nor may Congress delegate responsibility for the conduct of a military campaign to an officer insulated from presidential direction or removal.[25] These limitations marked a significant change from the power that the Articles of Confederation had given to Congress to appoint officers of the armed forces.[26]

It is less clear, however, that the President's authority as Commander in Chief precludes congressional enactments that substantively direct the conduct of military campaigns. In an exhaustive survey of evidence from Founding-era practices, the Constitutional Convention, and the state ratification process, David Barron and Martin Lederman conclude that historically "the legislature possessed the power to subject the Executive to control over all matters pertaining to warmaking," including "such clearly tactical matters as the movement of troops."[27] "[N]otwithstanding recent attempts to yoke the defense of executive defiance in wartime to original understandings," they explain, "there is surprisingly little Founding-era evidence supporting the notion that the conduct of military campaigns is beyond legislative control and a fair amount of evidence that affirmatively undermines it."[28]

During the Revolutionary War, for example, the Continental Congress exercised extensive authority over the strategies and tactics, including troop deployments, ordered by George Washington as Commander in Chief of the colonial army. Scrupulously deferential to congressional dictates, Washington never assumed that he had authority to disobey a legislative command, even when he believed Congress's judgment to be clearly wrong.[29] Similarly, there is no indication in early state constitutions that the Commander in Chief of the militia could act contrary to statutes governing military affairs. The constitutions of several states, including Massachusetts and New Hampshire, made clear that the war powers of the commander in chief were subject to legislative control.[30]

If we look beyond original understandings, we find little evidence in our constitutional practice of any widely shared understanding that the President's authority as Commander in Chief precludes congressional regulation of military operations. Even during the Civil War, a reference point often invoked by contemporary defenders of robust executive power, "Lincoln himself never once asserted a broad power to disregard statutory limits, not even during his well-known exercise of expansive executive war powers at the onset of hostilities or when confronted with statutes that challenged his own tactical choices later in the war."[31] In particular, when President Lincoln in April 1861 authorized his generals to suspend habeas corpus in response to rioting in various states, he defended his action on two grounds: first, that the suspension was a necessary response to a genuine emergency at a time when Congress was not in session, and second, that the Article I Suspension Clause empowers the President, in Congress's absence, to suspend habeas corpus when the nation faces rebellion. Whatever the merits of these arguments, they were "a far cry from a claim of general power pursuant to the Commander in Chief Clause to defy statutes regulating the conduct of war."[32] Indeed, President Lincoln conceded that the suspension was subject to congressional override, and when Congress passed the Habeas Corpus Act of 1863 limiting the President's suspension power, neither he nor his administration argued that the statute would be unconstitutional if it constrained the President's detention policies during war.[33]

Equally relevant is President Lincoln's acquiescence to the Second Confiscation Act, which Congress passed in 1862. Despite his concern that seizing rebel property and emancipating certain slaves as tactics for ending the war risked alienating the border states, "no executive branch official—including the President and his Attorney General—contended at any point in the extensive debate that the Act unconstitutionally interfered with the President's constitutional war authority" even though that argument had been thoroughly aired in Congress.[34]

The history of our constitutional practice reveals no longstanding tradition of preclusive executive power to control the conduct of war, although the claim has surfaced more often since the mid-twentieth century. President Truman invoked preclusive as well as inherent power as Commander in Chief in deploying forces to Europe in 1951 to counter the Soviet threat,[35] but it does not appear that the deployment actually violated any federal statutes. And while many believe Truman exceeded his inherent powers when he committed troops to the Korean War without prior congressional authorization,[36] his action did not rely on preclusive power to disregard a statutory prohibition. Over the next fifty years, Congress passed numerous laws restricting the President's power to conduct military operations, including legislation in 1971 prohibiting U.S. deployment of ground troops in Cambodia, the War Powers Resolution in 1973, the Foreign Intelligence Surveillance Act in 1978, and the Boland Amendments in the 1980s restricting military aid to the Contras in Nicaragua.[37] Although nearly all of President Truman's successors claimed preclusive power in one or more circumstances, the practice was not consistent and often left unclear whether the claim was made in anticipation of future circumstances or in response to an applicable law on the books. "Certainly there was no sustained practice of actually disregarding statutes similar to that we have seen since September 11, 2001."[38] Further, it is worth noting that, from the Founding to the present day, the Supreme Court has never invalidated a federal statute on the ground that it improperly interfered with the President's constitutional prerogative to conduct a military campaign.

Faced with this history, recent defenders of preclusive presidential power have argued that new constitutional understandings are required in order to meet new threats to national security. The principal author of the Office of Legal Counsel's August 2002 memorandum on torture has explained that traditional checks and balances "might have been more appropriate at the end of the Cold War, when conventional warfare between nation-states remained the chief focus of concern and few threats seemed to challenge American national security."[39] Today, however, "it certainly is no longer clear that the constitutional system ought to be fixed so as to make it difficult to use force" given the emergence of rogue nations, the easy availability of weapons of mass destruction, and the rise of international terrorism.[40] Instead of maintaining "a warmaking system that place[s] a premium on consensus, time for deliberation, and the approval of multiple institutions," the argument goes, now "[t]he United States must have the option to use force earlier and more quickly than in the past."[41]

Although arguments for preclusive power based on societal change can hold no sway among those who believe in an originalism of expected applications, they nonetheless merit careful consideration because our Constitution's text and principles were meant to be adapted to new challenges and not frozen in time. In the war on terrorism, we face an asymmetrical conflict where the enemy is not a nation-state but a diffuse and hidden network, where enemy tactics include the targeting of civilian populations, where armed struggle is not confined to a traditional battlefield, and where the enemy's sources of financing and support are largely secret and not rooted in a territorial homeland. These conditions differ in many ways from past conflicts with nation-states that have agreed to abide by laws of war, and the unconventional nature of the enemy and its tactics may call for novel responses. The question is whether effective responses to terrorist threats require an allocation of decision-making authority that departs from original understandings of separation of powers and its actual practice throughout our history—in particular, the long-standing power of Congress to regulate the President's conduct of military campaigns.

It may be too soon to answer the question definitively, given the recency of the war on terrorism. But the argument for unchecked presidential power based on changed conditions should be viewed with skepticism. As an initial matter, we ought not to assume too quickly that the threat of terrorism is entirely different from security threats that our nation has confronted in the past. "The United States has long been troubled by substate actors engaged in nontraditional tactics to undermine U.S. interests," beginning with the Barbary pirates during the Founding era.[42] But even acknowledging the important differences between today's threats and those of the past, it is not obvious that effective responses require an enlargement of presidential power up to and including the power to disregard federal statutes constraining the exercise of executive war powers.

As a functional matter, our nation's "history undermines assertions about the inherent or inevitable unmanageability or dangers of recognizing legislative control over the conduct of war."[43] In the war on terrorism, there is little evidence so far to suggest that complying with existing laws or engaging Congress in passing new legislation has hampered the President's prosecution of the war. Where the President has asked Congress for greater authority, Congress has generally been willing to provide it.[44]

For example, after the National Security Agency's secret warrantless surveillance program came to light in 2005, the Attorney General argued that the program was a proper exercise of the President's power as Commander in Chief because existing statutory authority for government wiretapping was inadequate to meet national security needs. The secret program was justified, the Attorney General claimed, despite procedures in the Foreign Intelligence Surveillance Act that comprised "the exclusive means" for conducting domestic electronic surveillance.[45] The President, however, had never asked Congress for additional authority. Once the national security needs were made clear to Congress, legislators enacted the authorizations necessary to put the surveillance within a legal framework that balances effective intelligence-gathering with important privacy concerns.[46]

As this example and others suggest, there are good reasons to believe that the development of sound antiterrorism policies requires more, not less, interbranch consultation and cooperation.[47] By contrast, the Bush administration's torture and interrogation policies showed how a claim of preclusive power—lacking the public deliberation, scrutiny, and consensus-building that the lawmaking process affords—could be self-defeating by compromising the effective prosecution of terrorist suspects, by undermining the collection of reliable intelligence, and by alienating potential allies throughout the world.

Notably, the Supreme Court has shown no inclination to endorse claims of preclusive power in the war on terrorism. Every major decision by the Court in this area has invoked traditional understandings of checks and balances. In *Rasul v. Bush*, for example, the Court held that federal courts have jurisdiction under the federal habeas statute to hear suits by Guantánamo detainees challenging the legality of their detention, effectively rejecting the President's argument that reading the habeas statute this way would unconstitutionally interfere with his Commander in Chief power.[48]

Similarly, in *Hamdi v. Rumsfeld*, the President claimed "plenary authority" to detain indefinitely an American citizen captured as an enemy combatant in Afghanistan despite a federal statute prohibiting the detention of citizens.[49] In a plurality opinion joined by Chief Justice Rehnquist, Justice Kennedy, and Justice Breyer, Justice O'Connor declined to reach the President's broad claim, instead upholding the detention on the ground that the Authorization of the Use of Military Force enacted by Congress after September 11, 2001, provided sufficient authorization for the detention. Rather than endorse a broad construction of the Commander in Chief power, the plurality situated the President's action within the confines of a duly enacted statute. Further, the plurality elaborated the due process requirements applicable to the detention. In doing so, Justice O'Connor reaffirmed our settled understanding of separation of powers:

> [The President's argument] serves only to condense power into a single branch of government. We have long since made clear that a state of war is not a blank check for the President when it comes to the rights of the Nation's citizens. Whatever power the United States Constitution envisions for the Executive in its exchanges with other nations or with enemy organizations in

times of conflict, it most assuredly envisions a role for all three branches when individual liberties are at stake.[50]

Subsequently, the Court in *Hamdan v. Rumsfeld* held that military tribunals created by President Bush purportedly through his inherent power as Commander in Chief were not authorized by statute and violated the Uniform Code of Military Justice and the Geneva Conventions.[51] In reaching its holding, the Court rejected the notion of preclusive presidential power by saying: "Whether or not the President has independent power, absent congressional authorization, to convene military commissions, he may not disregard limitations that Congress has, in proper exercise of its own war powers, placed on his powers."[52] As Justice Breyer observed, "[n]othing prevents the President from returning to Congress to seek the authority he believes necessary."[53] After *Hamdan*, the President did precisely that, and Congress responded by enacting legislation authorizing military commissions for aliens detained as enemy combatants.[54]

Although it is fair to say that the statutes examined in *Rasul*, *Hamdi*, and *Hamdan* are not models of legislative clarity or foresight, the decisions in those cases ultimately reflect the Court's adherence to Justice Jackson's dictum that "[w]ith all its defects, delays and inconveniences, men have discovered no technique for long preserving free government except that the Executive be under the law, and that the law be made by parliamentary deliberations."[55] Neither original understandings nor the lessons of constitutional practice, including our most recent experiences in the war on terrorism, provide reason to question that wisdom. In sum, fidelity to the Constitution requires that we preserve, not abandon, the core principle of checks and balances by working within our system of divided power to meet new challenges through democratic means.

CHAPTER SEVEN

Democracy

ASK THE AVERAGE person what democracy means and she is likely to reply "majority rule." Ask her what political equality means and she is likely to reply "one person, one vote." But neither majority rule nor one person, one vote has the kind of historical or constitutional pedigree that most people assume. To the contrary, most states until the 1960s flouted the principle of one person, one vote either by design or through inaction. Many states retained legislative district boundaries first drawn at the turn of the twentieth century long after their populations had shifted dramatically. Still other states, even if they went through the motions of redrawing legislative district boundaries after each census, crafted the new districts to perpetuate the existing allocation of power, often relying on state constitutional provisions that deliberately diminished the voting strength of urban areas.[1]

In 1962, when the Supreme Court launched what came to be known as the reapportionment revolution, typical examples of how seats were allocated include the following: in Maryland, a majority of the state senate could be elected from districts containing only 14.1% of the state's population; in Colorado and New York, a majority of the lower house of the state legislature could be elected from districts containing roughly a third of those states' populations; in Connecticut, each of the state's sixty-nine towns had equal representation in the state house, which meant that Colebrook (population 592 in 1960) elected two representatives, as did Hartford (population 177,397).[2]

The systematic effects of malapportionment permeated the political system. Across the country, legislatures controlled by representatives from small towns failed to respond fairly to the needs of urban and suburban residents. In the South, government remained firmly in the grip of reactionary legislators from rural hamlets who formed the backbone of the movement against school integration known as Massive Resistance. Chief Justice Earl Warren remarked that if the Supreme Court had completed the reapportionment revolution a decade earlier, *Brown v. Board of Education* might have been unnecessary, since more progressive elements in the South could have dismantled Jim Crow through the political process.[3] At the national level, power within Congress was distorted by the fact that many of the most senior members of the House of Representatives were elected from underpopulated districts drawn by unrepresentative state legislatures. Under these circumstances, it is no small irony that 1962—the year the Warren Court turned in earnest to the problem of apportionment—also marked the publication of Alexander Bickel's book *The Least Dangerous Branch*, whose influential critique of judicial review rested on claims about the "countermajoritarian difficulty" of courts overriding legislatures. When Bickel wrote, there was ample reason to question whether legislative judgments in fact reflected the views of contemporary popular majorities.

Today the reapportionment cases are widely accepted as faithful interpretations of the constitutional principles of self-government and equality. They have even won praise from conservative judges and scholars who criticize the Warren and Burger Courts' interventions into other legal and social institutions.[4] Yet the decisions cannot be explained by appealing to clear textual commands or by invoking original applications of the Constitution. Instead, the decisions illustrate how courts properly interpret the Constitution's text and principles when confronted with changing social conditions and practical circumstances of inequality. Further, the Court's efforts were part of an evolving conversation that ultimately engaged the political branches in providing greater democracy through legislation to enforce the Reconstruction Amendments.

When the Warren Court confronted congressional and state legislative malapportionment, it was well aware of the practice's pedigree. In 1946, the Court in *Colegrove v. Green* had confronted disparities as large as eight to one in the population of congressional districts within a state but had refused to intervene in what Justice Frankfurter memorably called "this political thicket."[5] Noting that "[t]hroughout our history...the most glaring disparities have prevailed as to the contours and the population of districts," the Court held that malapportionment raised a nonjusticiable political question under the Guarantee Clause and that responsibility for addressing the problem belonged to Congress.[6]

By the 1960s, it had become clear that the political process was incapable of fixing itself. Elected officials at the state and federal levels proved largely impervious to appeals from people they did not represent in the first place. Thus, in *Baker v. Carr*,[7] the Supreme Court revisited whether there was a role for judicial review in overseeing the creation of legislative districts. *Baker* challenged Tennessee's state legislative apportionment. Crafted in 1901 and resistant to revision ever since, the plan created legislative districts that by midcentury encompassed wildly different populations. For example, Decatur County's 5,563 citizens had the same number of representatives as Carter County's 23,303 citizens, and while Moore County had one representative for every 1,170 citizens, Rutherford County had one representative for every 12,658 citizens.[8] Tennessee's initial bias against urban areas, together with population growth and movement over the intervening sixty years, resulted in what Justice Clark described as "a topsy-turvical of gigantic proportions" and "a crazy quilt without rational basis."[9]

In *Baker*, the Court sidestepped the Guarantee Clause and instead relied on the Equal Protection Clause. That clause, the Court explained, protects individuals against arbitrary state discrimination, and "the right to relief under the equal protection clause is not diminished by the fact that the discrimination relates to political rights."[10] This conclusion itself marked a refusal to be limited to original applications, as the Fourteenth Amendment was not generally understood at the time of its drafting to reach political rights through the Equal Protection Clause. Indeed, part of the reason for the reduction-of-representation clause in Section 2 of the Fourteenth Amendment and for the Fifteenth Amendment's prohibition on racial discrimination in voting was the Framers' concern that the Equal Protection Clause alone did not protect the voting rights of freedmen.

The *Baker* Court also knew that allocation of political power on criteria other than population was common in our nation's experience. The U.S. Senate, for example, allocates two seats to each state regardless of its population. Moreover, at the time the Fourteenth Amendment was ratified, a majority of states used factors other than population to allocate seats in their legislative bodies. Even among the ten readmitted southern states, whose new constitutions might be thought to illustrate the requirements of the Reconstruction Amendments, only four used population as the sole determinant of apportionment.[11] The Court's decision to permit constitutional challenges to malapportionment thus depended on an interpretation of the Equal Protection Clause that went beyond the original understanding of the Fourteenth Amendment's applicability. In order to apply the equal protection principle barring "discrimination [that] reflects no policy, but simply arbitrary and capricious action,"[12] the Court had to determine whether geography, protection of rural interests, or other criteria besides population equality comprise arbitrary bases for apportionment, notwithstanding their assumed validity when the Fourteenth Amendment was ratified.

Over the next two years, the Court interpreted the Constitution to establish apportionment criteria that we take for granted today. In *Wesberry v. Sanders*, the Court construed Article I, Section 2, which provides that members of the House of Representatives be chosen "by the People of the several States," to require that "as nearly as is practicable one man's vote in a congressional election is to be worth as much as another's."[13] According to the Court, "[t]o say that a vote is worth more in one district than in another would...run counter to our fundamental ideas of democratic government."[14] This conclusion, the Court explained, follows from Article I, Section 2 even though its text does not expressly command a particular apportionment rule:

> No right is more precious in a free country than that of having a voice in the election of those who make the laws under which, as good citizens, we must live. Other rights, even the most basic, are illusory if the right to vote is undermined. Our Constitution leaves no room for classification of people in a way that unnecessarily abridges this right. In urging the people to adopt the Constitution, Madison said in No. 57 of *The Federalist:*
>
> Who are to be the electors of the Federal Representatives? Not the rich more than the poor; not the learned more than the ignorant; not the haughty heirs of distinguished names, more than the humble sons of obscure and unpropitious

fortune. The electors are to be the great body of the people
of the United States.

Readers surely could have fairly taken this to mean, "one person,
one vote."[15]

Four months later, in *Reynolds v. Sims*, the Court interpreted the
Equal Protection Clause to require a similar equalization of population in state legislative districts.[16] The Court again reached its
conclusion by invoking fundamental principles of democracy and
equality rather than the original understanding of the Fourteenth
Amendment:

> [R]epresentative government is in essence self-government
> through the medium of elected representatives of the people,
> and each and every citizen has an inalienable right to full and
> effective participation in the political processes of his State's
> legislative bodies. Most citizens can achieve this participation
> only as qualified voters through the election of legislators to
> represent them. Full and effective participation by all citizens in
> state government requires, therefore, that each citizen have an
> equally effective voice in the election of members of his state
> legislature. Modern and viable state government needs, and the
> Constitution demands, no less.[17]

Despite Justice Stewart's complaint that legislative apportionment "is far too subtle and complicated a business to be resolved as
a matter of constitutional law in terms of sixth-grade arithmetic,"[18]
the principle of one person, one vote had an elegant simplicity that
quickly garnered widespread support. Like other constitutional
rules (such as *Miranda*)[19] that conservatives have decried as judicial
activism, one person, one vote reflects the pragmatic wisdom of the
Warren Court. The declaration of a bright-line rule enabled the

political branches to understand their obligations and to respond to the principle of political equality in a more systematic way. By focusing on the mathematical weight of individual voters' ballots, the Court avoided the murkier political thicket in which questions regarding the allocation of political power lurked. Yet, by tying the constitutionality of districting schemes to population data, the Court effectively motivated periodic review of how political power is allocated. The decennial census compels reapportionment of virtually every legislative body in response to population shifts every ten years, and legislators' instincts for self-preservation create powerful incentives for them to address malapportionment before the courts intervene.

The idea behind one person, one vote was not merely to ensure abstract equality among individual voters. Whereas malapportionment often gave numerical minorities a stranglehold on government decision-making, one person, one vote was intended to assure that "in a society ostensibly grounded on representative government,...a majority of the people of a State could elect a majority of that State's legislators."[20] Moreover, Chief Justice Warren thought that one person, one vote would help ensure that "henceforth elections would reflect the collective public interest...rather than the machinations of special interests."[21] To be sure, this ambition has not been fully realized. Increasingly sophisticated redistricting techniques soon gave rise to the "equipopulous gerrymander"—an apportionment plan that complies with one person, one vote but carves lines with surgical precision to create districts designed to elect or defeat candidates from particular parties or constituencies.

Nevertheless, the Court's reinvigoration of the Equal Protection Clause as a source of political values spurred a national dialogue on the meaning of political equality. In *Reynolds v. Sims*, the Court observed that "the right of suffrage can be denied by a debasement or dilution of the weight of a citizen's vote just as effectively as by wholly prohibiting the free exercise of the franchise."[22] Soon thereafter, the Court acknowledged that even where a redistricting plan complied with one person, one vote, "[i]t might well be that, designedly or otherwise, a [particular] apportionment scheme, under the circumstances of a particular case, would operate to minimize or cancel out the voting strength of racial or political elements of the voting population."[23] Thus, the reapportionment cases prompted the Court and eventually Congress to address not only quantitative but also qualitative vote dilution.[24]

The Court initially took the lead in developing a theory of qualitative vote dilution. In *White v. Regester*, the Court struck down a Texas state redistricting plan even though it complied with one person, one vote because the way districts were drawn in black and Latino areas meant that minority voters "had less opportunity than did other residents in the district to participate in the political processes and to elect legislators of their choice."[25] In *City of Mobile v. Bolden*, however, a four-Justice plurality offered a narrow interpretation of the constitutional provisions that prohibit racial discrimination in voting, construing the Fifteenth Amendment to protect only the right to "register and vote without hindrance" and reading the Equal Protection Clause to require that plaintiffs prove that the challenged election was "conceived or operated as a purposeful device to further racial discrimination."[26]

Two years later, Congress responded to *Bolden*'s limited focus on intentional discrimination with an amended version of Section 2 of the Voting Rights Act that embraced a group-disadvantaging conception of political equality. The 1982 amendments to Section 2 provide that a voting rights violation is established when a plaintiff shows that the challenged practice "results in" discrimination.[27] Thus Congress made clear that not only discriminatory intent but also discriminatory *results* undermine the Fourteenth and Fifteenth Amendment guarantees of equal voting rights.[28] In its final Term, the Burger Court ratified this group-disadvantaging perspective when it acknowledged that Congress, in amending Section 2, had "dispositively reject[ed] the position of the plurality in [*Bolden*], which required proof that the contested electoral practice or mechanism was adopted or maintained with the intent to discriminate against minority voters."[29] The Court accepted Congress's directive that adjudication of Section 2 claims must proceed from "a functional view of the political process" and must undertake "a searching practical evaluation of the past and present reality" within the defendant jurisdiction.[30] Factors that are probative of voting discrimination include (but are not limited to) racial bloc voting, the responsiveness of elected officials to a minority group's concerns, and socioeconomic disparities that might impair a minority group's ability to participate effectively in the political process.[31]

The 1982 amendments had a transformative effect on representative democracy. At the time Section 2 was amended, a sizeable majority of municipal elections were conducted on an at-large basis, and most southern states elected at least some state legislators from multimember districts. Within a decade, most jurisdictions with substantial minority populations had switched to a system with at least some single-member districts, and state legislatures were elected entirely from single-member districts, some of which were majority black or Hispanic. By the post-1990 round of redistricting, blacks and Hispanics had progressed from being all but locked out of the political process to serving as key members of state redistricting committees, many of which produced more representative state legislatures and congressional delegations. Elected bodies across the nation now have minority legislative caucuses and minority governing officials. Minority legislators, in turn, have enhanced the responsiveness of our laws and policies to the needs and interests of minority communities, further enabling those communities to participate effectively in the political process.

Although many challenges remain in ensuring fairness at all levels of the political process, judicial interpretation of the Constitution has facilitated significant progress toward the development of truly representative political institutions. The Supreme Court has played this important role not by adhering to strict construction of constitutional text or by applying constitutional provisions as they would have been applied when ratified. In applying the textual command of equal protection of the laws and the underlying principles of representative democracy, the Court's reapportionment decisions are primarily concerned with giving the Constitution practical meaning in a society of shifting demographics as well as historic and contemporary inequality. When the Court unduly narrowed the constitutional principle of political equality in *City of Mobile v. Bolden*, Congress supplied a necessary corrective to which the Court subsequently deferred. This trajectory of interpretation illustrates the evolutionary process by which our courts, together with the political branches, faithfully apply the Constitution's text and principles to a changing world.

CHAPTER EIGHT

. . .

Criminal Justice

STORIES OF ABUSE and mistreatment in the criminal justice system have long held the nation's fascination. The most egregious examples include the 1931 Scottsboro trials; the 1961 conviction of Clarence Earl Gideon, who was later retried and acquitted after winning the right to counsel; and more recently the round-up in Tulia, Texas, of forty-six men and women, most of whom were African American, in a purported drug sting orchestrated by a rogue undercover officer in 1999. Such high-profile cases serve as occasional reminders that the accused in our system stand innocent before the law until proven guilty and that such proof must conform to specific constitutional limits on government power as well as the broad guarantee of due process of law.

Historically, although such incidents may not have been the norm across the country, they occurred more frequently than many people wished to accept. For much of the twentieth century, coerced confessions, police brutality, and other abuses were not necessarily common, but they were not rare either. In many southern states, the criminal justice system reflected the divisive and denigrating ideology of Jim Crow. And throughout the country, the most basic protections afforded by the system were often illusory in practice for poor or minority individuals accused of crime.

In the 1960s, the Supreme Court began to revolutionize the constitutional rights of individuals within the criminal justice system. The Court held that defendants are entitled to have an attorney present during custodial interrogations and lineups.[1] It required the state to provide an indigent criminal defendant with a lawyer if he or she could not afford one.[2] It extended the warrant requirements of the Fourth Amendment to cover electronic surveillance,[3] administrative inspections,[4] and the search of a home following an arrest.[5] Moreover, as discussed in more detail below, the Court in *Miranda v. Arizona* replaced case-by-case inquiry into the voluntariness of confessions with a prophylactic requirement that custodial interrogations be preceded with a warning notifying the defendant of the right to remain silent and to have a lawyer present during questioning.[6] And in *Mapp v. Ohio*, the Court extended the exclusionary rule to the states, barring prosecutors from using evidence obtained through any search that violates the Fourth Amendment.[7] Many of these decisions drew criticism for supposedly having no basis in the Constitution and for tilting the criminal justice system too heavily in favor of the accused. The criticism reached a crescendo when Richard Nixon made it a centerpiece of his 1968 presidential campaign, pledging to appoint judges who believed in "strict construction" and "law and order" (which Nixon understood to be the same things). President Nixon's successful campaign marked the beginning of the end of the Warren Court, as he and his Republican successors appointed several Justices who were more conservative on criminal justice issues than the Warren Court had been.

Tellingly, however, the landmark criminal procedure decisions of the Warren Court, while not extended in later doctrine and in some cases weakened by exceptions, remain largely intact today. Their endurance as settled law indicates that their constitutional grounding is more sound and their holdings more widely accepted than the attacks on them would suggest. Over the years, *Miranda* has been subjected to especially vigorous criticism, as conservatives have argued that the warnings are not constitutionally compelled and that voluntariness is the only true constitutional requirement for use of a confession in court. According to this view, the *Miranda* rule could be supplanted by a federal or state statute. But when the Supreme Court finally heard a case testing the constitutionality of a statute purporting to supersede *Miranda* in federal prosecutions, Chief Justice Rehnquist, an early critic of *Miranda*, wrote a seven-to-two opinion holding that "*Miranda* announced a constitutional rule that Congress may not supersede legislatively."[8] The Court declined to overrule *Miranda* on the ground that "*Miranda* has become embedded in routine police practice to the point where the warnings have become part of our national culture."[9]

The legitimacy of *Miranda* does not rest simply on long usage and familiarity. The decision itself is faithful to the Constitution in the way it interprets the document's text and principles to sustain their vitality as our society and institutions change over time. In particular, *Miranda* adapts the Fifth Amendment privilege against self-incrimination to important transformations of the criminal justice system that have occurred since the Founding era.

On an initial reading, the privilege against self-incrimination— "nor shall [any person] be compelled in any criminal case to be a witness against himself"[10]—appears limited to the principle that no one may be compelled to testify against himself in a criminal proceeding in which he is a defendant.[11] On this view, *Miranda*'s extension of the privilege to custodial interrogation by the police seems unauthorized by the text. But in order to properly construe the text, it is essential to understand the historical context in which the Fifth Amendment was ratified. As Yale Kamisar has explained, a criminal defendant was not permitted to testify at trial at all, either for or against himself, at the time of the Fifth Amendment's adoption.[12] Thus, the original importance of the privilege was not to protect against self-incrimination in a criminal trial. It was instead "to bar pretrial examination by magistrates, the only form of pretrial interrogation known at the time."[13]

Given this history, how does the privilege apply to pretrial questioning by the police? The problem is one that the Framers never contemplated for the simple reason that at the time "there was no generalized bureaucracy of investigation of the sort we know today as the police.... '[T]here were simply no "police interrogators" to whom the privilege could be applied.' "[14] What the Court eventually called "the advent of modern custodial police interrogation"[15] did not occur until the late nineteenth century. Yet the application of the privilege to police interrogation flows logically from the constitutional principle because "if the police are permitted to interrogate an accused under the pressure of compulsory detention to secure a confession...they are doing the very same acts which historically the judiciary was doing in the seventeenth century but which the privilege against self-incrimination abolished."[16] In other words, "[t]he function which the police have assumed in interrogating an accused is exactly that of the early committing magistrates, and the opportunities for imposition and abuse are fraught with much greater danger."[17] Chief Justice Warren described those dangers at length in *Miranda* en route to observing that the privilege, as it developed historically, "has always been 'as broad as the mischief against which it seeks to guard.' "[18] The Court's conclusion that "all the principles embodied in the privilege apply to informal compulsion exerted by law-enforcement officers during in-custody questioning"[19] is thus a sensible adaptation of the Fifth Amendment to new and unforeseen circumstances. "This is, indeed, a broad construction of the constitutional language"—and one that was not part of the original understanding—"but it is a construction which has seemed to be required if the basic objective of that language is to be realized."[20]

The specific warnings prescribed by *Miranda* have been more controversial. They are, critics say, a prime example of judicial legislation. Yet the warnings are fully consistent with a judicial role attentive to the practical efficacy of the Constitution's protections and to the lessons of experience in crafting workable rules. The Court in *Miranda* "came to [the issue of compulsion in custodial interrogation] after decades of experience with case-by-case assessment of all the circumstances" to determine the voluntariness of confessions.[21] As Stephen Schulhofer has explained, the totality-of-the-circumstances test

> had left lower courts without usable standards and thus had created disproportionate demands for case-by-case review in the federal courts. The problems of judicial review also meant that intense interrogation pressures were inadequately controlled in practice. The case-by-case approach even failed to prevent, and in subtle ways actually encouraged, outright physical brutality.... Finally, case-by-case review left police themselves without adequate guidance.[22]

Similarly, the Court in *Dickerson* noted *Miranda*'s concern that "reliance on the traditional totality-of-the-circumstances test raised a risk of overlooking an involuntary custodial confession"[23] and also observed that "experience suggests that the totality-of-the-circumstances test...is more difficult than *Miranda* for law enforcement officers to conform to, and for courts to apply in a consistent manner."[24] Against this backdrop, the *Miranda* warnings reflect the Court's attempt to develop a practical rule for the accused, the police, and the courts to ensure the efficacy of the Fifth Amendment privilege. Notably, although *Dickerson* held that "*Miranda* announced a constitutional rule,"[25] the Court there, as in *Miranda* itself, declined to hold that "the *Miranda* warnings are required by the Constitution, in the sense that nothing else will suffice to satisfy constitutional requirements."[26] The Court thus continues to leave open the possibility that a legislative solution, informed by experience with evolving interrogation practices, could be at least as effective as *Miranda* warnings in protecting Fifth Amendment rights.[27]

In the Fourth Amendment area as well, key Warren Court decisions reflect a judicial approach that faithfully interprets the Constitution by giving practical effect to its text and principles in the face of societal change. In chapter 2, we saw this methodology at work in *Katz v. United States*,[28] where the Court construed the right against unreasonable searches and seizures to cover not only physical trespass but also electronic surveillance. Although the protections of the Fourth Amendment were originally tied to common-law protections of physical spaces and tangible objects, new communication technologies and the expectations of privacy we have when using them have outstripped the original understanding of the amendment's reach. *Katz* illustrates how an approach to interpretation that relies too heavily on original understandings of the reach of a constitutional principle would defy our own understanding of the Constitution as a document meant to retain, not lose, its significance over time. In reading the terms "search" and "seizure" to cover nonphysical intrusions such as wiretapping, the Court famously declared that "the Fourth Amendment protects people, not places,"[29] and effectively heeded Justice Brandeis's admonition that the Constitution "must have a...capacity of adaptation to a changing world" if "[r]ights declared in words [are not to] be lost in reality."[30]

The application of the exclusionary rule to the states also illustrates the adaptation of constitutional principle to societal change. Although the text of the Fourth Amendment does not prescribe a remedy for violations, the principal remedy available during the Founding era was the common law of trespass, which threatened strict liability for law enforcement officials who conducted warrantless searches but granted immunity to officials acting pursuant to a warrant. By imposing probable cause and specificity requirements on when a warrant may issue, the Fourth Amendment eliminated general warrants and, in so doing, narrowed the grounds on which an official could claim immunity in a trespass action. Personal liability thus gave law enforcement authorities a strong incentive to comply with the Fourth Amendment in its original historical setting.[31]

By the time the Supreme Court decided *Mapp v. Ohio*,[32] years of experience had shown that civil remedies and other alternatives were inadequate to deter Fourth Amendment violations. The Court in *Mapp* noted that "while in 1949...almost two-thirds of the States were opposed to the use of the exclusionary rule, now...more than half of those since passing upon it, by their own legislative or judicial decision, have wholly or partly adopted or adhered to [it]."[33] Citing California as a prominent example, the Court observed that "[t]he experience of California that such other remedies have been worthless and futile is buttressed by the experience of other States."[34] Immunity doctrines, the difficulty of proving official misconduct before a jury, and other obstacles meant that civil remedies did "little, if anything, to reduce the likelihood of the vast majority of [F]ourth [A]mendment violations—the frequent infringements motivated by commendable zeal, not condemnable malice."[35] Other remedies, such as criminal prosecution or injunctive relief against continuing violations, "are rarely brought and rarely succeed."[36] As Justice Ginsburg recently explained, "a forceful exclusionary rule" continues to be "the only effectively available way" to deter and remedy Fourth Amendment violations, especially in an age of increasing bureaucratization and technological sophistication of law enforcement.[37]

Thus the exclusionary rule, though not a perfect remedy, reflects a judicial adaptation of the Fourth Amendment's principles to contemporary realities. Far from unprincipled judicial legislation, the rule is designed to "merely place[] the government in the same position as if it had not conducted the illegal search and seizure in the first place."[38] Although the Framers did not contemplate the modern inefficacy of civil remedies for wrongful searches and seizures, the amendment was plainly intended to set effective limits on law enforcement and not to be "reduced to a 'form of words.' "[39] In light of its historical backdrop, the exclusionary rule makes sense as "a translation [of constitutional principle] aimed to preserve old protections in a new legal context."[40]

In recent years, the Supreme Court's treatment of the exclusionary rule has been rather inhospitable, with narrow majorities agreeing to limit its reach.[41] The Court should not continue this trend unless it finds a more effective way to prevent or remedy unlawful searches and seizures. If the Court finds such a solution, then the evolution of doctrine, far from subverting the Constitution or the judicial role, would serve to keep faith with the Constitution's text and principles over time.

CHAPTER NINE

. . .

Liberty

FOR THE PAST quarter century, debate over constitutional interpretation has often been summed up by reference to a single case: *Roe v. Wade*.[1] When the public thinks about the constitutional implications of presidential elections or Supreme Court vacancies, discussion quickly devolves into a variant of the question "Does this candidate or nominee support or seek to overturn *Roe?*" *Roe* has come to serve as shorthand not just for an individual's position on whether the Due Process Clauses of the Fifth and Fourteenth Amendments protect a woman's decision whether to terminate her pregnancy, but also for the broader question of how an individual approaches constitutional interpretation.

For all the focus on *Roe* itself, it is important first to locate *Roe* within the broader constellation of cases extending constitutional protection to individual decision-making on intimate questions of family life, sexuality, and reproduction. These cases, which deal with intimate and private activities, are often grouped under the rubric of the "right to privacy," a phrase derided by critics because the word "privacy" does not appear in the Constitution.[2] Privacy, however, is simply shorthand for a dimension of individual liberty, and the protection of "liberty" is a principle that not only appears in the Constitution's text but is central to the document's overall meaning. As such, the right to privacy reflects a widely shared understanding that certain activities involve private decision-making that ought to be free from government control. As Justice Kennedy said in *Lawrence v. Texas*:

> Liberty protects the person from unwarranted government intrusions into a dwelling or other private places. In our tradition the State is not omnipresent in the home. And there are other spheres of our lives and existence, outside the home, where the State should not be a dominant presence. Freedom extends beyond spatial bounds. Liberty presumes an autonomy of self that includes freedom of thought, belief, expression, and certain intimate conduct.[3]

The Constitution protects "liberty of the person both in its spatial and in its more transcendent dimensions."[4]

The rights affirmed in the cases from *Griswold v. Connecticut*, which struck down a law prohibiting married couples from using contraceptives,[5] to *Lawrence v. Texas*, which invalidated a law criminalizing same-sex sodomy,[6] enjoy widespread support and acceptance. They cannot be reconciled with an arid textualism or an originalism that asks how the Framing generation would have resolved the precise issues. But they are wholly consistent with an approach to constitutional interpretation that reads original commitments and contemporary social contexts together. The evolution of constitutional protection for individual autonomy in certain areas of intimate decision-making reflects precisely the rich form of constitutional interpretation this book envisions. In order to keep faith with the text and principles of the Constitution, judicial decisions have interpreted its guarantee of liberty in light of our society's evolving traditions and shared understandings of personal identity, privacy, and autonomy.

Perhaps the first case in this line of doctrine is the Supreme Court's 1942 decision in *Skinner v. Oklahoma*.[7] That case involved an Oklahoma statute that provided for the sterilization of certain "habitual" criminals. Justice Douglas's opinion for the Court recognized that the state was entitled to make distinctions among offenders without raising questions under the Equal Protection Clause. But the law at issue in *Skinner* was different:

> We are dealing here with legislation which involves one of the basic civil rights of man. Marriage and procreation are fundamental to the very existence and survival of the race. The power to sterilize, if exercised, may have subtle, far-reaching and devastating effects. In evil or reckless hands it can cause races or types which are inimical to the dominant group to wither and disappear. There is no redemption for the individual whom the law touches. Any experiment which the State conducts is to his irreparable injury. He is forever deprived of a basic liberty.[8]

Applying heightened scrutiny, the Court concluded that Oklahoma's law was unconstitutional.

Skinner was decided against the backdrop of several competing considerations. On the one hand, the Supreme Court had earlier upheld state sterilization of allegedly unfit individuals in *Buck v. Bell*, the notorious "[t]hree generations of imbeciles is enough" case in which Justice Holmes dismissively referred to the Equal Protection Clause as "the usual last resort of constitutional argument."[9] And the Court was hesitant to rule out government control over procreation altogether in light of its view of current scientific knowledge on the heritability of criminal traits. But by 1942, it was clear that "evil or reckless hands" in Nazi Germany and elsewhere were using sterilization as a technique to extinguish entire peoples. Just as our war against racism in Germany and Japan informed the Supreme Court's decisions in the *White Primary Cases*, which overruled earlier cases allowing political parties to exclude black voters, that war also shaped the Court's understanding of the individual liberty interest at stake in *Skinner*. Notably, in unanimously finding the Oklahoma statute unconstitutional, not a single Justice in *Skinner* asked whether forced sterilization would have been permitted in 1868 when the Fourteenth Amendment was adopted.

Moreover, *Skinner* illustrates an idea that arises repeatedly in the decisional autonomy cases, and that is the mutually supportive interaction between liberty and equality. As Justice Jackson understood, liberty is more secure when government is required to legislate evenhandedly: "The framers of the Constitution knew, and we should not forget today, that there is no more effective practical guaranty against arbitrary and unreasonable government than to require that the principles of law which officials would impose upon a minority must be imposed generally."[10] Similarly, equality is more secure when government may not deprive any group of a fundamental liberty interest without a compelling justification. In this way, equality and liberty arguments backstop each other, and this point has informed both contemporary understandings and judicial doctrine on decisional autonomy.[11]

The Court's next major foray in this area came in the Connecticut contraceptive cases. Like many other states, Connecticut adopted criminal prohibitions on the use of contraceptives in the late nineteenth century. But unlike virtually every other state in the nation, Connecticut maintained those statutes in their most sweeping form into the latter half of the twentieth century. Although Connecticut rarely enforced the prohibition against private physicians and their married clients, the law had an important chilling effect: it deterred the opening of public birth-control clinics that would have provided services to less affluent individuals or to women who were reluctant, for whatever reason, to consult their family doctor. In *Poe v. Ullman*, the Court dismissed a challenge to the Connecticut statute on the ground that the state's apparent failure to enforce the law meant there was no justiciable case or controversy.[12] But Justice Douglas and Justice Harlan dissented, finding in the Due Process Clause's protection of "liberty" a right for married couples to use contraception.

Justice Harlan's dissent in *Poe* is justly recognized as one of the best expositions of the proper method for interpreting the guarantee of liberty in the Fifth and Fourteenth Amendments. Observing that the constitutional text is "not self-explanatory," Justice Harlan explained:

> Due process has not been reduced to any formula; its content cannot be determined by reference to any code. The best that can be said is that through the course of this Court's decisions it has represented the balance which our Nation, built upon postulates of respect for the liberty of the individual, has struck between that liberty and the demands of organized society. If the supplying of content to this Constitutional concept has of necessity been a rational process, it certainly has not been one where judges have felt free to roam where unguided speculation might take them. The balance of which I speak is the balance struck by this country, having regard to what history teaches are the traditions from which it developed as well as the traditions from which it broke. That tradition is a living thing. A decision of this Court which radically departs from it could not long survive, while a decision which builds on what has survived is

likely to be sound. No formula could serve as a substitute, in this area, for judgment and restraint.

It is this outlook which has led the Court continuingly to perceive distinctions in the imperative character of constitutional provisions, since that character must be discerned from a particular provision's larger context. And inasmuch as this context is one not of words, but of history and purposes, the full scope of the liberty guaranteed by the Due Process Clause cannot be found in or limited by the precise terms of the specific guarantees elsewhere provided in the Constitution. This "liberty" is not a series of isolated points pricked out in terms of the taking of property; the freedom of speech, press, and religion; the right to keep and bear arms; the freedom from unreasonable searches and seizures; and so on. It is a rational continuum which, broadly speaking, includes a freedom from all substantial arbitrary impositions and purposeless restraints, and which also recognizes, what a reasonable and sensitive judgment must, that certain interests require particularly careful scrutiny of the state needs asserted to justify their abridgment....

Each new claim to Constitutional protection must be considered against a background of Constitutional purposes, as they have been rationally perceived and historically developed. Though we exercise limited and sharply restrained judgment, yet there is no "mechanical yardstick," no "mechanical answer." The decision of an apparently novel claim must depend on grounds which follow closely on well-accepted principles and criteria. The new decision must take "its place in relation to what went before and further [cut] a channel for what is to come."[13]

Applying these principles to the issue at hand, Justice Harlan concluded that Connecticut's decision to enforce its moral judgment through a criminal statute directed at married couples violated due process. He noted that the "aspect of liberty which embraces the concept of the privacy of the home receives explicit Constitutional protection at two places only"—in the Third Amendment, which regulates the quartering of troops, and the Fourth Amendment, which prohibits unreasonable searches and seizures.[14] However, he explained, limiting the right of privacy "to what is explicitly provided in the Constitution" would improperly "divorce[] [the concept] from the rational purposes, historical roots, and subsequent developments of the relevant provisions."[15] The Connecticut statute, while not involving a physical intrusion into the home, nonetheless intruded "on the life which characteristically has its place in the home."[16] Indeed, the statute regulated the "private realm of family life," no aspect of which "is more private or more intimate than a husband and wife's marital relations."[17] Thus, Justice Harlan interpreted the constitutional guarantee of "liberty" to encompass not only the spatial but also the decisional aspects of individual privacy. Although the constitutional provisions that secure a right to privacy do not mention its nonphysical dimensions, Justice Harlan understood that a constitutional "principle, to be vital, must be capable of wider application than the mischief which gave it birth."[18]

To be sure, Justice Harlan identified limits on the principle he advanced, some of which we no longer recognize today. For example, he did not question the state's right to enact laws against fornication, adultery, or homosexual conduct.[19] But, as Justice Harlan himself acknowledged, each constitutional claim must be considered against the backdrop of our evolving traditions and the principles developed in prior cases; there is "no mechanical answer."[20]

Four years later, the Court revisited the constitutionality of the Connecticut statute, this time reaching the merits and striking it down.[21] The Court's seven-to-two decision in *Griswold* produced multiple rationales. Justice Douglas's opinion for the Court did not locate the right of married couples to use contraception within a single constitutional provision. Rather, he pointed to a "zone of privacy created by several fundamental constitutional guarantees" including the First, Third, Fourth, and Fifth Amendments, all of which "have penumbras, formed by emanations from those guarantees that help give them life and substance."[22] Justice Goldberg, along with Chief Justice Warren and Justice Brennan, joined Justice Douglas's opinion for the Court but wrote separately to emphasize the Ninth Amendment's recognition of unenumerated rights. Justice Harlan and Justice White would have decided the case solely under the Due Process Clause on the reasoning that Justice Harlan had set forth in *Poe*.

In light of the fractured reasoning of the Court majority, it is notable that *Griswold* has become, in Jack Balkin's words, part of the "constitutional catechism"[23] widely accepted by the American people. Its privileged place in the constitutional canon is best demonstrated by the defeat of Judge Robert Bork's Supreme Court nomination in 1987. A major issue in the confirmation hearings was Bork's analysis of *Griswold*.[24] The Court had drawn a sharp distinction between the Connecticut anticontraception laws and "the wisdom, need, and propriety of laws that touch economic problems, business affairs, or social conditions."[25] But Bork, a self-proclaimed originalist, maintained there was no constitutionally significant difference between "the facts in *Griswold*," which involved the prosecution of a doctor and clinic director who provided contraceptives to a married couple, and "a hypothetical suit by an electric utility company and one of its customers to void a smoke pollution ordinance as unconstitutional."[26] He declared the two cases "*identical*."[27] He saw no constitutionally significant difference between the "sexual gratification" that a married couple would obtain from the use of contraception and the "economic gratification" that the utility company and its customers would get from cheaper power.[28] The defeat of

Bork's nomination signaled a strong public understanding that the Constitution protects a broad right to privacy. More fundamentally, it marked the failure of originalism to withstand public scrutiny as a methodology for faithfully interpreting the Constitution's text and principles.

Most historical accounts of the development of the right to privacy jump from *Griswold* to the 1972 decision *Eisenstadt v. Baird*,[29] another case concerning access to contraceptives. But between *Griswold* and *Eisenstadt*, the Supreme Court issued yet another canonical opinion, *Loving v. Virginia*,[30] that bears importantly on constitutional protection of individual decision-making. *Loving* struck down Virginia's law against interracial marriage on the ground that it reflected "arbitrary and invidious discrimination.... designed to maintain White Supremacy" in violation of the Equal Protection Clause.[31] But in the opinion's final two paragraphs, *Loving* marked a turn toward substantive due process. Virginia, the Court said, had "deprive[d] the Lovings of liberty without due process of law" by denying them the "freedom to marry [that] has long been recognized as one of the vital personal rights essential to the orderly pursuit of happiness by free men."[32] Citing *Skinner*, the Court again braided equality and liberty concerns by explaining that "[t]o deny this fundamental freedom on so unsupportable a basis as the racial classifications embodied in these statutes, classifications so directly subversive of the principle of equality at the heart of the Fourteenth Amendment, is surely to deprive all the State's citizens of liberty without due process of law."[33]

While *Griswold* and *Loving* were cases about marriage, *Eisenstadt* decoupled the autonomy interest from a traditional institution. There the Court held that the Equal Protection Clause precluded states from denying unmarried individuals the same access to contraception that *Griswold* had provided to married persons. While recognizing that "in *Griswold* the right of privacy in question inhered in the marital relationship," the Court went on to say that

> the marital couple is not an independent entity with a mind and heart of its own, but an association of two individuals each with a separate intellectual and emotional makeup. If the right of privacy means anything, it is the right of the individual, married or single, to be free from unwarranted governmental intrusion into matters so fundamentally affecting a person as the decision whether to bear or beget a child.[34]

Thus, the Court moved from recognizing the importance of a social institution to recognizing the centrality of intimate decision-making to an individual's identity and self-determination.

Today, our constitutional culture has so internalized the principles of *Griswold* and *Eisenstadt* that it is hard to imagine a legislature enacting, let alone a court upholding, a statute that criminalizes the distribution or use of contraceptives by adults. What accounts for that success? In part, as Justice Harlan suggested, it reflects the Court's wisdom in identifying "the decision whether to bear or beget a child" as one within the scope of liberty protected by the Due Process Clause. Whatever the understanding at the time of the framing or ratification of the Reconstruction Amendments, Americans now recognize that control over the number and timing of children is critical to the ability of men and women to participate fully in the political, economic, and social life of the nation. Any constitutional theory that either rejects that view or endorses it only grudgingly as a matter of stare decisis cannot achieve widespread acceptance or legitimacy.

To be sure, the right to choose abortion has been more controversial than the right to obtain and use contraceptives. But nothing about the Court's interpretive method distinguishes the core right affirmed in *Roe v. Wade* from its doctrinal forerunners. In *Roe*, as in *Meyer v. Nebraska*,[35] *Pierce v. Society of Sisters*,[36] *Skinner, Griswold*, and *Eisenstadt*, the Court reasoned from constitutional text, principles, and precedent to the conclusion that the "right of privacy...founded in the Fourteenth Amendment's concept of personal liberty and restrictions upon state action...is broad enough to encompass a woman's decision whether or not to terminate her pregnancy."[37]

Despite the controversy surrounding *Roe*, the joint opinion in *Planned Parenthood v. Casey* was correct to note in 1992 that "[a]n entire generation has come of age free to assume *Roe*'s concept of liberty in defining the capacity of women to act in society, and to make reproductive decisions."[38] Nearly another entire generation has come of age since *Casey*. Today, no woman of reproductive age in the United States has ever lived under a regime where she did not have the constitutional right to control her fertility. Judges, no less than the people themselves, have lived their lives in a post-*Roe* world. They have family members, friends, neighbors, and colleagues who have assumed *Roe*'s concept of liberty.

Over the decades since *Roe*, our society has deepened its understanding of the constitutional underpinnings of the right to reproductive autonomy. Some judges and commentators, most notably Justice Ginsburg, have sought to locate the right not only in the liberty protected by the Due Process Clause but also in the gender equality component of the Equal Protection Clause.[39] Indeed, the Court decided *Roe* at the beginning of a period of popular mobilization, lawmaking, and constitutional interpretation that transformed the national understanding of gender equality. Still others have sought to reinforce the right by arguing for a revival of the Privileges or Immunities Clause of the Fourteenth Amendment[40] or by relying on First Amendment–based protections for freedom of conscience.[41] The reasons for this evolution are not just, or even primarily, a tactical desire to shore up what might otherwise seem a vulnerable result. Whatever the virtues of these alternative rationales, it is unlikely that antiabortion forces will be convinced to abandon their opposition by a shift in doctrine. Rather, these additional defenses of reproductive autonomy reflect a richer understanding of the social, political, and economic context in which decisions about childbearing are made. That context, in turn, affects our constitutional understanding.

Social changes also underpin the recent extension of the privacy right to the protection of intimate decision-making by gay people. In *Lawrence v. Texas*, the Court struck down a Texas statute criminalizing private homosexual activity between consenting adults.[42] Justice Kennedy's opinion captures the Court's modern approach to due process:

> Had those who drew and ratified the Due Process Clauses of the Fifth Amendment or the Fourteenth Amendment known the components of liberty in its manifold possibilities, they might have been more specific. They did not presume to have this insight. They knew times can blind us to certain truths and later generations can see that laws once thought necessary and proper in fact serve only to oppress. As the Constitution endures, persons in every generation can invoke its principles in their own search for greater freedom.[43]

Lawrence marks a healthy rejection of a late Rehnquist Court dictate that substantive due process analysis should focus on a narrow "description of the asserted fundamental liberty interest."[44] The *Lawrence* Court firmly rejected the view that the liberty interest at issue was "simply the right to engage in certain sexual conduct."[45] That view, the Court explained, "demeans the claim the individual put forward, just as it would demean a married couple were it to be said marriage is simply about the right to have sexual intercourse."[46] The Court instead described the liberty at issue as gay people's right to "control their destiny,"[47] reaffirming that " '[a]t the heart of liberty is the right to define one's own concept of existence, of meaning, of the universe, and of the mystery of human life.' "[48]

By conceiving of liberty in broader terms than the specific conduct at issue, the Court recast the right as involving not only liberty but equality as well. As a practical matter, the effect of the Texas law was not oppressive interference with the intimate lives of gay people, as the law was virtually never enforced. Instead, the real problem with the Texas law was its primary collateral consequence: "When homosexual conduct is made criminal by the law of the State, that declaration in and of itself is an invitation to subject homosexual persons to discrimination both in the public and in the private spheres."[49] In worrying that criminalization of private homosexual conduct invites public discrimination against homosexual persons, the Court understood that the lives and identities of gay people transcend what they do in their bedrooms to encompass who they are in civil society. Protecting gay people's choices within the intimacy of their homes serves essentially as a safeguard of their dignity in a more public sphere. With this reasoning, the Court again demonstrated that "[e]quality of treatment and the due process right to demand respect for conduct protected by the substantive guarantee of liberty are linked in important respects, and a decision on the latter point advances both interests."[50]

. . .

Among critics of the Court's doctrine in this area, it is often said that constitutional interpretation becomes undisciplined and unguided once the term "liberty" is understood to mean more than what the Bill of Rights expressly provides or more than what the Framers of the Fifth and Fourteenth Amendments intended. Yet when one considers the Court's liberty decisions in their totality, an unmistakable characteristic that emerges is their incremental quality. Far from opening the floodgates to a torrent of new fundamental rights, the Court's decisions have built carefully and gradually on a limited and consistent set of core themes, with scrupulous attention to the historic and evolving traditions of our nation. As Justice Harlan said, "[t]hat tradition is a living thing."[51] The freedoms we enjoy today have been forged through the application of his insight that there is "no mechanical formula" for striking the proper balance between the guarantee of liberty and the demands of organized society.[52] The lived experiences, social understandings, and deeply held values of the American people rightly inform the meaning of constitutionally protected "liberty" and, in so doing, comprise an interpretive approach that enables our courts to faithfully and meaningfully apply the Constitution's enduring principles from one generation to the next.

CHAPTER TEN

. . .

Progress and Possibilities

SINCE 1789, OTHER NATIONS' constitutions have come and gone. By one recent estimate, national constitutions last only an average of seventeen years.[1] The U.S. Constitution, by contrast, not only endures—it thrives. Why? As this book suggests, a major reason for its continued vitality is its capacity for growth and adaptation, not only through formal amendment under Article V but also through interpretation and use by generations of ordinary citizens, elected officials, and judges. As an earlier professor-turned-President wrote, "the Constitution of the United States is not a mere lawyers' document: it is a vehicle of life, and its spirit is always the spirit of the age."[2]

In chapter 2, we quoted at length from Justice Brandeis's dissenting opinion in *Olmstead v. United States*, in which he said:

"Time works changes, brings into existence new conditions and purposes. Therefore a principle to be vital must be capable of wider application than the mischief which gave it birth. This is peculiarly true of constitutions. They are not ephemeral enactments, designed to meet passing occasions. They are, to use the words of Chief Justice Marshall, 'designed to approach immortality as nearly as human institutions can approach it.' The future is their care and provision for events of good and bad tendencies of which no prophecy can be made. In the application of a constitution, therefore, our *contemplation* cannot be only of what has been but of what may be."[3]

Justice Brandeis was himself quoting from Justice McKenna's opinion for the Court in *Weems v. United States*, a case that illustrates our central theme.

Weems involved the application of the Eighth Amendment's prohibition on cruel and unusual punishment to a situation outside the experience or expectations of the Framers. The case arose in the Philippines, which was then under U.S. sovereignty as a result of the Spanish-American War. A government officer had been duly convicted of falsifying two modest payments in a cash account, and the local court had sentenced him to a punishment called *cadena temporal*, which required, among other things, that the defendant's wrists be chained to his ankles "night and day," that he perform "hard and painful labor," that he be entirely isolated "from friend or relative," and that he suffer "a perpetual limitation of his liberty" in the form of official surveillance for the rest of his life.[4] In assessing the validity of the punishment, the Supreme Court held the principles of the Eighth Amendment applicable to the Philippines and noted that "[w]hat constitutes a cruel and unusual punishment has not been exactly decided."[5] But the Court went on to explain, in a discussion culminating in the passage quoted above, that the scope of the Eighth Amendment's protection cannot be confined to the abuses of the English monarchs or to the prevailing norms of cruelty or proportionality in the Founding era.[6] The Court interpreted the

Eighth Amendment to express "a precept of justice that punishment for crime should be graduated and proportioned to offense" and held the punishment unconstitutional.[7]

A century later, Americans continue to face the task of applying our Constitution to new contexts. William Faulkner famously wrote: "The past is never dead. It's not even past."[8] And so we still face some of the questions raised by *Weems*. How does the Constitution apply to United States–controlled territory overseas—for example, the naval station at Guantánamo Bay in Cuba or the Bagram Air Force Base in Afghanistan? Does the Eighth Amendment forbid repeat offender laws that impose draconian punishments for minor offenses? Are there punishments that may not be imposed under any circumstances, beyond the punishments already forbidden under existing case law?

More broadly, the Constitution's text and principles must be adapted to changes in the world. Constitutional law has only begun to consider the array of issues arising from the omnipresence of computers. How should First Amendment principles of free speech apply in cyberspace? To what extent do constitutional principles restrict government surveillance of electronic communications? Should the various doctrines governing campaign finance law apply to candidates' use of the Internet? Or should campaign finance law be reconsidered in light of changes in modern communications and media?

Moreover, how should changes in scientific understanding inform constitutional law? The Constitution has long recognized principles of liberty and autonomy with respect to intimate matters of family life. How do those principles apply to abortion and end-of-life issues in light of medical advances and our evolving understanding of human development and cognition? Scientists have managed to sequence the entire human genome and are now poised to elucidate the genetic bases of disease, behavior, and even cognition. What constraints does the Constitution impose on the government's collection and use of human DNA? What powers does Congress have under the enforcement clause of the Fourteenth Amendment to regulate state use of genetic testing? Advances in neuroscience may one day enable us to decode, model, and record the processes of human thought and decision-making. How should constitutional protections for individual privacy be adapted to the potential uses and abuses of such research?

How should constitutional interpretation respond to changes in our understanding of the environment? The current Supreme Court is divided over the scope of federal power to enact environmental protection statutes, with several Justices inclined to distinguish between environmental regulations that affect interstate commerce or navigable waters and those that bear only upon intrastate territory.[9] As our understandings of ecology deepen, that distinction may become untenable. More fundamentally, in a world of physical and economic global interdependence, how should legislatures, executive branch officials, and the courts think about questions of enumerated powers and federalism?

The changes that inform constitutional interpretation are not limited to scientific developments. As we have seen, changes in social understandings often, and rightly, change how constitutional principles are applied. Consider, for example, the history of litigation over the right to marry. State and local governments have always limited the right to certain people under certain circumstances. Not until 1948, when the California Supreme Court decided *Perez v. Sharp*,[10] did any court hold that the Equal Protection Clause forbids states from refusing to recognize interracial marriages, and it took an additional generation before the U.S. Supreme Court reached that conclusion in *Loving v. Virginia*.[11] In subsequent years, the Court came to recognize the marriage rights of prisoners and indigent individuals.[12] Today there is a vigorous debate over the right of same-sex couples to marry. That debate, fueled by a 2004 decision of the Massachusetts Supreme Judicial Court and subsequent judicial and legislative activity,[13] would have been unthinkable a half century ago, just as a debate over the right of interracial couples to marry would have seemed pointless a half century before that. Here, as in other areas, constitutional understandings have changed as the norms and values of our society have changed.

Just as the Framers could not have imagined the internet, DNA testing, global warming, or women's equality, there are undoubtedly social developments and constitutional questions that we cannot imagine today. But if our national experience is any guide, we can be confident that the Constitution's text and principles will endure—and they will endure because of their adaptability to new conditions and new challenges through an ongoing process of interpretation. Throughout our history, this process of interpretation has sustained the vitality of the Constitution and its democratic legitimacy. Whatever allure there may be in theories that would reduce constitutional interpretation to a simpler, more mechanical process, those theories ultimately fail to explain our actual constitutional practice and its remarkable achievements over time. The American people adopted the Constitution in order to "establish Justice, insure domestic Tranquility, provide for the common defence, promote the general Welfare, and secure the Blessings of Liberty." As our nation and the world continue to change, constitutional interpretation that is faithful to those purposes enables and motivates each generation of Americans to keep faith with the Constitution.

The Constitution of the United States

We the People of the United States, in Order to form a more perfect Union, establish Justice, insure domestic Tranquility, provide for the common defence, promote the general Welfare, and secure the Blessings of Liberty to ourselves and our Posterity, do ordain and establish this Constitution for the United States of America.

ARTICLE I

Section 1. All legislative Powers herein granted shall be vested in a Congress of the United States, which shall consist of a Senate and House of Representatives.

Section 2. The House of Representatives shall be composed of Members chosen every second Year by the People of the several States, and the Electors in each State shall have the Qualifications requisite for Electors of the most numerous Branch of the State Legislature.

No Person shall be a Representative who shall not have attained to the Age of twenty five Years, and been seven Years a Citizen of the United States, and who shall not, when elected, be an Inhabitant of that State in which he shall be chosen.

Representatives and direct Taxes shall be apportioned among the several States which may be included within this Union, according to their respective Numbers, which shall be determined by adding to the whole Number of free Persons, including those bound to Service for a Term of Years, and excluding Indians not taxed, three fifths of all other Persons. The actual Enumeration shall be made within three Years after the first Meeting of the Congress of the United States, and within every subsequent Term of ten Years, in such Manner as they shall by Law direct. The Number of Representatives shall not exceed one for every thirty Thousand, but each State shall have at Least one Representative; and until such enumeration shall be made, the State of New Hampshire shall be entitled to chuse three, Massachusetts eight, Rhode Island and Providence Plantations one, Connecticut five, New York six, New Jersey four, Pennsylvania eight, Delaware one, Maryland six, Virginia ten, North Carolina five, South Carolina five and Georgia three.

When vacancies happen in the Representation from any State, the Executive Authority thereof shall issue Writs of Election to fill such Vacancies.

The House of Representatives shall chuse their Speaker and other Officers; and shall have the sole Power of Impeachment.

Section 3. The Senate of the United States shall be composed of two Senators from each State, chosen by the Legislature thereof, for six Years; and each Senator shall have one Vote.

Immediately after they shall be assembled in Consequence of the first Election, they shall be divided as equally as may be into three Classes. The Seats of the Senators of the first Class shall be vacated at the Expiration of the second Year, of the second Class at the Expiration of the fourth Year, and of the third Class at the Expiration of the sixth Year, so that one third may be chosen every second Year; and if Vacancies happen by Resignation, or otherwise, during the Recess of the Legislature of any State, the Executive thereof may make temporary Appointments until the next Meeting of the Legislature, which shall then fill such Vacancies.

No person shall be a Senator who shall not have attained to the Age of thirty Years, and been nine Years a Citizen of the United States, and who shall not, when elected, be an Inhabitant of that State for which he shall be chosen.

The Vice President of the United States shall be President of the Senate, but shall have no Vote, unless they be equally divided.

The Senate shall chuse their other Officers, and also a President pro tempore, in the absence of the Vice President, or when he shall exercise the Office of President of the United States.

The Senate shall have the sole Power to try all Impeachments. When sitting for that Purpose, they shall be on Oath or Affirmation. When the President of the United States is tried, the Chief Justice shall preside: And no Person shall be convicted without the Concurrence of two thirds of the Members present.

Judgment in Cases of Impeachment shall not extend further than to removal from Office, and disqualification to hold and enjoy any Office of honor, Trust or Profit under the United States: but the Party convicted shall nevertheless be liable and subject to Indictment, Trial, Judgment and Punishment, according to Law.

Section 4. The Times, Places and Manner of holding Elections for Senators and Representatives, shall be prescribed in each State by the Legislature thereof; but the Congress may at any time by Law make or alter such Regulations, except as to the Places of chusing Senators.

The Congress shall assemble at least once in every Year, and such Meeting shall be on the first Monday in December, unless they shall by Law appoint a different Day.

Section 5. Each House shall be the Judge of the Elections, Returns and Qualifications of its own Members, and a Majority of each shall constitute a Quorum to do Business; but a smaller Number may adjourn from day to day, and may be authorized to compel the Attendance of absent Members, in such Manner, and under such Penalties as each House may provide.

Each House may determine the Rules of its Proceedings, punish its Members for disorderly Behaviour, and, with the Concurrence of two thirds, expel a Member.

Each House shall keep a Journal of its Proceedings, and from time to time publish the same, excepting such Parts as may in their Judgment require Secrecy; and the Yeas and Nays of the Members of either House on any question shall, at the Desire of one fifth of those Present, be entered on the Journal.

Neither House, during the Session of Congress, shall, without the Consent of the other, adjourn for more than three days, nor to any other Place than that in which the two Houses shall be sitting.

Section 6. The Senators and Representatives shall receive a Compensation for their Services, to be ascertained by Law, and paid out of the Treasury of the United States. They shall in all Cases, except Treason, Felony and Breach of the Peace, be privileged from Arrest during their Attendance at the Session of their respective Houses, and in going to and returning from the same; and for any Speech or Debate in either House, they shall not be questioned in any other Place.

No Senator or Representative shall, during the Time for which he was elected, be appointed to any civil Office under the Authority of the United States, which shall have been created, or the Emoluments whereof shall have been encreased during such time; and no Person holding any Office under the United States, shall be a Member of either House during his Continuance in Office.

Section 7. All bills for raising Revenue shall originate in the House of Representatives; but the Senate may propose or concur with Amendments as on other Bills.

Every Bill which shall have passed the House of Representatives and the Senate, shall, before it become a Law, be presented to the President of the United States; If he approve he shall sign it, but if not he shall return it, with his Objections to that House in which it shall have originated, who shall enter the Objections at large on their Journal, and proceed to reconsider it. If after such Reconsideration two thirds of that House shall agree to pass the Bill, it shall be sent, together with the Objections, to the other House, by which it shall likewise be reconsidered, and if approved by two thirds of that House, it shall become a Law. But in all such Cases the Votes of both Houses shall be determined by yeas and Nays, and the Names of the Persons voting for and against the Bill shall be entered on the Journal of each House respectively. If any Bill shall not be returned by the President within ten Days (Sundays excepted) after it shall have been presented to him, the Same shall be a Law, in like Manner as if he had signed it, unless the Congress by their Adjournment prevent its Return, in which Case it shall not be a Law.

Every Order, Resolution, or Vote to which the Concurrence of the Senate and House of Representatives may be necessary (except on a question of Adjournment) shall be presented to the President of the United States; and before the Same shall take Effect, shall be approved by him, or being disapproved by him, shall be repassed by two thirds of the Senate and House of Representatives, according to the Rules and Limitations prescribed in the Case of a Bill.

Section 8. The Congress shall have Power To lay and collect Taxes, Duties, Imposts and Excises, to pay the Debts and provide for the common Defence and general Welfare of the United States; but all Duties, Imposts and Excises shall be uniform throughout the United States;

To borrow money on the credit of the United States;

To regulate Commerce with foreign Nations, and among the several States, and with the Indian Tribes;

To establish an uniform Rule of Naturalization, and uniform Laws on the subject of Bankruptcies throughout the United States;

To coin Money, regulate the Value thereof, and of foreign Coin, and fix the Standard of Weights and Measures;

To provide for the Punishment of counterfeiting the Securities and current Coin of the United States;

To establish Post Offices and Post Roads;

To promote the Progress of Science and useful Arts, by securing for limited Times to Authors and Inventors the exclusive Right to their respective Writings and Discoveries;

To constitute Tribunals inferior to the supreme Court;

To define and punish Piracies and Felonies committed on the high Seas, and Offences against the Law of Nations;

To declare War, grant Letters of Marque and Reprisal, and make Rules concerning Captures on Land and Water;

To raise and support Armies, but no Appropriation of Money to that Use shall be for a longer Term than two Years;

To provide and maintain a Navy;

To make Rules for the Government and Regulation of the land and naval Forces;

To provide for calling forth the Militia to execute the Laws of the Union, suppress Insurrections and repel Invasions;

To provide for organizing, arming, and disciplining, the Militia, and for governing such Part of them as may be employed in the Service of the United States, reserving to the States respectively, the Appointment of the Officers, and the Authority of training the Militia according to the discipline prescribed by Congress;

To exercise exclusive Legislation in all Cases whatsoever, over such District (not exceeding ten Miles square) as may, by Cession of particular States, and the Acceptance of Congress, become the Seat of the Government of the United States, and to exercise like Authority over all Places purchased by the Consent of the Legislature of the State in which the Same shall be, for the Erection of Forts, Magazines, Arsenals, dock-Yards, and other needful Buildings;—And

To make all Laws which shall be necessary and proper for carrying into Execution the foregoing Powers, and all other Powers vested by this Constitution in the Government of the United States, or in any Department or Officer thereof.

Section 9. The Migration or Importation of such Persons as any of the States now existing shall think proper to admit, shall not be prohibited by the Congress prior to the Year one thousand eight hundred and eight, but a Tax or duty may be imposed on such Importation, not exceeding ten dollars for each Person.

The Privilege of the Writ of Habeas Corpus shall not be suspended, unless when in Cases of Rebellion or Invasion the public Safety may require it.

No Bill of Attainder or ex post facto Law shall be passed.

No capitation, or other direct, Tax shall be laid, unless in Proportion to the Census or Enumeration herein before directed to be taken.

No Tax or Duty shall be laid on Articles exported from any State.

No Preference shall be given by any Regulation of Commerce or Revenue to the Ports of one State over those of another: nor shall Vessels bound to, or from, one State, be obliged to enter, clear, or pay Duties in another.

No Money shall be drawn from the Treasury, but in Consequence of Appropriations made by Law; and a regular Statement and Account of the Receipts and Expenditures of all public Money shall be published from time to time.

No Title of Nobility shall be granted by the United States: And no Person holding any Office of Profit or Trust under them, shall, without the Consent of the Congress, accept of any present, Emolument, Office, or Title, of any kind whatever, from any King, Prince, or foreign State.

Section 10. No State shall enter into any Treaty, Alliance, or Confederation; grant Letters of Marque and Reprisal; coin Money; emit Bills of Credit; make any Thing but gold and silver Coin a Tender in Payment of Debts; pass any Bill of Attainder, ex post facto Law, or Law impairing the Obligation of Contracts, or grant any Title of Nobility.

No State shall, without the Consent of the Congress, lay any Imposts or Duties on Imports or Exports, except what may be absolutely necessary for executing it's inspection Laws: and the net Produce of all Duties and Imposts, laid by any State on Imports or Exports, shall be for the Use of the Treasury of the United States; and all such Laws shall be subject to the Revision and Controul of the Congress.

No State shall, without the Consent of Congress, lay any Duty of Tonnage, keep Troops, or Ships of War in time of Peace, enter into any Agreement or Compact with another State, or with a foreign Power, or engage in War, unless actually invaded, or in such imminent Danger as will not admit of delay.

ARTICLE II

Section 1. The executive Power shall be vested in a President of the United States of America. He shall hold his Office during the Term of four Years, and, together with the Vice President, chosen for the same Term, be elected, as follows:

Each State shall appoint, in such Manner as the Legislature thereof may direct, a Number of Electors, equal to the whole Number of Senators and Representatives to which the State may be entitled in the Congress: but no Senator or Representative, or Person holding an Office of Trust or Profit under the United States, shall be appointed an Elector.

The Electors shall meet in their respective States, and vote by Ballot for two persons, of whom one at least shall not be an Inhabitant of the same State with themselves. And they shall make a List of all the Persons voted for, and of the Number of Votes for each; which List they shall sign and certify, and transmit sealed to the Seat of the Government of the United States, directed to the President of the Senate. The President of the Senate shall, in the Presence of the Senate and House of Representatives, open all the Certificates, and the Votes shall then be counted. The Person having the greatest Number of Votes shall be the President, if such Number be a Majority of the whole Number of

Electors appointed; and if there be more than one who have such Majority, and have an equal Number of Votes, then the House of Representatives shall immediately chuse by Ballot one of them for President; and if no Person have a Majority, then from the five highest on the List the said House shall in like Manner chuse the President. But in chusing the President, the Votes shall be taken by States, the Representation from each State having one Vote; a quorum for this Purpose shall consist of a Member or Members from two-thirds of the States, and a Majority of all the States shall be necessary to a Choice. In every Case, after the Choice of the President, the Person having the greatest Number of Votes of the Electors shall be the Vice President. But if there should remain two or more who have equal Votes, the Senate shall chuse from them by Ballot the Vice-President.

The Congress may determine the Time of chusing the Electors, and the Day on which they shall give their Votes; which Day shall be the same throughout the United States.

No Person except a natural born Citizen, or a Citizen of the United States, at the time of the Adoption of this Constitution, shall be eligible to the Office of President; neither shall any Person be eligible to that Office who shall not have attained to the Age of thirty five Years, and been fourteen Years a Resident within the United States.

In Case of the Removal of the President from Office, or of his Death, Resignation, or Inability to discharge the Powers and Duties of the said Office, the Same shall devolve on the Vice President, and the Congress may by Law provide for the Case of Removal, Death, Resignation or Inability, both of the President and Vice President, declaring what Officer shall then act as President, and such Officer shall act accordingly, until the Disability be removed, or a President shall be elected.

The President shall, at stated Times, receive for his Services, a Compensation, which shall neither be increased nor diminished during the Period for which he shall have been elected, and he shall not receive within that Period any other Emolument from the United States, or any of them.

Before he enter on the Execution of his Office, he shall take the following Oath or Affirmation: "I do solemnly swear (or affirm) that I will faithfully execute the Office of President of the United States, and will to the best of my Ability, preserve, protect and defend the Constitution of the United States."

Section 2. The President shall be Commander in Chief of the Army and Navy of the United States, and of the Militia of the several States, when called into the actual Service of the United States; he may require the Opinion, in writing, of the principal Officer in each of the executive Departments, upon any Subject relating to the Duties of their respective Offices, and he shall have Power to grant Reprieves and Pardons for Offences against the United States, except in Cases of Impeachment.

He shall have Power, by and with the Advice and Consent of the Senate, to make Treaties, provided two thirds of the Senators present concur; and he shall nominate, and by and with the Advice and Consent of the Senate, shall appoint Ambassadors, other public Ministers and Consuls, Judges of the supreme Court, and all other Officers of the United States, whose Appointments are not herein otherwise provided for, and which shall be established by Law: but the Congress may by Law vest the Appointment of such inferior

Officers, as they think proper, in the President alone, in the Courts of Law, or in the Heads of Departments.

The President shall have Power to fill up all Vacancies that may happen during the Recess of the Senate, by granting Commissions which shall expire at the End of their next Session.

Section 3. He shall from time to time give to the Congress Information of the State of the Union, and recommend to their Consideration such Measures as he shall judge necessary and expedient; he may, on extraordinary Occasions, convene both Houses, or either of them, and in Case of Disagreement between them, with Respect to the Time of Adjournment, he may adjourn them to such Time as he shall think proper; he shall receive Ambassadors and other public Ministers; he shall take Care that the Laws be faithfully executed, and shall Commission all the Officers of the United States.

Section 4. The President, Vice President and all civil Officers of the United States, shall be removed from Office on Impeachment for, and Conviction of, Treason, Bribery, or other high Crimes and Misdemeanors.

ARTICLE III

Section 1. The judicial Power of the United States, shall be vested in one supreme Court, and in such inferior Courts as the Congress may from time to time ordain and establish. The Judges, both of the supreme and inferior Courts, shall hold their Offices during good Behaviour, and shall, at stated Times, receive for their Services, a Compensation, which shall not be diminished during their Continuance in Office.

Section 2. The judicial Power shall extend to all Cases, in Law and Equity, arising under this Constitution, the Laws of the United States, and Treaties made, or which shall be made, under their Authority;—to all Cases affecting Ambassadors, other public Ministers and Consuls;—to all Cases of admiralty and maritime Jurisdiction;—to Controversies to which the United States shall be a Party;—to Controversies between two or more States;—between a State and Citizens of another State;—between Citizens of different States;—between Citizens of the same State claiming Lands under Grants of different States, and between a State, or the Citizens thereof, and foreign States, Citizens or Subjects.

In all Cases affecting Ambassadors, other public Ministers and Consuls, and those in which a State shall be Party, the supreme Court shall have original Jurisdiction. In all the other Cases before mentioned, the supreme Court shall have appellate Jurisdiction, both as to Law and Fact, with such Exceptions, and under such Regulations as the Congress shall make.

The Trial of all Crimes, except in Cases of Impeachment, shall be by Jury; and such Trial shall be held in the State where the said Crimes shall have been committed; but when not committed within any State, the Trial shall be at such Place or Places as the Congress may by Law have directed.

Section 3. Treason against the United States, shall consist only in levying War against them, or in adhering to their Enemies, giving them Aid and Comfort. No Person shall be convicted of Treason unless on the Testimony of two Witnesses to the same overt Act, or on Confession in open Court.

The Congress shall have Power to declare the Punishment of Treason, but no Attainder of Treason shall work Corruption of Blood, or Forfeiture except during the Life of the Person attainted.

ARTICLE IV

Section 1. Full Faith and Credit shall be given in each State to the public Acts, Records, and judicial Proceedings of every other State. And the Congress may by general Laws prescribe the Manner in which such Acts, Records and Proceedings shall be proved, and the Effect thereof.

Section 2. The Citizens of each State shall be entitled to all Privileges and Immunities of Citizens in the several States.

A Person charged in any State with Treason, Felony, or other Crime, who shall flee from Justice, and be found in another State, shall on Demand of the executive Authority of the State from which he fled, be delivered up, to be removed to the State having Jurisdiction of the Crime.

No Person held to Service or Labour in one State, under the Laws thereof, escaping into another, shall, in Consequence of any Law or Regulation therein, be discharged from such Service or Labour, but shall be delivered up on Claim of the Party to whom such Service or Labour may be due.

Section 3. New States may be admitted by the Congress into this Union; but no new States shall be formed or erected within the Jurisdiction of any other State; nor any State be formed by the Junction of two or more States, or Parts of States, without the Consent of the Legislatures of the States concerned as well as of the Congress.

The Congress shall have Power to dispose of and make all needful Rules and Regulations respecting the Territory or other Property belonging to the United States; and nothing in this Constitution shall be so construed as to Prejudice any Claims of the United States, or of any particular State.

Section 4. The United States shall guarantee to every State in this Union a Republican Form of Government, and shall protect each of them against Invasion; and on Application of the Legislature, or of the Executive (when the Legislature cannot be convened) against domestic Violence.

ARTICLE V

The Congress, whenever two thirds of both Houses shall deem it necessary, shall propose Amendments to this Constitution, or, on the Application of the Legislatures of two thirds of the several States, shall call a Convention for proposing Amendments, which, in either Case, shall be valid to all Intents and Purposes, as part of this Constitution, when ratified by the Legislatures of three fourths of the several States, or by Conventions in three fourths thereof, as the one or the other Mode of Ratification may be proposed by the Congress; Provided that no Amendment which may be made prior to the Year One thousand eight hundred and eight shall in any Manner affect the first and fourth Clauses in the Ninth Section of the first Article; and that no State, without it's Consent, shall be deprived of its equal Suffrage in the Senate.

ARTICLE VI

All Debts contracted and Engagements entered into, before the Adoption of this Constitution, shall be as valid against the United States under this Constitution, as under the Confederation.

This Constitution, and the Laws of the United States which shall be made in Pursuance thereof; and all Treaties made, or which shall be made, under the Authority of the United States, shall be the supreme ^{Law} of the Land; and the Judges in every State shall be bound thereby, any Thing in the Constitution or Laws of any State to the Contrary notwithstanding.

The Senators and Representatives before mentioned, and the Members of the several State Legislatures, and all executive and judicial Officers, both of the United States and of the several States, shall be bound by Oath or Affirmation, to support this Constitution; but no religious Test shall ever be required as a Qualification to any Office or public Trust under the United States.

ARTICLE VII

The Ratification of the Conventions of nine States, shall be sufficient for the Establishment of this Constitution between the States so ratifying the Same.

Done in Convention by the Unanimous Consent of the States present the Seventeenth Day of September in the Year of our Lord one thousand seven hundred and Eighty seven and of the Independence of the United States of America the Twelfth In witness whereof We have hereunto subscribed our Names.

GEORGE WASHINGTON—President and deputy from Virginia

[Signed also by the deputies of twelve States.]

Deleware	George Read
	Gunning Bedford, Jr.
	John Dickinson
	Richard Bassett
	Jacob Broom
Maryland	James McHenry
	Daniel of St. Thomas Jenifer
	Daniel Carroll
Virginia	John Blair
	James Madison Jr.
North Carolina	William Blount
	Richard Dobbs Spaight
	Hugh Williamson
South Carolina	John Rutledge
	Charles Cotesworth Pinckney
	Charles Pinckney
	Pierce Butler
Georgia	William Few
	Abraham Baldwin
New Hampshire	John Langdon
	Nicholas Gilman
Massachusetts	Nathaniel Gorham
	Rufus King
Connecticut	William Samuel Johnson
	Roger Sherman

New York	Alexander Hamilton
New Jersey	William Livingston
	David Brearley
	William Paterson
	Jonathan Dayton
Pennsylvania	Benjamin Franklin
	Thomas Mifflin
	Robert Morris
	George Clymer
	Thomas FitzSimons
	Jared Ingersoll
	James Wilson
	Gouverneur Morris

Attest William Jackson Secretary

Amendments to the Constitution of the United States of America

AMENDMENT I

(Ratified December 15, 1791)

Congress shall make no law respecting an establishment of religion, or prohibiting the free exercise thereof; or abridging the freedom of speech, or of the press; or the right of the people peaceably to assemble, and to petition the Government for a redress of grievances.

AMENDMENT II

(Ratified December 15, 1791)

A well regulated Militia, being necessary to the security of a free State, the right of the people to keep and bear Arms, shall not be infringed.

AMENDMENT III

(Ratified December 15, 1791)

No Soldier shall, in time of peace be quartered in any house, without the consent of the Owner, nor in time of war, but in a manner to be prescribed by law.

AMENDMENT IV

(Ratified December 15, 1791)

The right of the people to be secure in their persons, houses, papers, and effects, against unreasonable searches and seizures, shall not be violated, and no Warrants shall issue, but upon probable cause, supported by Oath or affirmation, and particularly describing the place to be searched, and the persons or things to be seized.

AMENDMENT V

(Ratified December 15, 1791)

No person shall be held to answer for a capital, or otherwise infamous crime, unless on a presentment or indictment of a Grand Jury, except in cases arising in the land or naval forces, or in the Militia, when in actual service in time of War or public danger; nor shall any person be subject for the same offence to be twice put in jeopardy of life or limb; nor shall be compelled in any criminal case to be a witness against himself, nor be deprived of life, liberty, or property, without due process of law; nor shall private property be taken for public use, without just compensation.

AMENDMENT VI

(Ratified December 15, 1791)

In all criminal prosecutions, the accused shall enjoy the right to a speedy and public trial, by an impartial jury of the State and district wherein the crime shall have been committed, which district shall have been previously ascertained by law, and to be informed of the nature and cause of the accusation; to be confronted with the witnesses against him; to have compulsory process for obtaining witnesses in his favor, and to have the Assistance of Counsel for his defence.

AMENDMENT VII

(Ratified December 15, 1791)

In Suits at common law, where the value in controversy shall exceed twenty dollars, the right of trial by jury shall be preserved, and no fact tried by a jury, shall be otherwise re-examined in any Court of the United States, than according to the rules of the common law.

AMENDMENT VIII

(Ratified December 15, 1791)

Excessive bail shall not be required, nor excessive fines imposed, nor cruel and unusual punishments inflicted.

AMENDMENT IX

(Ratified December 15, 1791)

The enumeration in the Constitution, of certain rights, shall not be construed to deny or disparage others retained by the people.

AMENDMENT X

(Ratified December 15, 1791)

The powers not delegated to the United States by the Constitution, nor prohibited by it to the States, are reserved to the States respectively, or to the people.

AMENDMENT XI

(Ratified February 7, 1795)

The Judicial power of the United States shall not be construed to extend to any suit in law or equity, commenced or prosecuted against one of the United States by Citizens of another State, or by Citizens or Subjects of any Foreign State.

AMENDMENT XII

(Ratified June 15, 1804)

The Electors shall meet in their respective states, and vote by ballot for President and Vice-President, one of whom, at least, shall not be an inhabitant of the same state with themselves; they shall name in their ballots the person voted for as President, and in distinct ballots the person voted for as Vice-President, and they shall make distinct lists of all persons voted for as President, and of all persons voted for as Vice-President and of the number of votes for each, which lists they shall sign and certify, and transmit sealed to the seat of the government of the United States, directed to the President of the Senate;—The President of the Senate shall, in the presence of the Senate and House of Representatives, open all the certificates and the votes shall then be counted;—The person having the greatest Number of votes for President, shall be the President, if such number be a majority of the whole number of Electors appointed; and if no person have such majority, then from the persons having the highest numbers not exceeding three on the list of those voted for as President, the House of Representatives shall choose immediately, by ballot, the President. But in choosing the President, the votes shall be taken by states, the representation from each state having one vote; a quorum for this purpose shall consist of a member or members from two-thirds of the states, and a majority of all the states shall be necessary to a choice. And if the House of Representatives shall not choose a President whenever the right of choice shall devolve upon them, before the fourth day of March next following, then the Vice-President shall act as President, as in the case of the death or other constitutional disability of the President.— The person having the greatest number of votes as Vice-President, shall be the Vice-President, if such number be a majority of the whole number of Electors appointed, and if no person have a majority, then from the two highest numbers on the list, the Senate shall choose the Vice-President; a quorum for the purpose shall consist of two-thirds of the whole number of Senators, and a majority of the whole number shall be necessary to a choice. But no person constitutionally ineligible to the office of President shall be eligible to that of Vice-President of the United States.

AMENDMENT XIII

(Ratified December 6, 1865)

Section 1. Neither slavery nor involuntary servitude, except as a punishment for crime whereof the party shall have been duly convicted, shall exist within the United States, or any place subject to their jurisdiction.

Section 2. Congress shall have power to enforce this article by appropriate legislation.

AMENDMENT XIV

(Ratified July 9, 1869)

Section 1. All persons born or naturalized in the United States, and subject to the jurisdiction thereof, are citizens of the United States and of the State wherein they reside. No State shall make or enforce any law which shall abridge the privileges or immunities of citizens of the United States; nor shall any State deprive any person of life, liberty, or property, without due process of law; nor deny to any person within its jurisdiction the equal protection of the laws.

Section 2. Representatives shall be apportioned among the several States according to their respective numbers, counting the whole number of persons in each State, excluding Indians not taxed. But when the right to vote at any election for the choice of electors for President and Vice-President of the United States, Representatives in Congress, the Executive and Judicial officers of a State, or the members of the Legislature thereof, is denied to any of the male inhabitants of such State, being twenty-one years of age, and citizens of the United States, or in any way abridged, except for participation in rebellion, or other crime, the basis of representation therein shall be reduced in the proportion which the number of such male citizens shall bear to the whole number of male citizens twenty-one years of age in such State.

Section 3. No person shall be a Senator or Representative in Congress, or elector of President and Vice-President, or hold any office, civil or military, under the United States, or under any State, who, having previously taken an oath, as a member of Congress, or as an officer of the United States, or as a member of any State legislature, or as an executive or judicial officer of any State, to support the Constitution of the United States, shall have engaged in insurrection or rebellion against the same, or given aid or comfort to the enemies thereof. But Congress may by a vote of two-thirds of each House, remove such disability.

Section 4. The validity of the public debt of the United States, authorized by law, including debts incurred for payment of pensions and bounties for services in suppressing insurrection or rebellion, shall not be questioned. But neither the United States nor any State shall assume or pay any debt or obligation incurred in aid of insurrection or rebellion against the United States, or any claim for the loss or emancipation of any slave; but all such debts, obligations and claims shall be held illegal and void.

Section 5. The Congress shall have power to enforce, by appropriate legislation, the provisions of this article.

AMENDMENT XV

(Ratified February 3, 1870)

Section 1. The right of citizens of the United States to vote shall not be denied or abridged by the United States or by any State on account of race, color, or previous condition of servitude.

Section 2. The Congress shall have power to enforce this article by appropriate legislation.

AMENDMENT XVI

(Ratified February 3, 1913)

The Congress shall have power to lay and collect taxes on incomes, from whatever source derived, without apportionment among the several States, and without regard to any census or enumeration.

AMENDMENT XVII

(Ratified April 8, 1913)

The Senate of the United States shall be composed of two Senators from each State, elected by the people thereof, for six years; and each Senator shall have one vote. The electors in each State shall have the qualifications requisite for electors of the most numerous branch of the State legislatures.

When vacancies happen in the representation of any State in the Senate, the executive authority of such State shall issue writs of election to fill such vacancies: Provided, That the legislature of any State may empower the executive thereof to make temporary appointments until the people fill the vacancies by election as the legislature may direct.

This amendment shall not be so construed as to affect the election or term of any Senator chosen before it becomes valid as part of the Constitution.

AMENDMENT XVIII

(Ratified January 16, 1919)

Section 1. After one year from the ratification of this article the manufacture, sale, or transportation of intoxicating liquors within, the importation thereof into, or the exportation thereof from the United States and all territory subject to the jurisdiction thereof for beverage purposes is hereby prohibited.

Section 2. The Congress and the several States shall have concurrent power to enforce this article by appropriate legislation.

Section 3. This article shall be inoperative unless it shall have been ratified as an amendment to the Constitution by the legislatures of the several States, as provided in the Constitution, within seven years from the date of the submission hereof to the States by the Congress.

AMENDMENT XIX

(Ratified August 18, 1920)

The right of citizens of the United States to vote shall not be denied or abridged by the United States or by any State on account of sex.

Congress shall have power to enforce this article by appropriate legislation.

AMENDMENT XX

(Ratified January 23, 1933)

Section 1. The terms of the President and Vice President shall end at noon on the 20th day of January, and the terms of Senators and Representatives at noon on the 3d day of January, of the years in which such terms would have ended if this article had not been ratified; and the terms of their successors shall then begin.

Section 2. The Congress shall assemble at least once in every year, and such meeting shall begin at noon on the 3d day of January, unless they shall by law appoint a different day.

Section 3. If, at the time fixed for the beginning of the term of the President, the President elect shall have died, the Vice President elect shall become President. If a President shall not have been chosen before the time fixed for the beginning of his term, or if the President elect shall have failed to qualify, then the Vice President elect shall act as President until a President shall have qualified; and the Congress may by law provide for the case wherein neither a

President elect nor a Vice President elect shall have qualified, declaring who shall then act as President, or the manner in which one who is to act shall be selected, and such person shall act accordingly until a President or Vice President shall have qualified.

Section 4. The Congress may by law provide for the case of the death of any of the persons from whom the House of Representatives may choose a President whenever the right of choice shall have devolved upon them, and for the case of the death of any of the persons from whom the Senate may choose a Vice President whenever the right of choice shall have devolved upon them.

Section 5. Sections 1 and 2 shall take effect on the 15th day of October following the ratification of this article.

Section 6. This article shall be inoperative unless it shall have been ratified as an amendment to the Constitution by the legislatures of three-fourths of the several States within seven years from the date of its submission.

AMENDMENT XXI

(Ratified December 5, 1933)

Section 1. The eighteenth article of amendment to the Constitution of the United States is hereby repealed.

Section 2. The transportation or importation into any State, Territory, or possession of the United States for delivery or use therein of intoxicating liquors, in violation of the laws thereof, is hereby prohibited.

Section 3. The article shall be inoperative unless it shall have been ratified as an amendment to the Constitution by conventions in the several States, as provided in the Constitution, within seven years from the date of the submission hereof to the States by the Congress.

AMENDMENT XXII

(Ratified February 27, 1951)

Section 1. No person shall be elected to the office of the President more than twice, and no person who has held the office of President, or acted as President, for more than two years of a term to which some other person was elected President shall be elected to the office of the President more than once. But this Article shall not apply to any person holding the office of President, when this Article was proposed by the Congress, and shall not prevent any person who may be holding the office of President, or acting as President, during the term within which this Article becomes operative from holding the office of President or acting as President during the remainder of such term.

Section 2. This article shall be inoperative unless it shall have been ratified as an amendment to the Constitution by the legislatures of three-fourths of the several States within seven years from the date of its submission to the States by the Congress.

AMENDMENT XXIII

(Ratified March 29, 1961)

Section 1. The District constituting the seat of Government of the United States shall appoint in such manner as the Congress may direct: A number of electors of President and Vice President equal to the whole number of Senators and Representatives in Congress to which the District would be entitled if it were a State, but in no event more than the least populous State; they shall be in addition to those appointed by the States, but they shall be considered, for the purposes of the election of President and Vice President, to be electors appointed by a State; and they shall meet in the District and perform such duties as provided by the twelfth article of amendment.

Section 2. The Congress shall have power to enforce this article by appropriate legislation.

AMENDMENT XXIV

(Ratified January 23, 1964)

Section 1. The right of citizens of the United States to vote in any primary or other election for President or Vice President, for electors for President or Vice President, or for Senator or Representative in Congress, shall not be denied or abridged by the United States or any State by reason of failure to pay any poll tax or other tax.

Section 2. The Congress shall have power to enforce this article by appropriate legislation.

AMENDMENT XXV

(Ratified February 10, 1967)

Section 1. In case of the removal of the President from office or of his death or resignation, the Vice President shall become President.

Section 2. Whenever there is a vacancy in the office of the Vice President, the President shall nominate a Vice President who shall take office upon confirmation by a majority vote of both Houses of Congress.

Section 3. Whenever the President transmits to the President pro tempore of the Senate and the Speaker of the House of Representatives his written declaration that he is unable to discharge the powers and duties of his office, and until he transmits to them a written declaration to the contrary, such powers and duties shall be discharged by the Vice President as Acting President.

Section 4. Whenever the Vice President and a majority of either the principal officers of the executive departments or of such other body as Congress may by law provide, transmit to the President pro tempore of the Senate and the Speaker of the House of Representatives their written declaration that the President is unable to discharge the powers and duties of his office, the Vice President shall immediately assume the powers and duties of the office as Acting President.

Thereafter, when the President transmits to the President pro tempore of the Senate and the Speaker of the House of Representatives his written declaration that no inability exists, he shall resume the powers and duties of his office unless the Vice President and a majority of either the principal officers of the executive department or of such other body as Congress may by law provide, transmit within four days to the President pro tempore of the Senate and the Speaker of the House of Representatives their written declaration that the President is unable to discharge the powers and duties of his office. Thereupon Congress shall decide the issue, assembling within forty eight hours for that purpose if not in session. If the Congress, within twenty one days after receipt of the latter written declaration, or, if Congress is not in session, within twenty one days after Congress is required to assemble, determines by two thirds vote of both Houses that the President is unable to discharge the powers and duties of his office, the Vice President shall continue to discharge the same as Acting President; otherwise, the President shall resume the powers and duties of his office.

AMENDMENT XXVI

(Ratified July 1, 1971)

Section 1. The right of citizens of the United States, who are eighteen years of age or older, to vote shall not be denied or abridged by the United States or by any State on account of age.

Section 2. The Congress shall have power to enforce this article by appropriate legislation.

AMENDMENT XXVII

(Originally Proposed September 25, 1789. Ratified May 7, 1992)

No law, varying the compensation for the services of the Senators and Representatives, shall take effect, until an election of Representatives shall have intervened.

Notes

. . .

INTRODUCTION

1. Missouri v. Holland, 252 U.S. 416, 433 (1920).

2. *Id.* at 434.

3. OFFICE OF LEGAL POLICY, U.S. DEP'T OF JUSTICE, GUIDELINES ON CONSTITUTIONAL LITIGATION 3 (1988).

4. Poe v. Ullman, 367 U.S. 497, 540 (1961) (Harlan, J., dissenting) (citing McCulloch v. Maryland, 17 U.S. 316 (1819)).

5. *See* U.S. CONST. art. I, § 2 (House of Representatives), art. I, § 3 (Senate), art. II, § 1 (President).

6. *McCulloch*, 17 U.S. at 407.

7. *Id.*

8. *Id.* at 407, 415.

9. *Id.* at 407.

10. *Id.*

11. President Franklin D. Roosevelt, Address on Constitution Day (Sept. 17, 1937), *available at* www.presidency.ucsb.edu/ws/index. php?pid=15459.

12. Parents Involved in Cmty. Schs. v. Seattle Sch. Dist. No. 1, 551 U.S. 701, 867 (2007) (Breyer, J., dissenting).

13. *Id.* at 868.

CHAPTER 1

1. Martin Luther King, Jr., I Have a Dream, Keynote Address of the March on Washington, D.C., for Civil Rights (Aug. 28, 1963), *in* A TESTAMENT OF HOPE: THE ESSENTIAL WRITINGS OF MARTIN LUTHER KING, JR. 217, 217 (James M. Washington ed., 1986).

2. DECLARATION OF INDEPENDENCE para. 1 (U.S. 1776).

3. THE FEDERALIST No. 51 (James Madison).

4. *Id.*

5. *Id.*

6. Martin v. Hunter's Lessee, 14 U.S. 304, 324 (1816).

7. ARTICLES OF CONFEDERATION art. III (1781).

8. THE FEDERALIST No. 52 (James Madison).

9. BERNARD BAILYN, THE IDEOLOGICAL ORIGINS OF THE AMERICAN REVOLUTION 184–85 (1992); *see* THE DECLARATION OF INDEPENDENCE para. 1 (U.S. 1776) ("We hold these truths to be self-evident, that all men are created equal, that they are endowed by their Creator with certain unalienable Rights, that among these are Life, Liberty and the pursuit of Happiness.").

10. *See* GORDON S. WOOD, THE CREATION OF THE AMERICAN REPUBLIC, 1776–1787, at 293–94 (2d ed. 1998).

11. James Iredell, Speech in the North Carolina Ratification Convention (July 28, 1788), *in* JACK N. RAKOVE, DECLARING RIGHTS: A BRIEF HISTORY WITH DOCUMENTS 145, 146 (1998).

12. James Madison, Speech to the House of Representatives (June 8, 1789), *in* RAKOVE, *supra* note 11, at 170, 179; *see also* THE FEDERALIST No. 78 (Alexander Hamilton) ("This independence of the judges is equally requisite to guard the Constitution and the rights of individuals from the effects of those ill humors, which the arts of designing men, or the influence of particular conjunctures, sometimes disseminate among the people themselves, and

which...have a tendency...to occasion dangerous innovations in the government, and serious oppressions of the minor party in the community.").

13. Madison, Speech to the House of Representatives, *in* RAKOVE, *supra* note 11, at 178.

14. John Dickinson, An Address to the Committee of Correspondence in Barbados (Philadelphia 1766), *in* WRITINGS OF JOHN DICKINSON 261, 262 (Paul L. Ford ed., 1895), *quoted in* WOOD, *supra* note 10, at 293.

15. Letter from Thomas Jefferson to James Madison (March 15, 1789), *in* RAKOVE, *supra* note 11, at 165, 166.

16. *See* DANIEL A. FARBER, RETAINED BY THE PEOPLE: THE "SILENT" NINTH AMENDMENT AND THE CONSTITUTIONAL RIGHTS AMERICANS DON'T KNOW THEY HAVE 39–44 (2007). The Framers' premise in enumerating federal rights was the logical inverse of their premise in enumerating federal powers: "The powers not delegated to the United States by the Constitution, nor prohibited by it to the States, are reserved to the States respectively, or to the people." U.S. CONST. amend. X. Notably, however, the Framers were careful not to restrict the national government only to powers "*expressly* delegated" by the founding text, as Article II of the Articles of Confederation had done.

17. *See* Ableman v. Booth, 62 U.S. 506 (1858); Dred Scott v. Sandford, 60 U.S. 393 (1857); Prigg v. Pennsylvania, 41 U.S. 539 (1842).

18. Abraham Lincoln, Speech at Springfield, Illinois (June 16, 1858), *in* 3 THE COLLECTED WORKS OF ABRAHAM LINCOLN 461–62 (Roy P. Basler ed., 1953).

19. Proclamation Regarding the Status of Slaves in States Engaged in Rebellion Against the United States (Jan. 1, 1863), *available at* www.presidency.ucsb.edu/ws/index.php?pid=69880.

20. ERIC FONER, RECONSTRUCTION: AMERICA'S UNFINISHED REVOLUTION, 1863–1877, at 8 (1988).

21. The Slaughter-House Cases, 83 U.S. 36, 69 (1873); *see id.* ("It was very well understood that in the form of apprenticeship for long terms, as it had been practiced in the West India Islands, on the abolition of slavery by the English government, or by reducing the slaves to the condition of serfs attached to the plantation, the purpose of the article might have been evaded, if only the word slavery had been used.").

22. *See* The Civil Rights Cases, 109 U.S. 3, 20 (1883) ("By its own unaided force and effect [the Thirteenth Amendment] abolished slavery, and established universal freedom.... [T]he amendment is not a mere prohibition of state laws establishing or upholding slavery, but an absolute declaration that slavery or involuntary servitude shall not exist in any part of the United States.").

23. *See* United States v. Reynolds, 235 U.S. 133 (1914); Bailey v. Alabama, 219 U.S. 219 (1911).

24. *Slaughter-House Cases*, 83 U.S. at 72.

25. In addition to the Bill of Rights, the Eleventh Amendment denies federal courts jurisdiction over suits between a state and "Citizens of another State, or...Citizens or Subjects of any Foreign State." The Twelfth Amendment, which changed the presidential selection process set forth in Article I, reduced the likelihood that presidential elections would be decided by Congress.

26. Dred Scott v. Sandford, 60 U.S. 393 (1857) (invaliding the Missouri Compromise and holding that black people, whether free or slave, are not and cannot be citizens of the United States).

27. *See* U.S. Const. art. I, § 8, art. III, § 3, cl. 2, art. IV, § 3, cl. 2.

28. *See* McCulloch v. Maryland, 17 U.S. 316, 421 (1819) ("Let the end be legitimate, let it be within the scope of the constitution, and all means which are appropriate, which are plainly adapted to that end, which are not prohibited, but consist with the letter and spirit of the constitution, are constitutional."); *id.* at 357 ("The court, in inquiring whether congress had made a selection of constitutional means, is to...[see] whether they are appropriate means to an end.").

29. Jones v. Alfred H. Mayer Co., 392 U.S. 409, 438–40 (1968).

30. *See* Civil Rights Act of 1866, ch. 31, 14 Stat. 27.

31. Akhil Reed Amar, America's Constitution: A Biography 381 (2005) (emphasis in original).

32. *Id.*

33. *Id.* at 386–88 (discussing the views of Congressman John Bingham, the principal author of the Fourteenth Amendment, and Senator Jacob Howard, who introduced the Fourteenth Amendment to Congress as it emerged from the Joint Committee on Reconstruction); Foner, *supra* note 10, at 258–59 (same).

34. *See* Randy E. Barnett, *The Proper Scope of the Police Power*, 79 NOTRE DAME L. REV. 429, 457–64 (2004) (showing that key members of the Reconstruction Congress understood the Privileges or Immunities Clause to protect not only rights created by positive law, but also unspecified natural rights inherent to citizenship); *see also* FONER, *supra* note 10, at 257 ("The debate [over the Fourteenth Amendment] abounded in generalities such as 'the fundamental rights of citizens,' and Republicans rejected calls to define these with precision. Unlike the Civil Rights Act, which listed numerous rights a state could not abridge, the Amendment used only the broadest language.").

35. Katzenbach v. Morgan, 384 U.S. 641, 650 (1966) (citing McCulloch v. Maryland, 17 U.S. 316, 421 (1819)).

36. Cong. Globe, 42d Cong., 1st Sess. app. at 83 (1871) (statement of Rep. Bingham), *quoted in* FONER, *supra* note 10, at 258.

37. U.S. CONST. amend. XIV, § 2. The penalty does not apply to denial of the franchise "for participation in rebellion, or other crime." *Id.*

38. *See* AMAR, *supra* note 31, at 391; Akhil Reed Amar, *The Fifteenth Amendment and "Political Rights,"* 17 CARDOZO L. REV. 2225, 2228 (1996).

39. *See* St. Francis College v. Al-Khazraji, 481 U.S. 604, 610–13 (1987) (reviewing nineteenth-century texts and legislative histories of the Civil Rights Act of 1866 and the Voting Rights Act of 1870 to show that "race" discrimination was understood to include discrimination against Arabs, Jews, Germans, and other ethnic groups); Shaare Tefile Congregation v. Cobb, 481 U.S. 615 (1987) (holding that the ban on racial discrimination in Civil Rights Act of 1866 prohibits discrimination against Jews).

40. U.S. CONST. amend. XIV, § 2.

41. AMAR, *supra* note 31, at 419.

42. *See* Pollock v. Farmers' Loan & Trust Co., 158 U.S. 601 (1895).

CHAPTER 2

1. Marbury v. Madison, 5 U.S. 137, 177 (1803).

2. *Id.* at 180; *see* Larry D. Kramer, *The Supreme Court, 2000 Term— Foreword: We the Court*, 115 HARV. L. REV. 4, 88–89 (2001); William W. Van Alstyne, *A Critical Guide to* Marbury v. Madison, 1969 DUKE L.J. 1, 34–37.

3. Cooper v. Aaron, 358 U.S. 1, 18 (1958).

4. U.S. CONST. pmbl.

5. THE FEDERALIST NO. 78 (Alexander Hamilton).

6. *Id.*

7. ARCHIBALD COX, THE ROLE OF THE SUPREME COURT IN AMERICAN GOVERNMENT 117–18 (1976).

8. Jack Balkin, *Abortion and Original Meaning*, 24 CONST. COMMENT. 291, 307 (2007). The term "fidelity" has been variously used in writings on constitutional interpretation. *See, e.g.*, Frank I. Michelman, *Fidelity and Legitimacy*, ADVANCE, Fall 2007, at 69; Robin West, *Constitutional Fidelity and Democratic Legitimacy*, ADVANCE, Fall 2007, at 75; Symposium, *Fidelity in Constitutional Theory*, 65 FORDHAM L. REV. 1247 (1997); *see also* SANFORD LEVINSON, CONSTITUTIONAL FAITH (1988). Our use of the term most closely resembles the usage in Balkin, *supra*, and Lawrence Lessig, *Fidelity in Translation*, 71 TEX. L. REV. 1165 (1993).

9. Lessig, *supra* note 8, at 1169.

10. *See* U.S. CONST. art. I, §§ 7, 12, 16, amend. XXII, § 1.

11. *Id.* at 1217.

12. 277 U.S. 438, 471 (1928) (Brandeis, J., dissenting).

13. *See id.* at 463–66 (majority opinion).

14. *Id.* at 464.

15. *Id.* at 472–73 (Brandeis, J., dissenting) (quoting McCulloch v. Maryland, 17 U.S. 316, 407 (1819), and Weems v. United States, 217 U.S. 349, 373 (1910)) (other internal quotation marks and citations omitted).

16. *Id.* at 473–74 (internal quotation marks and citations omitted).

17. 389 U.S. 347 (1967) (holding that government interception of an individual's telephone calls constitutes a search within the meaning of the Fourth Amendment).

18. *Olmstead*, 277 U.S. at 472–73 (Brandeis, J., dissenting) (quoting *Weems*, 217 U.S. at 373) (internal quotation marks omitted).

19. United States v. Butler, 297 U.S. 1, 62 (1936).

20. *Confirmation Hearing on the Nomination of John G. Roberts, Jr. to Be Chief Justice of the United States: Hearing before the S. Comm. on the Judiciary*, 109th Cong. 55, 56 (2005) (statement of John G. Roberts, Jr.).

21. Officially, "[t]he Strike Zone is that area over homeplate the upper limit of which is a horizontal line at the midpoint between the top of the shoulders and the top of the uniform pants, and the lower level is a line at the hollow beneath the kneecap. The Strike Zone shall be determined from the batter's stance as the batter is prepared to swing at a pitched ball." MAJOR LEAGUE BASEBALL, OFFICIAL BASEBALL RULES (2008) (Rule 2.00). Despite its precision, the strike zone is understood to reflect a general concept—namely, the area where the batter is thought to have a fair opportunity to hit a pitched ball—whose interpretation has varied as the game has evolved. For example, when the transition from bulky outside chest protectors to compact inside vests enabled umpires to crouch lower behind the catcher, the lowered line of sight resulted in the calling of lower strikes. As pitches thrown high and inside became viewed as offensive to the batter, and as the league adopted stricter rules against intentionally hitting batters, the strike zone moved toward the outside. In addition, the evolution of norms in favor of more hitting in the game has tended to favor a smaller strike zone. For a discussion of how contemporary understandings of the game have affected interpretation of the strike zone, see Peter Gammons, *Whatever Happened to the Strike Zone?* SPORTS ILLUSTRATED, Apr. 6, 1987, at 36.

22. 128 S. Ct. 2783 (2008).

23. *See* J. Harvie Wilkinson III, *Of Guns, Abortions, and the Unraveling Rule of Law*, 95 VA. L. REV. 253 (2009); Reva B. Siegel, *Dead or Alive: Originalism as Popular Constitutionalism in* Heller, 122 HARV. L. REV. 191 (2008); Richard A. Posner, *In Defense of Looseness: The Supreme Court and Gun Control*, NEW REPUBLIC, Aug. 27, 2008, at 32.

24. *Heller*, 128 S. Ct. at 2801.

25. *See id.* at 2802–3.

26. *See id.* at 2833–36 (Stevens, J., dissenting).

27. *Id.* at 2836.

28. 307 U.S. 174, 178 (1939).

29. *Heller*, 128 S. Ct. at 2845 (Stevens, J., dissenting).

30. *Id.* at 2814, 2816 (majority opinion).

31. *See, e.g.*, McCreary County v. ACLU, 545 U.S. 844, 885, 896–99 (2005) (Scalia, J., dissenting).

32. *Heller*, 128 S. Ct. at 2791–92. *Reno v. ACLU* involved the application of the First Amendment to Internet speech, and *Kyllo* involved the application of the Fourth Amendment to a thermal-imaging device.

33. *Id.* at 2815, 2817 (internal quotation marks and citations omitted).

34. *See id.* at 2815–16.

35. *Id.* at 2818.

36. Olmstead v. United States, 277 U.S. 438, 472 (1928) (Brandeis, J., dissenting).

37. *Heller*, 128 S. Ct. at 2818.

38. *Id.* at 2816–17.

39. *Id.* at 2852 (Breyer, J., dissenting); *see* Wilkinson, *supra* note 23, at 296 ("[T]he Court's dicta on the likely constitutionality of commercial sale regulations and felon possession bans sure looks like balancing: because the history is ambiguous, the opinion seems to announce that some state interests in safety outweigh some personal interest in gun possession.").

40. Among the most basic examples, the Constitution protects freedom of speech, but not if someone "falsely shout[s] fire in a theatre and caus[es] a panic," Schenck v. United States, 249 U.S. 47, 52 (1919); it prohibits treating people differently on the basis of race, but not if the government has a compelling interest for doing so and adopts the least discriminatory means to further that interest, *see* Adarand Constructors, Inc. v. Peña, 515 U.S. 200, 227 (1995); and it protects free exercise of religion, but not if someone is motivated by religious conviction to harm another, *see* Reynolds v. United States, 98 U.S. 145, 166 (1878).

41. *See Heller*, 128 S. Ct. at 2852 (Breyer, J., dissenting) ("In applying this kind of standard the Court normally defers to a legislature's empirical judgment in matters where a legislature is likely to have greater expertise and greater institutional factfinding capacity.").

42. *See id.* at 2821.

43. *Id.* at 2852 (Breyer, J., dissenting).

44. *See* Lessig, *supra* note 8, at 1188 ("In at least some cases, the…originalist, by ignoring changes in context, changes rather than preserves meaning.").

45. *See infra* chapter 5.

46. *See infra* chapter 3.

47. *Heller*, 128 S. Ct. at 2816–17.

48. *Compare* David Strauss, *Principle and Its Perils*, 64 U. Chi. L. Rev. 373, 381 (1997) (reviewing Ronald Dworkin, Freedom's Law: The Moral Reading of the American Constitution (1996)) ("[T]he commitment to, or demand for, an abstract principle [from which specific doctrinal results can be logically derived] precipitates a kind of impatience with the sorts of judgments that controversial legal questions often require—fine-grained assessments of a variety of conflicting principles, rather than the deductive application of a single, decisive principle.").

49. *Heller*, 128 S. Ct. at 2868 (Breyer, J., dissenting).

50. Balkin, *supra* note 8, at 293; *see also* Kermit Roosevelt III, The Myth of Judicial Activism: Making Sense of Supreme Court Decisions 47–58 (2006) (drawing similar distinction between "meaning originalism" and "application originalism"); Randy E. Barnett, Restoring the Lost Constitution: The Presumption of Liberty 93–94 (2004) (drawing similar distinction between "original meaning originalism" and "original intention originalism" to parallel Ronald Dworkin's distinction between "semantic originalism" and "expectations originalism").

51. Lessig, *supra* note 8, at 1264.

52. Antonin Scalia, *Response*, *in* A Matter of Interpretation: Federal Courts and the Law 145 (Amy Gutmann ed., 1997) (emphasis in original); *see also* Antonin Scalia, *Originalism: The Lesser Evil*, 57 U. Cin. L. Rev. 849, 861–62 (1989).

53. *See* McCreary County v. ACLU, 545 U.S. 844, 885 (2005) (Scalia, J., dissenting); Elk Grove Unified Sch. Dist. v. Newdow, 542 U.S. 1, 45 (2004) (Thomas, J., concurring in the judgment).

54. *McCreary*, 545 U.S. at 896–97 (Scalia, J., dissenting) (emphasis in original).

55. *See* Eric Schnapper, *Affirmative Action and the Legislative History of the Fourteenth Amendment*, 71 Va. L. Rev. 753, 754 (1985) ("[The Reconstruction programs] were generally open to all blacks, not only to recently freed slaves, and were adopted over repeatedly expressed objections that such racially exclusive measures were unfair to whites."); *see also* Stephen A. Siegel, *The Federal Government's Power to Enact Color-conscious Laws: An Originalist Inquiry*, 92 Nw. U. L. Rev. 477 (1998).

56. *See infra* chapter 6.

57. *See* Paul Brest, *The Misconceived Quest for the Original Understanding*, 60 B.U. L. Rev. 204, 214–15 (1980).

58. *See id.* at 221 ("The act of translation required…involves the counterfactual and imaginary act of projecting the adopters' concepts and attitudes into a future they probably could not have envisioned. When the interpreter engages in this sort of projection, she is in a fantasy world more of her own than of the adopters' making.").

59. *See* Balkin, *supra* note 8, at 297–303.

60. The Federalist No. 37 (James Madison).

61. The Federalist No. 82 (Alexander Hamilton).

62. Kathleen M. Sullivan, *What's Wrong with Constitutional Amendments?* in The Constitution Project, "Great and Extraordinary Occasions": Developing Guidelines for Constitutional Change 40, 41 (1999).

63. The Federalist No. 49 (James Madison).

64. *See* David A. Strauss, *The Irrelevance of Constitutional Amendments*, 114 Harv. L. Rev. 1457 (2001).

65. *See* H. Jefferson Powell, *The Original Understanding of Original Intent*, 98 Harv. L. Rev. 885 (1985) (demonstrating that the Framers themselves did not expect the Constitution to be interpreted according to their original intent).

66. *See* Stephen Breyer, Active Liberty: Interpreting Our Democratic Constitution 118 (2005) ("Given the open-ended nature of *content*, why should one expect to find fixed views [among the Framers] about the nature of interpretive practices?") (emphasis in original).

67. *See* Michael J. Gerhardt, *The Rhetoric of Judicial Critique: From Judicial Restraint to the Virtual Bill of Rights*, 10 Wm. & Mary Bill Rts. J. 585, 587 (2002).

68. The categories of judicial activism listed in the next sentence are discussed in William P. Marshall, *Conservatives and the Seven Sins of Judicial Activism*, 73 U. Colo. L. Rev. 1217 (2002).

69. The Rehnquist Court invalidated more acts of Congress per year than any other Court in history, with Chief Justice Rehnquist and Justices O'Connor, Scalia, Kennedy, and Thomas voting to strike down federal legislation more often than Justice Stevens, Justice Souter, Justice Breyer,

or Justice Ginsburg. *See* Paul Gewirtz & Chad Golder, *So Who Are the Activists?* N.Y. TIMES, July 6, 2005, at A19. Some of those decisions purport to limit Congress's power under the Commerce Clause or Section 5 of the Fourteenth Amendment in the name of federalism. But other cases show that conservative Justices are selective in their deference to state or local decision-making. *See, e.g.,* District of Columbia v. Heller, 128 S. Ct. 2783 (2008); Parents Involved in Cmty. Sch. v. Seattle Sch. Dist. No. 1, 551 U.S. 701 (2007); Lorillard Tobacco Co. v. Reilly, 533 U.S. 525 (2001); Boy Scouts v. Dale, 530 U.S. 640 (2000); Phillips v. Washington Legal Found., 524 U.S. 156 (1998); Lucas v. S.C. Coastal Council, 505 U.S. 1003 (1992); City of Richmond v. J.A. Croson Co., 488 U.S. 469 (1989).

70. *See, e.g.,* Fed. Mar. Comm'n v. S.C. State Ports Auth., 535 U.S. 743 (2002); Alden v. Maine, 527 U.S. 706 (1999).

71. *See, e.g.,* Adarand Constructors, Inc. v. Peña, 515 U.S. 200 (1995); Lucas v. S.C. Coastal Council, 505 U.S. 1003 (1992).

72. *See, e.g.,* Hein v. Freedom from Religion Found., 551 U.S. 587 (2007); FEC v. Wis. Right to Life, Inc., 551 U.S. 449 (2007); Morse v. Frederick, 551 U.S. 393 (2007); Bowles v. Russell, 551 U.S. 205 (2007); Gonzales v. Carhart, 550 U.S. 124 (2007).

73. *Compare* Hein v. Freedom from Religion Found., 551 U.S. 587 (2007), Bowles v. Russell, 551 U.S. 205 (2007), Alexander v. Sandoval, 532 U.S. 275 (2001), *and* Lewis v. Casey, 518 U.S. 343 (1996), *with* Palazzolo v. Rhode Island, 533 U.S. 606 (2001), *and* Northeastern Fla. Chapter of Associated Gen. Contractors v. Jacksonville, 508 U.S. 656 (1993).

74. *See* Bush v. Gore, 531 U.S. 98 (2000).

75. *See supra* text accompanying notes 45–47.

76. *See* United States v. Carolene Prods. Co., 304 U.S. 144, 152 n.4 (1938) (noting that "whether prejudice against discrete and insular minorities may be a special condition, which tends seriously to curtail the operation of those political processes ordinarily to be relied upon to protect minorities, and which may call for a correspondingly more searching judicial inquiry"); McCulloch v. Maryland, 17 U.S. 31 (1819) (applying the principle of no taxation without representation to invalidate state taxation of a national bank).

77. *See* Harriet Chiang, *Election Could Shape Supreme Court for Years to Come,* S.F. CHRON., Oct. 24, 2000, at A4.

78. *See* Elisabeth Bumiller, *McCain Assures Conservatives of His Stance on Judges*, N.Y. TIMES, May 7, 2008, at A22.

79. *See* Miller v. California, 413 U.S. 15, 24 (1973) (defining standard for government regulation of obscenity); Brandenburg v. Ohio, 395 U.S. 444, 447 (1969) (permitting government regulation of speech that incites imminent lawless action).

80. *See* N.Y. Times Co. v. United States, 403 U.S. 713 (1971) (rejecting President's claim of executive authority to impose prior restraint on publication of the Pentagon Papers); Gitlow v. New York, 268 U.S. 652 (1925) (holding that the Fourteenth Amendment makes First Amendment freedoms applicable to the states).

81. *See* Gibbons v. Ogden, 22 U.S. 1, 187–89 (1824); McCulloch v. Maryland, 17 U.S. 316, 413–15 (1819).

82. *See* San Antonio Indep. Sch. Dist. v. Rodriguez, 411 U.S. 1 (1973); McCleskey v. Kemp, 481 U.S. 279 (1987).

83. Missouri v. Holland, 252 U.S. 416, 433 (1920).

84. *See* David A. Strauss, *Common Law Constitutional Interpretation*, 63 U. CHI. L. REV. 877, 884–90 (1996).

85. McCulloch v. Maryland, 17 U.S. 316, 407 (1819).

86. *See infra* chapter 3.

87. 22 U.S. 1, 188 (1824) (Marshall, C.J.).

88. Antonin Scalia, *Common-law Courts in a Civil-law System: The Role of United States Federal Courts in Interpreting the Constitution and Laws, in* A MATTER OF INTERPRETATION, *supra* note 52, at 3, 23.

89. *See* Hamdi v. Rumsfeld, 542 U.S. 507, 579 (2004) (Thomas, J., dissenting); Fed. Mar. Comm'n v. S.C. State Ports Auth., 535 U.S. 743 (2002).

90. *Fed. Mar. Comm'n*, 535 U.S. at 754; *see* Alden v. Maine, 527 U.S. 706 (1999).

91. STANLEY I. KUTLER, THE WARS OF WATERGATE: THE LAST CRISIS OF RICHARD NIXON 144 (1992) (quoting Nixon); *see* Engel v. Vitale, 370 U.S. 421 (1962).

92. Poe v. Ullman, 367 U.S. 497, 540 (1961) (Harlan, J., dissenting) (citing McCulloch v. Maryland, 17 U.S. 316 (1819)).

CHAPTER 3

1. 347 U.S. 483 (1954).

2. *Id.* at 489; *see* Gebhart v. Belton, 345 U.S. 972 (1953) (ordering reargument of *Brown* cases).

3. 347 U.S. at 489.

4. *Id.* at 490.

5. *Id.* at 492–93.

6. *See id.* at 493 ("Today, education is perhaps the most important function of state and local governments. Compulsory school attendance laws and the great expenditures for education both demonstrate our recognition of the importance of education to our democratic society. It is required in the performance of our most basic public responsibilities, even service in the armed forces. It is the very foundation of good citizenship. Today it is a principal instrument in awakening the child to cultural values, in preparing him for later professional training, and in helping him to adjust normally to his environment. In these days, it is doubtful that any child may reasonably be expected to succeed in life if he is denied the opportunity of an education. Such an opportunity, where the state has undertaken to provide it, is a right which must be made available to all on equal terms.").

7. *Id.* at 494.

8. *Id.* (internal quotation marks omitted). Although much criticism has been directed at the Court's citation of psychological research to support the latter proposition, *see id.* at 494 n.11, such critiques too often overlook the simple fact that the citation was "relegated to a footnote and treated as merely corroboratory of common sense." Charles L. Black, Jr., *The Lawfulness of the Segregation Decisions*, 69 YALE L.J. 421, 430 n.25 (1960).

9. Black, *supra* note 8, at 424.

10. *See, e.g.*, Baltimore v. Dawson, 350 U.S. 877 (1955) (per curiam) (beaches, bathhouses, and swimming pools); Holmes v. City of Atlanta, 350 U.S. 879 (1955) (per curiam) (golf courses); Gayle v. Browder, 352 U.S. 903 (1956) (per curiam) (buses); New Orleans City Park Improvement Ass'n v.

Detiege, 358 U.S. 54 (1958) (per curiam) (parks and recreational facilities).

11. *Compare* WHAT BROWN V. BOARD OF EDUCATION SHOULD HAVE SAID (Jack M. Balkin ed., 2001) (collecting alternative *Brown* opinions from nine scholars).

12. The Court dismissed the argument that "the enforced separation of the two races stamps the colored race with a badge of inferiority" by declaring that "[i]f this be so, it is not by reason of anything found in the act, but solely because the colored race chooses to put that construction upon it." Plessy v. Ferguson, 163 U.S. 537, 551 (1896). Further, the Court said, "[t]he argument assumes that social prejudices may be overcome by legislation, and that equal rights cannot be secured to the negro except by an enforced commingling of the two races. We cannot accept this proposition. If the two races are to meet upon terms of social equality, it must be the result of natural affinities, a mutual appreciation of each other's merits, and a voluntary consent of individuals.... If the civil and political rights of both races be equal, one cannot be inferior to the other civilly or politically. If one race be inferior to the other socially, the [C]onstitution of the United States cannot put them upon the same plane." *Id.* at 551–52.

13. *Brown*, 347 U.S. at 489 (emphasis added).

14. *See, e.g.,* RAOUL BERGER, GOVERNMENT BY JUDICIARY: THE TRANSFORMATION OF THE FOURTEENTH AMENDMENT 117–33, 241–45 (1977); ROBERT H. BORK, THE TEMPTING OF AMERICA: THE POLITICAL SEDUCTION OF THE LAW 75–76 (1990); LAURENCE H. TRIBE & MICHAEL C. DORF, ON READING THE CONSTITUTION 12–13 (1991); Alexander M. Bickel, *The Original Understanding and the Segregation Decision,* 69 HARV. L. REV. 1, 58 (1955); Thomas C. Grey, *Do We Have an Unwritten Constitution?,* 27 STAN. L. REV. 703, 712 (1975); Michael Klarman, *An Interpretive History of Modern Equal Protection,* 90 MICH. L. REV. 213, 252 (1991); Richard A. Posner, *Bork and Beethoven,* 42 STAN. L. REV. 1365, 1374–76 (1990); Mark V. Tushnet, *Following the Rules Laid Down: A Critique of Interpretivism and Neutral Principles,* 96 HARV. L. REV. 781, 790, 800 (1983).

15. *See* Michael W. McConnell, *Originalism and the Desegregation Decisions,* 81 VA. L. REV. 947 (1995).

16. *See* Michael J. Klarman, Brown, *Originalism, and Constitutional Theory: A Response to Professor McConnell,* 81 VA. L. REV. 1881 (1995).

17. Parents Involved in Cmty. Schs. v. Seattle Sch. Dist. No. 1, 551 U.S. 701, 747–48 (2007) (plurality opinion of Roberts, C.J.) (quoting Brown v. Bd. of Educ., 349 U.S. 294, 300–01 (1955)).

18. *Id.* at 799 (Stevens, J., dissenting); *see also* Plessy v. Ferguson, 163 U.S. 537, 557 (1896) (Harlan, J., dissenting) (refuting the claim that segregation "prescribes a rule applicable alike to white and colored citizens" by observing that "[e]very one knows that the statute in question had its origin in the purpose, not so much to exclude white persons from railroad cars occupied by blacks, as to exclude colored people from coaches occupied by or assigned to white persons.... No one would be so wanting in candor as to assert the contrary.").

19. Geoffrey R. Stone, *The Roberts Court, Stare Decisis, and the Future of Constitutional Law*, 82 TULANE L. REV. 1533, 1540 (2008) (emphases in original).

20. Washington v. Davis, 426 U.S. 229 (1976) (upholding employment qualifying test with racially disparate impact despite no evidence of the test's validity as a measure of subsequent job performance); *see also* McCleskey v. Kemp, 481 U.S. 279 (1987) (upholding state death penalty scheme despite large racial disparities in capital sentencing based on the victim's race).

21. Goodwin Liu, *"History Will Be Heard": An Appraisal of the* Seattle/Louisville *Decision*, 2 HARV. L. & POL'Y REV. 53, 65 (2008).

22. *Parents Involved*, 551 U.S. at 867–68 (Breyer, J., dissenting).

23. Minor v. Happersett, 88 U.S. 162, 174–77 (1875).

24. 83 U.S. 130 (1873).

25. 83 U.S. 36 (1873).

26. *Bradwell*, 83 U.S. at 141 (Bradley, J., concurring in the judgment, joined by Swayne & Field, JJ.). Chief Justice Chase, the fourth dissenter in *Slaughter-House*, dissented alone in *Bradwell* but was too ill to write an opinion. He died shortly after *Bradwell* was decided.

27. *Id.* at 141–42.

28. 154 U.S. 116 (1894).

29. *See, e.g.*, Commonwealth v. Welosky, 177 N.E. 656 (Mass. 1931); People *ex rel.* Fyfe v. Barnett, 150 N.E. 290 (Ill. 1925); State v. Kelley, 229 P. 659 (Idaho 1924); State v. Mittle, 113 S.E. 335 (S.C. 1922).

30. Hoyt v. Florida, 368 U.S. 57, 62 (1961).

31. 208 U.S. 412, 422, 423 (1908); *see also* Bosley v. McLaughlin, 236 U.S. 385 (1915); Miller v. Wilson, 236 U.S. 373 (1915); Riley v. Massachusetts, 232 U.S. 671 (1914).

32. 300 U.S. 379, 398 (1937). *West Coast Hotel* overruled *Adkins v. Children's Hospital*, 261 U.S. 525 (1923), which had invalidated minimum wage legislation for women on the ground that differences "in the contractual, political, and civil status of women" versus men "have now come almost, if not quite, to the vanishing point." *Id.* at 553.

33. 335 U.S. 464, 466 (1948).

34. *See, e.g.*, City of Milwaukee v. Piscuine, 119 N.W.2d 442 (Wis. 1963); Henson v. City of Chicago, 114 N.E.2d 778 (Ill. 1953); Randles v. Wash. State Liquor Control Bd., 206 P.2d 1209 (Wash. 1949).

35. Reva B. Siegel, *Constitutional Culture, Social Movement Conflict and Constitutional Change: The Case of the de facto ERA*, 94 CAL. L. REV. 1323, 1324 (2006).

36. 404 U.S. 71 (1971).

37. CASS R. SUNSTEIN, THE SECOND BILL OF RIGHTS: FDR'S UNFINISHED REVOLUTION AND WHY WE NEED IT MORE THAN EVER 126 (2004).

38. The history is recounted in numerous sources, including Siegel, *supra* note 35, and Robert C. Post & Reva B. Siegel, *Legislative Constitutionalism and Section Five Power: Policentric Interpretation of the Family and Medical Leave Act*, 112 YALE L.J. 1943, 1984–2004 (2003).

39. *See* Civil Rights Act of 1964, tit. VII, Pub. L. No. 88–352, § 703, 78 Stat. 241, 255 (codified as amended at 42 U.S.C. § 2000e-2(a)).

40. *See* Equal Employment Opportunity Act of 1972, Pub. L. No. 92–261, § 2, 86 Stat. 103, 103.

41. *See* Education Amendments of 1972, Pub. L. No. 92-318, § 901, 86 Stat. 235, 373–74.

42. *See* State and Local Fiscal Assistance Act of 1972, Pub. L. No. 92–512, § 122, 86 Stat. 919, 932; Federal Water Pollution Control Act Amendments of 1972, Pub. L. No. 92–500, § 13, 86 Stat. 816, 903; Nurses Training Act of 1971, Pub. L. No. 92–158, § 11, 85 Stat. 465, 479–80; Comprehensive Health Manpower Training Act of 1971, Pub. L. No. 92–157, § 101, 85 Stat. 431, 461.

43. 411 U.S. 677, 688 (1973) (plurality opinion).

44. *Id.* at 687.

45. *Id.* at 687–88 (citing Katzenbach v. Morgan, 384 U.S. 641, 648–49 (1966), and other cases).

46. *Id.* at 684.

47. *Id.* at 686.

48. *Id.*

49. 420 U.S. 636 (1975).

50. *Id.* at 643 (internal quotation marks and citation omitted).

51. 421 U.S. 7, 14–15 (1975) (internal quotation marks omitted).

52. 429 U.S. 190, 204 (1976).

53. 458 U.S. 718, 730 (1982).

54. 518 U.S. 532, 534 (1996) (hereafter *VMI*) (citation omitted).

55. *Hogan,* 458 U.S. at 725.

56. *VMI,* 518 U.S. at 531 (quoting *Hogan,* 458 U.S. at 724 (internal quotation marks omitted)).

57. Indeed, a significant reason why Robert Bork failed to win confirmation to the Supreme Court was his criticism of the Court's gender equality jurisprudence on originalist grounds. The Reagan Justice Department agreed with Bork that the Framers never intended the Fourteenth Amendment to prohibit gender discrimination. But it recognized that "the American public would not trust the constitutional judgment of a Supreme Court nominee" who took that view and, on the eve of the hearings, urged Bork to retract his criticism of precedents holding that the Equal Protection Clause applies to gender classifications. Siegel, *supra* note 35, at 1411; *see also* ETHAN BRONNER, BATTLE FOR JUSTICE: HOW THE BORK NOMINATION SHOOK AMERICA 251–60 (1989). Although Bork repudiated his earlier view, the Senate Judiciary Committee did not find his confirmation conversion to be credible. *See* S. EXEC. REP. NO. 100-7, at 45–47 (1987).

58. *See* Califano v. Webster, 430 U.S. 313, 318 (1977) (upholding statute allowing women to eliminate more low-earning years than men in computing Social Security benefits because it "operated directly to compensate women for past economic discrimination"); Schlesinger v. Ballard, 419 U.S. 498, 508 (1975) (upholding statute providing women in

the navy with a longer period to achieve mandatory promotion than men because women face restrictions on participation in combat and most sea duty); Kahn v. Shevin, 416 U.S. 351, 353–54 (1974) (upholding property tax exemption for widows but not widowers because of ongoing disadvantages facing widows seeking to enter the job market).

59. *See* Nguyen v. INS, 533 U.S. 53, 64 (2001) (citing "the unique relationship of the mother to the event of birth" in upholding a statute granting automatic U.S. citizenship to a child born abroad to unmarried parents if the mother is a U.S. citizen but not if only the father is a U.S. citizen); Michael M. v. Sonoma County Super. Ct., 450 U.S. 464, 471 (1981) (upholding statutory rape law punishing men, but not women, for sexual intercourse involving a female under age 18 on the ground that "young men and young women are not similarly situated with respect to the problems and the risks of sexual intercourse"). *But compare* Geduldig v. Aiello, 417 U.S. 484, 496 n.20 (1974) (concluding that exclusion of pregnancy-related disabilities from state disability insurance coverage is not "a sex-based classification" even though "only women can become pregnant"). *Geduldig* has been superseded by the Pregnancy Discrimination Act, 42 U.S.C. § 2000e(k), at least with respect to employment discrimination.

60. *See* 411 U.S. at 687–88.

61. 538 U.S. 721, 726–29 (2003) (upholding the twelve-week leave entitlement under the Family and Medical Leave Act as valid Section 5 legislation to remedy state practices that stereotype women as caregivers).

62. *See* David A. Strauss, *The Irrelevance of Constitutional Amendments*, 114 HARV. L. REV. 1457, 1476–77 (2001) ("[I]t is difficult to identify any respect in which constitutional law is different from what it would have been if the ERA had been adopted."); William N. Eskridge, Jr., *Channeling: Identity-based Social Movements and Public Law*, 150 U. PA. L. REV. 419, 502 (2001) ("[The women's movement] was able to do through the Equal Protection Clause virtually everything the ERA would have accomplished had it been ratified and added to the Constitution."); Jeffrey Rosen, *The New Look of Liberalism on the Court*, N.Y. TIMES, Oct. 5, 1997, § 6 (Magazine), at 60, 65 ("'There is no practical difference between what has evolved and the E.R.A.'" (quoting Justice Ruth Bader Ginsburg)).

63. Ruth Colker, *The Supreme Court's Historical Errors in* City of Boerne v. Flores, 43 B.C. L. REV. 783, 817 (2002); *see* Michael W. McConnell, *Institutions*

and Interpretation: A Critique of City of Boerne v. Flores, 111 HARV. L. REV. 153, 182–83 (1997).

64. *See* Virginia v. Rives, 100 U.S. 313 (1879); United States v. Reese, 92 U.S. 214 (1875).

65. *See* United States v. Harris, 106 U.S. 629 (1883); United States v. Cruikshank, 92 U.S. 542 (1875); *see generally* CHARLES LANE, THE DAY FREEDOM DIED: THE COLFAX MASSACRE, THE SUPREME COURT AND THE BETRAYAL OF RECONSTRUCTION (2008).

66. *See* The Civil Rights Cases, 109 U.S. 3 (1883).

67. *Id.* at 46–47 (Harlan, J., dissenting).

68. *See* Robert C. Post & Reva B. Siegel, *Equal Protection by Law: Federal Antidiscrimination Legislation after* Morrison *and* Kimel, 110 YALE L.J. 441, 515–18 (2000).

69. Pub. L. No. 89–110, 79 Stat. 437, 437 (pmbl.).

70. *See* Lassiter v. Northampton Election Bd., 360 U.S. 45 (1959) (upholding North Carolina literacy requirement against facial challenge under the Fifteenth Amendment); Breedlove v. Suttles, 302 U.S. 277 (1937) (upholding Georgia poll tax under the Fourteenth Amendment).

71. Pub. L. No. 89–110, § 4(a), 79 Stat. at 438.

72. Pub. L. No. 89–110, § 10(a), (b), 79 Stat. at 442.

73. Pub. L. No. 89–110, § 5, 79 Stat. at 439.

74. 384 U.S. 641, 648 (1966). The Court framed the inquiry as follows: "Without regard to whether the judiciary would find that the Equal Protection Clause itself nullifies New York's English literacy requirement as so applied, could Congress prohibit the enforcement of the state law by legislating under § 5 of the Fourteenth Amendment?" *Id.* at 649.

75. *Id.* at 650 (citing McCulloch v. Maryland, 17 U.S. 316, 421 (1819)); *see id.* at 650 (quoting *Ex parte* Virginia, 100 U.S. 339, 345–46 (1879) ("Whatever legislation is appropriate, that is, adapted to carry out the objects the amendments have in view, whatever tends to enforce submission to the prohibitions they contain, and to secure to all persons the enjoyment of perfect equality of civil rights and the equal protection of the laws against State denial or invasion, if not prohibited, is brought within the domain of congressional power.")).

76. 383 U.S. 301, 328 (1966) (footnote omitted).

77. *See* Harper v. Va. Bd. of Elections, 383 U.S. 663 (1966) (overruling Breedlove v. Suttles, 302 U.S. 277 (1937)).

78. *See* Heart of Atlanta Motel v. United States, 379 U.S. 241 (1964); Katzenbach v. McClung, 379 U.S. 294 (1964). *But compare Heart of Atlanta*, 379 U.S. at 280 (Douglas, J., concurring) ("A decision based on the Fourteenth Amendment would have a more settling effect, making unnecessary litigation over whether a particular restaurant or inn is within the commerce definitions of the Act or whether a particular customer is an interstate traveler.... And that construction would put an end to all obstructionist strategies and finally close one door on a bitter chapter in American history."); *id.* at 291, 293 (Goldberg, J., concurring) ("The primary purpose of the Civil Rights Act of 1964... is the vindication of human dignity and not mere economics.... [I]n my view, Congress clearly had authority under both § 5 of the Fourteenth Amendment and the Commerce Clause to enact the Civil Rights Act of 1964.").

79. Archibald Cox, *The Supreme Court, 1965 Term—Foreword: Constitutional Adjudication and the Promotion of Human Rights*, 80 HARV. L. REV. 91, 94 (1966).

80. Equal Employment Opportunity Act of 1972, Pub. L. No. 92–261, § 2, 86 Stat. 103, 103; *see* Fitzpatrick v. Bitzer, 427 U.S. 445 (1976) (upholding application of Title VII to the states as a legitimate exercise of Section 5 power).

81. Education Amendments of 1972, Pub. L. No. 92–318, § 901, 86 Stat. 235, 373–74 (adding Title IX to the Civil Rights Act of 1964).

82. *See* Craig v. Boren, 429 U.S. 190 (1976).

83. Pregnancy Discrimination Act of 1978, Pub. L. No. 95–555, 92 Stat. 2076. Congress overruled the Court's interpretation of Title VII of the Civil Rights Act of 1964 in *General Electric Co. v. Gilbert*, 429 U.S. 125 (1976), and, by making the PDA applicable to the states, challenged the Court's holding in *Geduldig v. Aiello*, 417 U.S. 484 (1974), that pregnancy discrimination is not sex discrimination under the Equal Protection Clause.

84. Family and Medical Leave Act of 1993, Pub. L. No. 103–3, 107 Stat. 7; Violence Against Women Act of 1994, Pub. L. No. 103–322, 108 Stat. 1902. On the role of the women's movement in shaping constitutional

gender equality norms, see generally Post & Siegel, *supra* note 38, at 1980–2020.

85. Age Discrimination in Employment Act of 1967, Pub. L. No. 90–202, 81 Stat. 602; Fair Labor Standards Amendments of 1974, Pub. L. No. 9–259, § 28, 88 Stat. 55, 74.

86. Americans with Disabilities Act, Pub. L. No. 101-336, 104 Stat. 327 (1990).

87. City of Boerne v. Flores, 521 U.S. 507, 536 (1997).

88. Bd. of Trs. of Univ. of Ala. v. Garrett, 531 U.S. 356, 368–74 (2001).

89. *Boerne*, 521 U.S. at 520.

90. *See id.* at 529, 533–34.

91. Kimel v. Fla. Bd. of Regents, 528 U.S. 62, 86 (2000).

92. United States v. Morrison, 529 U.S. 598, 621–24 (2000) (declining to overrule the *Civil Rights Cases*).

93. *Garrett*, 531 U.S. at 370, 372.

94. McConnell, *supra* note 63, at 183.

95. 538 U.S. 721 (2003).

96. *Id.* at 738 (quoting congressional committee reports).

97. *See* Personnel Adm'r v. Feeney, 442 U.S. 256, 279 (1979) (rejecting claim that civil service employment preference for veterans amounted to unconstitutional gender discrimination on the ground that "'[d]iscriminatory purpose'…implies more than intent as volition or intent as awareness of consequence. It implies that the decisionmaker…selected or reaffirmed a particular course of action at least in part 'because of,' not merely 'in spite of,' its adverse effects upon an identifiable group.") (footnotes omitted).

CHAPTER 4

1. Texas v. Johnson, 491 U.S. 397, 411 (1989).

2. *Id.* at 414.

3. 4 WILLIAM BLACKSTONE, COMMENTARIES *151–52; *see* 2 THE DOCUMENTARY HISTORY OF THE RATIFICATION OF THE CONSTITUTION 455 (Merrill Jensen ed., 1976) ("[W]hat is meant by liberty of the press is that there

should be no antecedent restraint upon it; but that every author is responsible when he attacks the security or welfare of the government...." (quoting James Wilson at the Pennsylvania ratifying convention of 1787)).

4. Madison's Report on the Virginia Resolutions (1800), *in* 4 THE DEBATES IN THE SEVERAL STATE CONVENTIONS ON THE ADOPTION OF THE FEDERAL CONSTITUTION 546, 569 (Jonathan Elliot ed., 1836).

5. Benjamin Franklin, An Account of the Supremest Court of Judicature in Pennsylvania, viz., The Court of the Press (Sept. 12, 1789), *reprinted in* 10 THE WRITINGS OF BENJAMIN FRANKLIN 37 (Albert Smyth ed., 1907).

6. Abrams v. United States, 250 U.S. 616, 630 (1919) (Holmes, J., dissenting).

7. *Id.*

8. New York Times Co. v. Sullivan, 376 U.S. 254, 270 (1964).

9. LEONARD W. LEVY, EMERGENCE OF A FREE PRESS 8 (1985).

10. *Id.*

11. *See* GEOFFREY R. STONE, PERILOUS TIMES: FREE SPEECH IN WARTIME 43 (2004); LEVY, *supra* note 9, at 11–12.

12. The Trial of John Tutchin, 14 HOWELL STATE TRIALS 1095, 1128 (1704).

13. LEVY, *supra* note 9, at x (internal quotation marks omitted).

14. *See id.* at 37–45 (describing the Zenger case).

15. Harold L. Nelson, *Seditious Libel in Colonial America*, 3 AM. J. LEGAL HIST. 160, 163 (1959). "Broad judicial functions lay with the colonial assemblies, in a day before separation of powers in democratic government had been worked out...." *Id.*

16. LEVY, *supra* note 9, at 48; *see id.* at 45 ("Had John Peter Zenger attacked the New York Assembly instead of a despised royal governor, he would have been summarily convicted at the bar of the house, jailed, and in all likelihood, forgotten by posterity."); *id.* at 45–61, 71–86 (providing examples of legislative prosecution for breach of parliamentary privilege or contempt).

17. *See id.* at 173–219.

18. ARTHUR M. SCHLESINGER, PRELUDE TO INDEPENDENCE: THE NEWSPAPER WAR ON BRITAIN, 1764–1776, at 189 (1971).

19. *See* LEVY, *supra* note 9, at 183.

20. *Id.* at 269.

21. *See, e.g.,* David M. Rabban, *The Ahistorical Historian: Leonard Levy on Freedom of Expression in Early American History*, 37 STAN. L. REV. 795 (1985).

22. An Act for the Punishment of Certain Crimes Against the United States, ch. 74, § 2, 1 Stat. 596, 596 (1798). For histories of the Sedition Act, see generally Communist Party v. Subversive Activities Control Bd., 367 U.S. 1, 155–61 (1961) (Black, J., dissenting); JOHN C. MILLER, CRISIS IN FREEDOM: THE ALIEN AND SEDITION ACTS (1951); and CLAUDE G. BOWERS, JEFFERSON AND HAMILTON: THE STRUGGLE FOR DEMOCRACY (1925).

23. Sedition Act, § 2, 1 Stat. at 597.

24. STONE, *supra* note 11, at 37.

25. For details on the congressional debate, see DAVID P. CURRIE, THE CONSTITUTION IN CONGRESS: THE FEDERALIST PERIOD, 1798–1801, at 260–68 (1997).

26. Sedition Act, §§ 2, 3, 1 Stat. at 596–97.

27. STONE, *supra* note 11, at 43.

28. AKHIL REED AMAR, THE BILL OF RIGHTS: CREATION AND RECONSTRUCTION 23 (1998); *see* Sedition Act, § 4, 1 Stat. at 597.

29. *See* STONE, *supra* note 11, at 63.

30. *See id.* at 68.

31. *See id.* at 67.

32. *See id.* at 73.

33. H.R. REP. NO. 26-86, at 2 (1840); *see* Act of July 4, 1840, ch. 45, 6 Stat. 802.

34. New York Times Co. v. Sullivan, 376 U.S. 254, 276 (1964).

35. *Id.* at 273.

36. *See generally* DAVID M. RABBAN, FREE SPEECH IN ITS FORGOTTEN YEARS (1997).

37. Patterson v. Colorado, 205 U.S. 454, 462 (1907). Justice Holmes, who wrote the opinion, later renounced this view. *See* Abrams v. United States, 250 U.S. 616, 630 (1919) (Holmes, J., dissenting).

38. *See Patterson*, 205 U.S. at 462 (upholding contempt conviction of defendant whose articles and cartoon criticizing the Colorado Supreme Court "tend to obstruct the administration of justice"); Turner v. Williams, 194 U.S. 279, 294 (1904) (upholding deportation of alien anarchist on the ground that "[e]ven if [the defendant]...only regarded the absence of government as a political ideal," his advocacy of that ideal supported an inference that "he contemplated the ultimate realization of his ideal by the use of force, or that his speeches were incitements to that end").

39. *See* STONE, *supra* note 11, at 153–58.

40. Act of June 15, 1917, ch. 30, tit. I, § 3, 40 Stat. 217, 219 (codified at 18 U.S.C. § 2388(a)).

41. *See id.*

42. Espionage Act, tit. XII, §§ 1–2, 40 Stat. at 230 (codified at 18 U.S.C. § 1717(a)).

43. *See* STONE, *supra* note 11, at 147–51; RABBAN, *supra* note 36, at 249–55.

44. RABBAN, *supra* note 36, at 257.

45. Shaffer v. United States, 255 F. 886, 889 (9th Cir. 1919).

46. *See* RABBAN, *supra* note 36, at 257–61 (discussing examples of Espionage Act convictions); STONE, *supra* note 11, at 170–73 (same).

47. Masses Publishing Co. v. Patten, 244 F. 535 (S.D.N.Y. 1917).

48. *Id.* at 536.

49. *See id.* at 544.

50. *Id.* at 539.

51. *Id.* at 539–40.

52. *See id.* at 540.

53. *Id.* at 540, 541.

54. *Id.* at 540.

55. Masses Publishing Co. v. Patten, 246 F. 24 (2d Cir. 1917). Judge Hand issued his opinion in *Masses* knowing that it might cost him a promotion to the Second Circuit. *See* GERALD GUNTHER, LEARNED HAND: THE MAN AND THE JUDGE 155 (1994). He was indeed passed over for the appointment in 1917 but was eventually elevated in 1924.

56. *See* Schenck v. United States, 249 U.S. 47 (1919); Frohwerk v. United States, 249 U.S. 47 (1919); Debs v. United States, 249 U.S. 47 (1919); *see also* Sugarman v. United States, 249 U.S. 182, 185 (1919) (dismissing appeal of Espionage Act conviction on jurisdictional grounds upon finding "no substantial constitutional question...presented by the defendant").

57. 249 U.S. at 49–51.

58. *Id.* at 52.

59. *See* 249 U.S. at 205, 207–8.

60. *Id.* at 208–09.

61. *Debs*, 249 U.S. at 216.

62. *See* RABBAN, *supra* note 36, at 293–98, 346–55 (discussing the transformation of Justice Holmes's views on free speech between *Schenck* and *Abrams*). For correspondence between Judge Hand and Justice Holmes, see Gerald Gunther, *Learned Hand and the Origins of Modern First Amendment Doctrine: Some Fragments of History*, 27 STAN. L. REV. 719, 758–61 (1975) (reprinting letters). For contemporaneous criticism of Justice Holmes's Espionage Act opinions, see Zechariah Chafee, Jr., *Freedom of Speech in War Time*, 32 HARV. L. REV. 932 (1919), and Ernst Freund, *The* Debs *Case and Freedom of Speech*, NEW REPUBLIC, May 3, 1919, at 13.

63. 250 U.S. 616 (1919); *see* Act of May 16, 1918, ch. 75, 40 Stat. 553.

64. *Id.* at 630–31(Holmes, J., dissenting). Although Holmes maintained that *Schenck*, *Frohwerk*, and *Debs* "were rightly decided," *id.* at 627, it is evident that he departed from the restrictive approach in those cases.

65. *See, e.g.,* Whitney v. California, 274 U.S. 357 (1927); Gitlow v. New York, 268 U.S. 652 (1925); Gilbert v. Minnesota, 254 U.S. 325 (1920); Pierce v. United States, 252 U.S. 239 (1920); Schaefer v. United States, 251 U.S. 466 (1920). The Court first recognized the applicability of the First Amendment to the states in *Gitlow*. *See* 268 U.S. at 666.

66. 268 U.S. at 673 (Holmes, J., dissenting); *see also* Schaefer, 251 U.S. at 486 (Brandeis, J., dissenting) (arguing that speech must be "immediately threaten[ing]" to establish "clear and present danger" and that "the remote or possible effect" of speech is not enough).

67. 274 U.S. at 377 (Brandeis, J., concurring in the judgment); *see id.* at 376 ("Fear of serious injury cannot alone justify suppression of free speech

and assembly. Men feared witches and burnt women. It is the function of speech to free men from the bondage of irrational fears.".). Justice Brandeis concurred in the judgment because the defendant "did not claim that…there was no clear and present danger of serious evil" and because "there was evidence on which the court or jury might have found that such danger existed." *Id.* at 379. In all other respects, the opinion is a dissent from the Court's narrow reading of the First Amendment.

68. *Id.*

69. *Id.* at 375.

70. *See* RABBAN, *supra* note 36, at 369 (Brandeis's opinion in *Whitney* "combined analytic brilliance with emotional power to create what is probably the most effective judicial interpretation of the First Amendment ever written").

71. R. G. BROWN ET AL., NATIONAL POPULAR GOVERNMENT LEAGUE, TO THE AMERICAN PEOPLE: REPORT UPON THE ILLEGAL PRACTICES OF THE UNITED STATES DEPARTMENT OF JUSTICE (1920).

72. *Id.* at 7; *see id.* at 11–67.

73. Editorial, CHRISTIAN SCIENCE MONITOR, June 25, 1920, at 16, *quoted in* STONE, *supra* note 11, at 226.

74. *See* RABBAN, *supra* note 36, at 304–16.

75. *See id.* at 316–41.

76. Act of Mar. 3, 1921, ch. 136, 41 Stat. 1359, 1360.

77. *See* STONE, *supra* note 11, at 231–32; Proclamation No. 2068, Christmas Amnesty Proclamation for Certain War-time Offenders Who Have Completed Their Prison Sentences (Dec. 23, 1933), *available at* www.presidency.ucsb.edu/ws/index.php?pid=14589.

78. 395 U.S. 444, 447 (1969). *Brandenburg* reversed the conviction of a Ku Klux Klan leader who had threatened racial violence in a speech at a cross-burning rally.

79. *Id.* at 449.

80. Their point was that there is no principled way to distinguish explicit advocacy of unlawful conduct from other forms of dissent that denounce existing law. *See* Whitney v. California, 274 U.S. 357, 376 (1927) (Brandeis, J., concurring in the judgment) ("Every denunciation of existing law tends in some measure to increase the probability that there will be violation of it.

Condonation of a breach enhances the probability. Expressions of approval add to the probability....Advocacy of lawbreaking heightens it still further. But even advocacy of violation, however reprehensible morally, is not a justification for denying free speech where the advocacy falls short of incitement and there is nothing to indicate that the advocacy would be immediately acted on."); Gitlow v. New York, 268 U.S. 652, 673 (1925) (Holmes, J., dissenting) ("Every idea is an incitement. It offers itself for belief and if believed it is acted on unless some other belief outweighs it or some failure of energy stifles the movement at its birth. The only difference between the expression of an opinion and an incitement in the narrower sense is the speaker's enthusiasm for the result.").

81. *Brandenburg*, 395 U.S. at 447.

82. *See* De Jonge v. Oregon, 299 U.S. 353 (1937); Near v. Minnesota, 283 U.S. 697 (1931); Stromberg v. California, 283 U.S. 359 (1931).

83. *See, e.g.,* Craig v. Harney, 331 U.S. 367, 377 (1947); Thomas v. Collins, 323 U.S. 516, 530 (1945); W. Va. State Bd. of Educ. v. Barnette, 319 U.S. 624, 633–34 (1943); Cantwell v. Connecticut, 310 U.S. 296, 311 (1940).

84. *See* Hartzel v. United States, 322 U.S. 680 (1944).

85. *See, e.g.,* Fisher v. Pace, 336 U.S. 155 (1949); Oklahoma v. U.S. Civil Serv. Comm'n, 330 U.S. 127 (1947); Prince v. Massachusetts, 321 U.S. 158 (1944).

86. 341 U.S. 494 (1951).

87. *See* Act of June 28, 1940, ch. 439, tit. I, § 2, 54 Stat. 670, 671 (codified at 18 U.S.C. § 2385).

88. *Dennis*, 341 U.S. at 507 (plurality opinion); *see id.* at 508 ("'[The First Amendment] requires that one be permitted to advocate what he will unless there is a clear and present danger that a substantial public evil will result therefrom.'" (quoting Am. Comm. Ass'n v. Douds, 339 U.S. 382, 412 (1950))).

89. *Id.* at 508.

90. *Id.* at 510 (quoting Dennis v. United States, 183 F.2d 201, 212 (2d Cir. 1950)). TheSecond Circuit opinion in *Dennis* was written by Judge Hand, who had been elevated to the court of appeals. For insights on how Judge Hand came to formulate this language in *Dennis*, see GUNTHER, *supra* note 55, at 598–605.

91. *Dennis*, 341 U.S. at 509 (plurality opinion).

92. *Id.* at 510.

93. *Id.* at 579 (Black, J., dissenting); *see also id.* at 585–86 (Douglas, J., dissenting). As Geoffrey Stone notes, information revealed in the 1990s showed links between the Soviet Union and the Communist Party of the United States that posed a real threat of espionage. But, he concludes, the fact that individuals who committed crimes should have been prosecuted "is quite different from prosecuting *other* people—the defendants in *Dennis*—for their advocacy of Marxist-Leninist doctrine." STONE, *supra* note 11, at 410.

94. Brandenburg v. Ohio, 395 U.S. 444, 454 (1969) (Douglas, J., concurring).

95. 354 U.S. 298 (1957).

96. *Id.* at 318.

97. *Id.* at 320.

98. *See* Lamont v. Postmaster General, 381 U.S. 301 (1965); Aptheker v. Sec'y of State, 378 U.S. 500 (1964); Speiser v. Randal, 357 U.S. 513 (1958); Maisenberg v. United States, 356 U.S. 670 (1958); Nowak v. United States, 356 U.S. 660 (1958).

99. *See* NAACP v. Alabama, 377 U.S. 288 (1964); Gibson v. Fla. Legislative Investigation Committee, 372 U.S. 539 (1963).

100. *See* Elfbrandt v. Russell, 384 U.S. 11 (1966); Scales v. United States, 367 U.S. 203 (1961).

101. 376 U.S. 254 (1964); *see* ANTHONY LEWIS, MAKE NO LAW: THE SULLIVAN CASE AND THE FIRST AMENDMENT (1991).

102. 393 U.S. 503 (1969).

103. New York Times Co. v. United States, 403 U.S. 713 (1971).

104. *See* United States v. Eichman, 496 U.S. 310 (1990); Texas v. Johnson, 491 U.S. 397 (1989).

105. *See* Dana Milbank & Emily Wax, *Bush Visits Mosque to Forestall Hate Crimes; President Condemns an Increase in Violence Aimed at Arab Americans*, WASH. POST, Sept. 18, 2001, at A1.

106. *Excerpts from Attorney General's Testimony before Senate Judiciary Committee*, N.Y. TIMES, Dec. 7, 2001, at B6.

107. STONE, *supra* note 11, at 42.

108. *Id.*

CHAPTER 5

1. *See* San Antonio Indep. Sch. Dist. v. Rodriguez, 411 U.S. 1 (1973); Jefferson v. Hackney, 406 U.S. 535 (1972); Lindsey v. Normet, 405 U.S. 56 (1972); Dandridge v. Williams, 397 U.S. 471 (1970); *see also* Town of Castle Rock v. Gonzales, 545 U.S. 748 (2005); DeShaney v. Winnebago County Dep't of Social Servs., 489 U.S. 189 (1989). *But cf.* Memorial Hosp. v. Maricopa County, 415 U.S. 250 (1974); U.S. Dep't of Agric. v. Moreno, 413 U.S. 528 (1973); Goldberg v. Kelly, 397 U.S. 254 (1970); Shapiro v. Thompson, 394 U.S. 618 (1969).

2. *See* CASS R. SUNSTEIN, THE SECOND BILL OF RIGHTS: FDR's UNFINISHED REVOLUTION AND WHY WE NEED IT MORE THAN EVER (2004); CHARLES L. BLACK, JR., A NEW BIRTH OF FREEDOM: HUMAN RIGHTS, NAMED AND UNNAMED 131–39 (1997); Robin West, *Unenumerated Duties*, 9 U. PA. J. CONST. L. 221 (2006); Laurence H. Tribe, *Unraveling* National League of Cities: *The New Federalism and Affirmative Rights to Essential Government Services*, 90 HARV. L. REV. 1065 (1977); Frank I. Michelman, *The Supreme Court, 1968 Term—Foreword: On Protecting the Poor through the Fourteenth Amendment*, 83 HARV. L. REV. 7 (1969).

3. *See* U.S. CONST. art. I, § 8, cl. 3 ("The Congress shall have Power...[t]o regulate Commerce...among the several States....").

4. United States v. Lopez, 514 U.S. 549, 585–86 (1995) (Thomas, J., concurring) (citing numerous Founding-era dictionaries, convention statements, and the Federalist Papers).

5. *See, e.g.,* Carter v. Carter Coal Co., 298 U.S. 238 (1936); Hammer v. Dagenhart, 247 U.S. 251 (1918); United States v. E.C. Knight Co., 156 U.S. 1 (1895).

6. *See* United States v. Butler, 297 U.S. 1 (1936) (invalidating federal tax on processors of agricultural commodities to subsidize farmers who agree to limit production).

7. 198 U.S. 45 (1905).

8. *See, e.g.*, Williams v. Standard Oil Co., 278 U.S. 235 (1929) (invalidating state regulation of gasoline prices); Louis K. Liggett Co. v. Baldridge, 278 U.S. 105 (1928) (invalidating state law limiting entry into the pharmacy business); Adkins v. Children's Hosp., 261 U.S. 525 (1923) (invalidating state minimum wage law for women); Coppage v. Kansas, 236 U.S. 1 (1915) (invalidating state law barring employment contracts that require employees to agree not to join a union); *Lochner*, 198 U.S. 45 (invalidating state law establishing maximum working hours for bakers).

9. Act of July 2, 1890, ch. 647, § 1, 26 Stat. 209 (codified at 15 U.S.C. § 1).

10. *E.C. Knight*, 156 U.S. at 9; *see id.* at 12 ("Commerce succeeds to manufacture, and is not a part of it.").

11. Hammer v. Dagenhart, 247 U.S. 251 (1918).

12. *See id.* at 273 ("There is no power vested in Congress to require the states to exercise their police power so as to prevent possible unfair competition.").

13. Some cases during the *Lochner* era upheld regulations deemed to have a legitimately protective purpose or to address activities "affected with a public interest." *See, e.g.*, Nebbia v. New York, 291 U.S. 502 (1934) (upholding price controls for milk); Block v. Hirsh, 256 U.S. 135 (1921) (upholding price regulation of rental housing); German Alliance Ins. Co. v. Lewis, 233 U.S. 389 (1914) (upholding price regulation of fire insurance); Muller v. Oregon, 208 U.S. 412 (1908) (upholding maximum hours law for women).

14. Morehead v. Tipaldo, 298 U.S. 587, 610–11 (1936).

15. Robert Rabin, *Federal Regulation in Historical Perspective*, 38 Stan. L. Rev. 1189, 1246 (1986).

16. Panama Refining Co. v. Ryan, 293 U.S. 388 (1935) (NIRA); Schechter Poultry v. United States, 295 U.S. 495 (1935) (same); United States v. Butler, 297 U.S. 1 (1936) (AAA).

17. U.S. Const. art. I, § 8, cl. 1.

18. William E. Leuchtenburg, *The Origins of Franklin D. Roosevelt's 'Court-Packing' Plan*, 1966 Sup. Ct. Rev. 347, 366.

19. Retirement Board v. Alton R. Co. 295 U.S. 330 (1935).

20. Carter v. Carter Coal, 298 U.S. 238 (1936).

21. 5 FRANKLIN D. ROOSEVELT, PUBLIC PAPERS AND ADDRESSES 191–92 (1936).

22. Under Article V, an amendment would have required a two-thirds vote in each House of Congress and then a three-fourths majority vote in the states. If states chose ratification by state legislatures, negative votes in one house of thirteen states would have been enough to defeat an amendment. President Roosevelt and his advisers thought it likely that big business and other well-heeled opponents of the New Deal would be able to muster the minority of negative votes required, perhaps by bribing critical legislators if necessary. Moreover, an amendment could have taken several years to ratify, and once ratified, it would have been interpreted by the same Court that had resisted the expansion of governmental responsibility for strengthening the economy.

23. West Coast Hotel Co. v. Parrish, 300 U.S. 379 (1937).

24. NLRB v. Jones & Laughlin Steel Corp., 301 U.S. 1 (1937).

25. Steward Machine Co. v. Davis, 301 U.S. 548 (1937).

26. *See, e.g.*, Wickard v. Filburn, 317 U.S. 111 (1942) (upholding application of federal quota on wheat production to wheat grown solely for home consumption as a valid exercise of Congress's commerce power); Olsen v. Nebraska, 313 U.S. 236 (1941) (upholding against due process challenge a state limitation on fees that employment agencies may charge employees and overruling Ribnik v. McBride, 277 U.S. 350 (1928)); United States v. Darby, 312 U.S. 100 (1941) (upholding Fair Labor Standards Act and overruling Hammer v. Dagenhart, 247 U.S. 251 (1918)); United States v. Carolene Prods. Co., 304 U.S. 144 (1938) (upholding federal ban on interstate shipment of filled milk against Commerce Clause and due process challenges).

27. 2 BRUCE ACKERMAN, WE THE PEOPLE: TRANSFORMATIONS 23–26, 342–44 (1998); *compare* Barry Cushman, *Formalism and Realism in Commerce Clause Jurisprudence*, 67 U. CHI. L. REV. 1089 (2000) (arguing that the evolution of interstate commerce doctrine between the Civil War and World War II was more intelligible and coherent than conventional accounts suggest).

28. McCulloch v. Maryland, 17 U.S. 316, 415 (1819).

29. Gibbons v. Ogden, 22 U.S. 1, 188 (1824).

30. While joining the Court in invalidating provisions of the NIRA in 1935, Justice Cardozo implicitly rejected the distinction between "direct" and "indirect" effects on commerce, instead observing that "[a] society such as ours 'is an elastic medium which transmits all tremors throughout its territory; the only question is of their size.'" A.L.A. Schechter Poultry Corp. v. United States, 295 U.S. 495, 554 (1935) (Cardozo, J., concurring) (quoting opinion below by Judge Learned Hand). For Justice Cardozo, whether an activity affects interstate commerce sufficiently to come within the ambit of federal regulatory power necessarily turns on "considerations of degree" rather than artificial categorization of direct versus indirect effects. *Id.* Justice Cardozo's insistence on constitutional judgment that acknowledges the true nature of underlying economic realities led him to dissent from the Court's decision the following year in *Carter v. Carter Coal Co.*, 298 U.S. 238 (1936). Noting the serious and widespread ills for workers, mine owners, and consumers resulting from overproduction of coal and collapse of coal prices, Justice Cardozo voted to uphold federally authorized price controls on the ground that "Congress was not condemned to inaction in the face of price wars and wage wars so pregnant with disaster." *Id.* at 331 (Cardozo, J., dissenting).

31. United States v. Morrison, 529 U.S. 598, 655 (2000) (Souter, J., dissenting) (quoting OLIVER WENDELL HOLMES, THE COMMON LAW 167 (Mark DeWolfe Howe ed., 1963)); *see id.* at 660 (Breyer, J., dissenting) (noting the "practical reality" that "[w]e live in a Nation knit together by two centuries of scientific, technological, commercial, and environmental change" and that those changes properly inform the scope of Congress's commerce power).

32. *See, e.g.*, Williams v. Standard Oil Co., 278 U.S. 235, 239 (1929) (holding that "a state Legislature is without constitutional power to fix prices at which commodities may be sold, services rendered, or property used, unless the business or property involved is 'affected with a public interest'") (internal citations omitted); Adair v. United States, 208 U.S. 161, 174–75 (1908) ("The right of a person to sell his labor upon such terms as he deems proper is, in its essence, the same as the right of the purchaser of labor to prescribe the conditions upon which he will accept such labor from the person offering to sell it....[T]he employer and the employee have equality of right, and any legislation that disturbs that equality is an

arbitrary interference with the liberty of contract which no government can legally justify in a free land."); Lochner v. New York, 1983 U.S. 45, 57 (1905) ("There is no contention that bakers as a class…are not able to assert their rights and care for themselves without the protecting arm of the state, interfering with their independence of judgment and of action.").

33. *See* Cass R. Sunstein, *Lochner's Legacy*, 87 COLUM. L. REV. 873, 876–81 (1987).

34. *Id.* at 882; *see also* Cass R. Sunstein, *Naked Preferences and the Constitution*, 84 COLUM. L. REV. 1689, 1718 (1984) ("Once it became clear that harms produced by the marketplace were also the products of public choices, efforts to alleviate those harms came to be regarded as permissible exercises of government power.").

35. United States v. Carolene Prods. Co., 304 U.S. 144, 152 & n.4 (1938).

36. Garcia v. San Antonio Metro. Transit Auth., 469 U.S. 528, 552 (1985).

37. United States v. Lopez, 514 U.S. 549, 608 (1995) (Souter, J., dissenting).

38. *See* United States v. Morrison, 529 U.S. 598, 613 (2000) (invalidating civil remedy provision of the Violence Against Women Act on the ground that "[g]ender-motivated crimes of violence are not, in any sense of the phrase, economic activity"); *Lopez*, 514 U.S. at 567 (invalidating the Gun-Free School Zones Act on the ground that "[t]he possession of a gun in a local school zone is in no sense an economic activity").

39. *Lopez*, 514 U.S. at 608 (Souter, J., dissenting); *see id.* ("[T]he act of calibrating the level of deference by drawing a line between what is patently commercial and what is less purely so will probably resemble the process of deciding how much interference with contractual freedom was fatal."); *see also Morrison*, 529 U.S. at 656–59 (Breyer, J., dissenting) (illuminating conceptual problems with the "economic" versus "noneconomic" distinction).

40. Gonzales v. Raich, 545 U.S. 1, 37 (2005) (qualifying *Morrison* and *Lopez* by holding that "Congress may regulate even noneconomic local activity if that regulation is a necessary part of a more general regulation of interstate commerce").

41. Carter v. Carter Coal Co., 298 U.S. 238, 327 (1936) (Cardozo, J., dissenting).

CHAPTER 6

1. THE FEDERALIST NO. 47 (James Madison).

2. U.S. CONST. art. II, § 3; *see* Christopher N. May, *Presidential Defiance of "Unconstitutional" Laws: Reviving the Royal Prerogative*, 21 HASTINGS CONST. L.Q. 865, 883–85 (1994).

3. *See* U.S. Dep't of Justice, Legal Authorities Supporting the Activities of the National Security Agency Described by the President 28–35 (Jan. 19, 2006) [hereinafter NSA Surveillance Memo], *available at* http://www.usdoj.gov/opa/whitepaperonnsalegalauthorities.pdf.

4. *See* Memorandum from Jay S. Bybee, Assistant Attorney General, Office of Legal Counsel, to Alberto R. Gonzales, Counsel to the President 36–39 (Aug. 1, 2002) (hereafter OLC Torture Memo), *reprinted in* THE TORTURE PAPERS: THE ROAD TO ABU GHRAIB 172, 204–07 (Karen J. Greenberg & Joshua L. Dratel eds., 2005). On his third day in office, President Obama "ordered his government not to rely on any legal opinions concerning interrogation produced by the Justice Department or other agencies between Sept. 11, 2001, and [January 20, 2009], when he assumed the presidency." Scott Shane et al., *Obama Reverses Key Bush Policy, But Questions on Detainees Remain*, N.Y. TIMES, Jan. 23, 2009, at A16.

5. *See* Brief for the Respondents at 42–45, Rasul v. Bush, 542 U.S. 466 (2004) (Nos. 03–334, 03–343).

6. *See* Statement on Signing the Department of Defense, Emergency Supplemental Appropriations to Address Hurricanes in the Gulf of Mexico, and Pandemic Influenza Act 2006, 41 WEEKLY COMP. PRES. DOC. 1918, 1919 (Dec. 30, 2005).

7. *See* OLC Torture Memo, *in* THE TORTURE PAPERS, *supra* note 4, at 206.

8. *See* Memorandum for the Files Re: Status of Certain OLC Opinions Issued in the Aftermath of the Terrorist Attacks of September 11, 2001, at 2 (Jan. 15, 2009) (stating that the "broad assertion of the President's Commander in Chief power that would deny Congress any role in regulating the detention, interrogation, prosecution, and transfer of enemy combatants captured in the global War on Terror" in prior memos "does not reflect the current views of OLC"), *available at* http://www.fas.org/irp/agency/doj/olc/olc011509.pdf.

9. OLC Torture Memo, *in* THE TORTURE PAPERS, *supra* note 4, at 206; *see also* Memorandum Opinion for the Deputy Counsel to the President from John C. Yoo, Deputy Assistant Attorney General, Office of Legal Counsel, The President's Constitutional Authority to Conduct Military Operations Against Terrorists and Nations Supporting Them (Sept. 25, 2001) ("[No] statute…can place any limits on the President's determinations as to any terrorist threat, the amount of military force to be used in response, or the method, timing, and nature of the response. These decisions, under our Constitution, are for the President alone to make."), *available at* www.usdoj.gov/olc/warpowers925.htm.

10. OLC Torture Memo, *in* THE TORTURE PAPERS, *supra* note 4, at 207.

11. *See* Bob Woodward, *CIA Told to Do 'Whatever Necessary' to Kill Bin Laden*, WASH. POST, Oct. 21, 2001, at A1 (quoting Vice President Cheney as saying that the war on terrorism "may never end. At least, not in our lifetime.").

12. THE FEDERALIST NO. 47 (James Madison).

13. THE FEDERALIST NO. 48 (James Madison).

14. U.S. CONST. art. I, § 8, cls. 10–16.

15. U.S. CONST. art. II, § 2, cl. 1.

16. 2 THE RECORDS OF THE FEDERAL CONVENTION OF 1787, at 318 (Max Farrand ed., 1937).

17. OLC Torture Memo, *in* THE TORTURE PAPERS, *supra* note 4, at 203.

18. *Id.*

19. *Id.* at 207.

20. Youngstown Sheet & Tube Co. v. Sawyer, 343 U.S. 579, 637 (1952) (Jackson, J., concurring).

21. *Id.* In Justice Jackson's familiar typology, Category One cases are those where the President's "authority is at its maximum" because he "acts pursuant to an express or implied authorization of Congress." *Id.* at 635.

22. *Id.* at 637–38.

23. *Id.* at 637.

24. *Id.* at 638.

25. *See* David J. Barron & Martin S. Lederman, *The Commander in Chief at the Lowest Ebb—Framing the Problem, Doctrine, and Original Understanding*, 121 HARV. L. REV. 689, 767–70 (2008) (explaining that the Commander in Chief designation grants the President preclusive power to superintend the military).

26. *See* ARTICLES OF CONFEDERATION art. IX, para. 4 (1781).

27. Barron & Lederman, *supra* note 23, at 800.

28. *Id.* at 696.

29. *See id.* at 773–80. Although the Continental Congress eventually recognized the inefficiency of micromanaging the prosecution of war and delegated to General Washington broad discretionary powers, the integration of such powers into the original understanding of "Commander in Chief" suggests that the President has inherent power to act in the absence of specific congressional direction, not necessarily that the President has preclusive power to disregard pertinent statutes. *See id.* at 778–80.

30. *See id.* at 780–85.

31. Barron & Lederman, *Constitutional History*, *supra* note 23, at 941, 993.

32. *Id.* at 1000.

33. *See id.* at 999–1000, 1005–08.

34. *Id.* at 1016.

35. *See id.* at 1060–61.

36. President Truman purported to rely on the United Nations Charter, although there is evidence that he committed American troops to the conflict before the Security Council had authorized the use of force. *See* Jane E. Stromseth, *Rethinking War Powers: Congress, the President, and the United Nations*, 81 GEO. L.J. 597, 622–35 (1993).

37. *See* Barron & Lederman, *Constitutional History*, *supra* note 23, at 1064–99 (reviewing legislative restrictions on the President's war powers and executive claims of preclusive power from the Nixon administration to the second Bush administration).

38. *Id.* at 1099.

39. JOHN YOO, THE POWERS OF WAR AND PEACE: THE CONSTITUTION AND FOREIGN AFFAIRS AFTER 9/11, at x (2005).

40. *Id.* at ix.

41. *Id.* at x; *see also* John Yoo, *War, Responsibility, and the Age of Terrorism*, 57 STAN. L. REV. 793, 813–22 (2004).

42. Deborah Pearlstein, *The Constitution and Executive Competence in the Post–Cold War World*, 38 COLUM. HUM. RTS. L. REV. 547, 570 (2007). Although scholars have debated the legality of the military action that President Jefferson initiated against the pirates in 1801 without congressional approval, Jefferson never claimed that his authority as Commander in Chief would trump duly enacted legislation regulating his conduct of war. After Jefferson reported his actions to Congress, Congress delegated broad authority to Jefferson to fight the pirates. *See* Act of Feb. 6, 1802, ch. 4, §§ 1–2, 2 Stat. 129, 130.

43. Barron & Lederman, *Constitutional History, supra* note 23, at 1101.

44. *See, e.g.*, Military Commissions Act of 2006, Pub. L. No. 109–366, 120 Stat. 2600; Uniting and Strengthening America by Providing Appropriate Tools Required to Intercept and Obstruct Terrorism (USA PATRIOT) Act Additional Reauthorizing Amendments Act of 2006, Pub. L. No. 109–178, 120 Stat. 278; USA PATRIOT Improvement and Reauthorization Act of 2005, Pub. L. No. 109–177, 120 Stat. 192 (2006); Intelligence Reform and Terrorism Prevention Act of 2004, Pub. L. No. 108–458, 118 Stat. 3638; USA PATRIOT Act of 2001, Pub. L. No. 107–56, 115 Stat. 272; Authorization for Use of Military Force, Pub. L. No. 107–40, 115 Stats. 224 (2001).

45. 18 U.S.C. § 2511(2)(f) (2000); *see* NSA Surveillance Memo, *supra* note 3, at 28–35.

46. *See* Protect America Act of 2007, Pub. L. No. 110-55, 121 Stat. 552; *see also* Foreign Intelligence Surveillance Act of 1978 Amendments Act of 2008, Pub. L. No. 110-261, 122 Stat. 2436.

47. *See* Pearlstein, *supra* note 40, at 571–78; Deborah Pearlstein, *Form and Function in the National Security Constitution*, 41 CONN. L. REV. (forthcoming 2009); *see also* Hamdan v. Rumsfeld, 548 U.S. 557, 636 (2006) (Breyer, J., concurring) ("Where...no emergency prevents consultation with Congress, judicial insistence upon that consultation does not weaken our Nation's ability to deal with danger. To the contrary, that insistence strengthens the Nation's ability to determine—through democratic means—how best to do so.").

48. 542 U.S. 466 (2004); *see* Brief for the Respondents at 42–45, Rasul v. Bush, 542 U.S. 466 (2004) (Nos. 03–334, 03–343).

49. 542 U.S. 507, 516 (2004); *see* Brief for the Respondents at 22, Hamdi v. Rumsfeld, 542 U.S. 507 (2004) (No. 03–6696).

50. *Hamdi*, 542 U.S. at 536 (plurality opinion) (citing Youngstown Sheet & Tube Co. v. Sawyer, 343 U.S. 579, 587 (1952)).

51. 548 U.S. 557 (2006).

52. *Id.* at 593 n.23 (citing *Youngstown*, 343 U.S. at 637 (Jackson, J., concurring)).

53. *Id.* at 636 (Breyer, J., concurring).

54. *See* Military Commissions Act of 2006, Pub. L. No. 109–366, 120 Stat. 2600. In *Boumediene v. Bush*, 128 S. Ct. 2229 (2008), the Court held the Military Commission Act unconstitutional insofar as it stripped the federal courts of jurisdiction to hear habeas corpus actions by aliens detained as enemy combatants.

55. *Youngstown*, 343 U.S. at 655 (Jackson, J., concurring).

CHAPTER 7

1. *See* Lani Guinier & Pamela S. Karlan, *The Majoritarian Difficulty: One Person, One Vote, in* REASON AND PASSION: JUSTICE BRENNAN'S ENDURING INFLUENCE 207 (E. Joshua Rosenkranz & Bernard Schwartz eds., 1997).

2. *See* Md. Comm. for Fair Representation v. Tawes, 377 U.S. 656, 665–66 (1964) (Maryland); Lucas v. Forty-Fourth Gen. Assembly of Colo., 377 U.S. 713, 725 (1964) (Colorado); WMCA, Inc. v. Lomenzo, 377 U.S. 633, 647 (1964) (New York); Baker v. Carr, 362 U.S. 186, 322 (1962) (Frankfurter, J., dissenting) (Connecticut).

3. *See* JOHN HART ELY, ON CONSTITUTIONAL GROUND 4 (1996).

4. *See* Bush v. Gore, 531 U.S. 98, 104–05 (2000) (per curiam); Vieth v. Jubelirer, 541 U.S. 267, 290 (2004) (plurality opinion of Scalia, J.) (describing one person, one vote as an "easily administrable standard" for courts to apply); Robert J. Pushaw, Jr., Bush v. Gore: *Looking at* Baker v. Carr *in a Conservative Mirror*, 18 CONST. COMMENT. 359, 379 (2001) (describing how the reapportionment cases became part of the constitutional canon).

5. 328 U.S. 549, 556 (1946).

6. *Id.* at 555, 556.

7. 369 U.S. 186 (1962).

8. *See id.* at 255 (Clark, J., concurring).

9. *Id.* at 254.

10. *Id.* at 210 (internal quotation marks and citation omitted).

11. *See* Reynolds v. Sims, 377 U.S. 533, 606 (1964) (Harlan, J., dissenting).

12. *Baker*, 369 U.S. at 226.

13. 376 U.S. 1, 7–8 (1964).

14. *Id.* at 8.

15. *Id.* at 17–18 (footnote and citation omitted).

16. 377 U.S. 533 (1964).

17. *Id.* at 565.

18. Avery v. Midland County, 390 U.S. 474, 510 (1968) (Stewart, J., dissenting).

19. Miranda v. Arizona, 384 U.S. 436 (1966); *see infra* chapter 8.

20. *Reynolds*, 377 U.S. at 565.

21. G. Edward White, Earl Warren: A Public Life 337 (1982).

22. *Reynolds*, 377 U.S. at 555.

23. Fortson v. Dorsey, 379 U.S. 433, 439 (1965).

24. *See* Daniel P. Tokaji, *The Sordid Business of Democracy*, 34 Ohio N.U. L. Rev. 341, 346 (2008) (explaining that "qualitative vote dilution" occurs when "redistricting practices...effectively weaken[] the voting strength of a group within the equi-populated district constraints").

25. 412 U.S. 755, 766 (1973).

26. 446 U.S. 55, 65, 66 (1980) (plurality opinion) (internal quotation marks and citations omitted).

27. Pub. L. No. 97-205, § 3, 96 Stat. 131, 134 (1982) (codified as amended at 42 U.S.C. § 1973(a)).

28. The primary purpose of the Voting Rights Act of 1965, unchanged by the 1982 amendments, is "[t]o enforce the [F]ifteenth [A]mendment to the Constitution of the United States." Pub. L. No. 89-110, 79 Stat. 437, 437.

29. Thornburg v. Gingles, 478 U.S. 30, 43–44 (1986).

30. *Id.* at 45 (quoting Senate Committee report) (internal quotation marks and citations omitted).

31. *See id.* at 49–77.

CHAPTER 8

1. *See* United States v. Wade, 388 U.S. 218 (1967); Miranda v. Arizona, 384 U.S. 436 (1966).

2. *See* Gideon v. Wainwright, 372 U.S. 335 (1963).

3. *See* Katz v. United States, 389 U.S. 347 (1967).

4. *See* See v. City of Seattle, 387 U.S. 541 (1967); Camara v. Mun. Court, 387 U.S. 523 (1967).

5. *See* Chimel v. California, 395 U.S. 752 (1969).

6. 384 U.S. 436 (1966).

7. 367 U.S. 643 (1961).

8. Dickerson v. United States, 530 U.S. 428, 444 (2000).

9. *Id.* at 443.

10. U.S. CONST. amend. V.

11. Justice White, dissenting in *Miranda*, read the text this way. *See* Miranda v. Arizona, 384 U.S. 436, 526–27 (1966) (White, J., dissenting).

12. *See* Yale Kamisar, *A Dissent from the* Miranda *Dissents: Some Comments on the "New" Fifth Amendment and the Old "Voluntariness" Test*, 65 MICH. L. REV. 59, 70–71 (1966) (citing Edward S. Corwin, *The Supreme Court's Construction of the Self-incrimination Clause*, 29 MICH. L. REV. 1 (1930), and Lewis Mayers, *The Federal Witness' Privilege Against Self-Incrimination: Constitutional or Common-Law?* 4 AM. J. LEGAL HIST. 107 (1960)).

13. Stephen J. Schulhofer, Reconsidering *Miranda*, 54 U. CHI. L. REV. 435, 438 (1987); *see* Kamisar, *supra* note 12, at 71 (quoting Mayers, *supra* note 12, at 114 n.20); *id.* at 72–73 (describing the practice of pretrial questioning by colonial magistrates).

14. Lawrence Lessig, *Fidelity in Translation*, 71 Tex. L. Rev. 1165, 1235 (1993) (quoting Yale Kamisar, *Equal Justice in the Gatehouses and Mansions of American Criminal Procedure, in* Criminal Justice in Our Time 1, 29 (A. E. Dick Howard ed., 1965)); *see* Kamisar, *supra* note 12, at 71 (noting that "there were no professional police either in England or America when the privilege was drafted and ratified, or at least the police had not yet assumed the functions of criminal investigation"); *compare* Carol S. Steiker, *Second Thoughts about First Principles*, 107 Harv. L. Rev. 820, 824 (1994) (identifying "two crucial changes between colonial times and the present that must inform our current readings" of constitutional criminal protections: first, the fact that "nothing even remotely resembling modern law enforcement existed" during the Founding era, and second, "the intensification of inter-racial conflict in our society during the Civil War and Reconstruction, and the myriad ways in which this conflict has intersected with law enforcement").

15. Dickerson v. United States, 530 U.S. 428, 434 (2000).

16. Albert R. Beisel, Control over Illegal Enforcement of the Criminal Law: Role of the Supreme Court 104 (1955), *quoted in* Kamisar, *supra* note 12, at 73–74.

17. Edmund M. Morgan, *The Privilege Against Self-Incrimination*, 34 Minn. L. Rev. 1, 27 (1949).

18. Miranda v. Arizona, 384 U.S. 436, 459–60 (1966) (quoting Counselman v. Hitchcock, 142 U.S. 547, 562 (1892)); *see id.* at 445–48 (discussing coercive police interrogation practices).

19. *Id.* at 461.

20. Erwin N. Griswold, The Fifth Amendment Today 55 (1955), *quoted in* Kamisar, *supra* note 12, at 81–82.

21. Schulhofer, *supra* note 13, at 451.

22. *Id.*

23. Dickerson v. United States, 530 U.S. 428, 442 (2000) (citing *Miranda*, 384 U.S. at 457).

24. *Id.* at 444.

25. *Id.*

26. *Id.* at 442; *see Miranda*, 384 U.S. at 490 ("[T]he Constitution does not require any specific code of procedures for protecting the privilege against

self-incrimination during custodial interrogation. Congress and the States are free to develop their own safeguards for the privilege, so long as they are fully as effective as those described [in *Miranda*].”); *id.* at 467 (same).

27. *Compare* Charles D. Weisselberg, *Mourning* Miranda, 96 CAL. L. REV. 1519 (2008) (arguing that judicial decisions and evolving police practices have eroded the efficacy of *Miranda* warnings in protecting Fifth Amendment rights); *id.* at 1597–98 (discussing legislative alternatives to *Miranda* warnings, including videotaping of interrogations).

28. 389 U.S. 347 (1967).

29. *Id.* at 351.

30. Olmstead v. United States, 277 U.S. 438, 472–73 (1928) (Brandeis, J., dissenting) (internal quotation marks and citation omitted).

31. *See* Lessig, *supra* note 14, at 1228–30.

32. 367 U.S. 643 (1961).

33. *Id.* at 651. In 1949, the Court in *Wolf v. Colorado*, 338 U.S. 25 (1949), held the obligations of the Fourth Amendment applicable to the states under the Due Process Clause but declined to incorporate the exclusionary rule.

34. *Mapp*, 367 U.S. at 652; *see id.* at 651 (noting that the California Supreme Court was “‘compelled to [adopt the exclusionary rule] because other remedies have completely failed to secure compliance with the constitutional provisions’” (quoting People v. Cahan, 282 P.2d 905, 911 (Cal. 1955))); *id.* at 670 (Douglas, J., concurring) (“The truth is that trespass actions against officers who make unlawful searches and seizures are mainly illusory remedies.”).

35. Potter Stewart, *The Road to* Mapp v. Ohio *and Beyond: The Origins, Development and Future of the Exclusionary Rule in Search-and-seizure Cases*, 83 COLUM. L. REV. 1365, 1389 (1983); *see id.* at 1388 (describing civil damage actions for Fourth Amendment violations as “expensive, time-consuming, not readily available, and rarely successful”).

36. *Id.* at 1388.

37. Herring v. United States, 129 S. Ct. 695, 706, 707 (2009) (Ginsburg, J., dissenting) (internal quotation marks and citation omitted); *compare* Arizona v. Evans, 514 U.S. 1, 17–18 (1995) (O’Connor, J., concurring) (“In recent years, we have witnessed the advent of powerful, computer-based recordkeeping systems that facilitate arrests in ways that have never before

been possible. The police, of course, are entitled to enjoy the substantial advantages this technology confers. They may not, however, rely on it blindly. With the benefits of more efficient law enforcement mechanisms comes the burden of corresponding constitutional responsibilities.").

38. *Evans*, 514 U.S. at 19 (Stevens, J., dissenting).

39. *Mapp*, 367 U.S. at 648 (quoting Silverthorne Lumber Co. v. United States, 251 U.S. 385, 392 (1920) (Holmes, J.)).

40. Lessig, *supra* note 14, at 1232.

41. *See* Herring v. United States, 129 S. Ct. 695 (2009) (refusing to apply the exclusionary rule to contraband found during an illegal arrest prompted by an invalid warrant arising from negligent police bookkeeping); Hudson v. Michigan, 547 U.S. 586 (2006) (refusing to apply the exclusionary rule to contraband found during an illegal search of a home that occurred in violation of the knock-and-announce rule).

CHAPTER 9

1. 410 U.S. 113 (1973).

2. Many state constitutions do contain a privacy clause. *See, e.g.,* ARIZ. CONST. art. II, § 8 ("No person shall be disturbed in his private affairs, or his home invaded, without authority of law."); CAL. CONST. art. I, § 1 (including "privacy" in the list of "inalienable rights" guaranteed to all people); FLA. CONST. art. I, § 23 ("Every natural person has the right to be let alone and free from governmental intrusion into the person's private life except as otherwise provided herein."); HAW. CONST. art. I, § 6 ("The right of the people to privacy is recognized and shall not be infringed without the showing of a compelling state interest."); MONT. CONST. art. II, § 10 ("The right of individual privacy is essential to the well-being of a free society and shall not be infringed without the showing of a compelling state interest.").

3. 539 U.S. 558, 562 (2003).

4. *Id.*

5. 381 U.S. 479 (1965).

6. 539 U.S. 558 (2003).

7. 316 U.S. 535 (1942).

8. *Id.* at 541.

9. 274 U.S. 200, 207–08 (1927).

10. Ry. Express Agency, Inc. v. New York, 336 U.S. 106, 112–13 (1949). In *Skinner*, Justice Jackson wrote separately to register his agreement with both Justice Douglas's equal protection rationale and Chief Justice Stone's due process rationale. *See Skinner*, 316 U.S. at 546 (Jackson, J., concurring).

11. *See* Pamela S. Karlan, *Loving* Lawrence, 102 MICH. L. REV. 1447 (2004); Pamela S. Karlan, *Equal Protection, Due Process, and the Stereoscopic Fourteenth Amendment*, 33 MCGEORGE L. REV. 472 (2002).

12. 367 U.S. 497 (1961).

13. *Id.* at 540, 542–43 (Harlan, J., dissenting) (quoting Irvine v. California, 347 U.S. 128, 147 (1954) (Frankfurter, J., dissenting)) (all other citations omitted).

14. *Id.* at 549.

15. *Id.*

16. *Id.* at 551.

17. *Id.* at 552.

18. *Id.* at 551 (quoting Weems v. United States, 217 U.S. 349, 373 (1910)) (internal quotation marks omitted).

19. *Id.* at 546.

20. *Id.* at 544 (internal quotation marks and citation omitted).

21. Griswold v. Connecticut, 381 U.S. 479 (1965).

22. *Id.* at 484, 485.

23. Jack Balkin, The Constitutional Catechism, http://balkin.blogspot.com/2006/01/constitutional-catechism.html (Jan. 11, 2006).

24. *See* Robert H. Bork, *Neutral Principles and Some First Amendment Problems*, 47 IND. L.J. 1 (1971).

25. *Griswold*, 381 U.S. at 482.

26. Bork, *supra* note 24, at 9.

27. *Id.*

28. *Id.* at 10.

29. 405 U.S. 438 (1972).

30. 388 U.S. 1 (1967).

31. *Id.* at 10, 11.

32. *Id.* at 12.

33. *Id.*

34. *Eisenstadt*, 405 U.S. at 453.

35. 262 U.S. 390 (1923) (invalidating state law that prohibited schools from teaching foreign languages). In interpreting the term "liberty" in the Due Process Clause, the unanimous Court said: "Without doubt, it denotes not merely freedom from bodily restraint but also the right of the individual to contract, to engage in any of the common occupations of life, to acquire useful knowledge, to marry, establish a home and bring up children, to worship God according to the dictates of his own conscience, and generally to enjoy those privileges long recognized at common law as essential to the orderly pursuit of happiness by free men." *Id.* at 399.

36. 268 U.S. 510, 534–35 (1925) (invalidating under the Due Process Clause a state law requiring parents to send their children to public schools because it "unreasonably interferes with the liberty of parents and guardians to direct the upbringing and education of children under their control").

37. 410 U.S. 113, 153 (1973).

38. 505 U.S. 833, 860 (1992) (joint opinion of O'Connor, Kennedy, & Souter, JJ.).

39. *See* Ruth Bader Ginsburg, *Some Thoughts on Autonomy and Equality in Relation to* Roe v. Wade, 63 N.C. L. Rev. 375 (1985); *see also* Catharine MacKinnon, *Reflections on Sex Equality under Law*, 100 Yale L.J. 1281, 1308–24 (1991); Sylvia A. Law, *Rethinking Sex and the Constitution*, 132 U. Pa. L. Rev. 955 (1984).

40. *See* Jack Balkin, *Abortion and Original Meaning*, 24 Const. Comment. 291, 328–36 (2007); *see also* David H. Gans & Douglas T. Kendall, The Gem of the Constitution: The Text and History of the Privileges or Immunities Clause of the Fourteenth Amendment 27, 33 (2008).

41. *See, e.g.*, Ronald Dworkin, Life's Dominion: An Argument about Abortion, Euthanasia, and Individual Freedom 160–66 (1993).

42. 539 U.S. 558 (2003).

43. *Id.* at 578–79.

44. Washington v. Glucksberg, 521 U.S. 702, 721 (1997) (internal quotation marks and citation omitted).

45. *Lawrence*, 539 U.S. at 567.

46. *Id.*

47. *Id.* at 578.

48. *Id.* at 574 (quoting Planned Parenthood v. Casey, 505 U.S. 833, 851 (1992) (joint opinion)).

49. *Id.* at 575.

50. *Id.*

51. Poe v. Ullman, 367 U.S. 497, 542 (1961) (Harlan, J., dissenting).

52. *Id.* at 543 (internal quotation marks and citation omitted).

CHAPTER 10

1. *See* Tom Ginsburg et al., The Lifespan of Written Constitutions 1 (Dec. 26, 2007) (unpublished manuscript), *available at* http://escholarship. org/uc/item/6jw9domf.

2. WOODROW WILSON, CONSTITUTIONAL GOVERNMENT IN THE UNITED STATES 69 (1908).

3. 277 U.S. 438, 472–73 (1928) (Brandeis, J., dissenting) (quoting Weems v. United States, 217 U.S. 349, 373 (1910)).

4. *Weems*, 217 U.S. at 366.

5. *Id.* at 367–68.

6. *See id.* at 368–73.

7. *Id.* at 367.

8. WILLIAM FAULKNER, REQUIEM FOR A NUN 92 (1951).

9. *See* Rapanos v. United States, 547 U.S. 715, 737–38 (2006); Solid Waste Agency of N. Cook County v. U.S. Army Corps of Eng'rs, 531 U.S. 159, 172–74 (2001).

10. 198 P.2d 17 (Cal. 1948).

11. 388 U.S. 1 (1967).

12. *See* Turner v. Safley, 482 U.S. 78 (1987); Zablocki v. Redhail, 434 U.S. 374 (1978).

13. *See* Goodridge v. Dep't of Pub. Health, 798 N.E.2d 941 (Mass. 2003) (holding under the state constitution that same-sex couples may not be excluded from marriage); *see also* Varnum v. Brien, 763 N.W.2d 862 (Iowa 2009); Kerrigan v. Comm'r of Pub. Health, 957 A.2d 407 (Conn. 2008) (same); *In re* Marriage Cases, 183 P.3d 384 (Cal. 2008) (same), *superseded by* CAL. CONST. art. I, § 7.5 ("Only marriage between a man and a woman is valid or recognized in California."). For discussion of recent legislative activity, see Maria Sacchetti, *Maine Voters Overturn State's New Same-sex Marriage Law*, BOSTON GLOBE, Nov. 4, 2009, at A1, and Abby Goodnough, *Gay Rights Groups Celebrate Victories in Marriage Push*, N.Y. TIMES, Apr. 8, 2009, at A1.

Index

...

DATE DUE

HIGHSMITH 45230